METAMORPHOSIS

Driving Effective Leadership Amid
Unpredictable Change

Suzzette Harriott, Ph.D.
Anthony Solomon, BS

Kindle Direct Publishing

kindle
direct
publishing

For Isabelle,
who lights up the world with every smile—
you are my inspiration every day.
— Suzzette

And for my father, Hugh,
and Uncles Jerome, Gregory, and Roger,
whose wisdom and support guide me always.
— Anthony

CONTENTS

PROLOGUE

In the intricate tapestry of life and work, leadership's role is in a transformative phase. As we navigate through an age marked by abundant challenges and fleeting certainties, the guiding principles of leadership are being reshaped. The traditional pillars of stern control and inflexible hierarchy are being phased out in favor of adaptability, collaboration, and creativity. We stand at a seminal moment in the global leadership story, heralding the rise of a leader who is agile, transformative, and, above all, ready for the unknown.

"Metamorphosis: Driving Effective Leadership Amid Unpredictable Change" encapsulates years of insight, observations, and learnings about steering leadership in a fluid world. It's a compass for those in or aspiring to leadership roles - be it in small teams, global corporations, nonprofits, or personal leadership. If the allure of transformation resonates with you and you believe in leadership's power to catalyze change, you are in the right place.

Recent global events, from the profound shifts instigated by COVID-19 to the complex geopolitics exemplified by situations like the Ukraine War, have crafted a fresh blueprint for global leadership. These events underline the demand for leaders equipped with resilience, empathy, and a knack for navigating ambiguity.

In such tumultuous times, the essence of leadership is paramount. Leaders now shoulder the responsibility of not just navigating the storm but also charting courses into uncertain futures. They must offer clarity amidst chaos, sow hope amidst despair, and kindle unity amidst divisions.

Leadership now transcends traditional roles, evolving into a guiding light amidst swirling mists.

Our book serves as a beacon for those feeling adrift in these turbulent waters. Crafted to aid leaders in steering their organizations through change, this guide is your ally in adapting, evolving, and fostering transformative cultures.

Embracing change is pivotal. After all, metamorphosis fuels evolution and progress. In this fast-paced world, adaptability is the cornerstone. Leaders must champion this metamorphic spirit, both personally and organizationally. Our aim? To be your guiding star on this transformative journey.

In a world that thrives on interconnectedness, leadership demands inclusivity, cherishing diverse views and ensuring every voice finds an echo. We explore the intricate dance of inclusive leadership, offering actionable insights to nurture a culture rooted in mutual respect.

True leadership success transcends mere profits or market shares; it's about tangible impact, enduring legacies, and the ripples of positive change within and beyond organizational boundaries. Our book assists in recalibrating your leadership compass, syncing it with the demands of a dynamic world.

The leadership horizon is awash with change, unpredictability, and opportunities. As leaders, the onus is on us to rise, seize these opportunities, and pioneer leadership amidst uncharted terrains. "Metamorphosis: Driving Effective Leadership Amid Unpredictable Change" is your collaborator in this voyage. Dive in for insights, resources, and strategies designed for this new leadership epoch. Welcome to the transformative age. Welcome to the metamorphosis.

P.S. For hands-on tools and exercises, refer to our accompanying workbook, and for personal reflections, our curated journal is replete with profound quotes from the text and prompts to deepen your leadership introspection. This journey is not just about navigating the new normal but also a quest of self-discovery, enhancing your inherent leadership prowess.

PART I: FOUNDATIONS OF LEADERSHIP

CHAPTER 1 - PILLARS OF LEADERSHIP

Imagine stepping into a colossus teetering on the edge of obsolescence. That's precisely where Satya Nadella found himself in 2014 when he took the helm of Microsoft. Once the indomitable force of the tech world, Microsoft had grown sluggish, struggling to keep up with the frenetic pace of innovation. Shareholders were antsy, employees were disengaged, and the public narrative was far from flattering.

Rather than chart a course dictated solely by profits and losses, Nadella dared to ask questions that probed the very soul of the organization. "What is our core mission? What do we want to achieve?" He recognized that the key to Microsoft's resurgence lay in redefining its leadership ethos, a task that was part mindset shift and part methodological revamp.

Within months, Nadella initiated a company-wide leadership self-assessment, one that sought to dissect the anatomy of leadership itself. This wasn't a superficial check-the-box exercise but an earnest quest to understand how leadership could serve as the critical component for organizational success. The results were eye-opening, sparking dialogues around empathy, growth mindsets, and the broader impact of leadership on business performance.

Then, a test came that was unlike any other—a global crisis, the COVID-19 pandemic. Just as businesses worldwide were grappling with lockdowns, remote work, and unpredictable market fluctuations, Microsoft demonstrated something remarkable. Under Nadella's leadership, the organization didn't merely aim to survive; it pivoted with grace, ensuring seamless service provision and pioneering tools that helped other businesses stay afloat. The leadership's response to this global crisis became a case study in adaptability, resilience, and ingenuity.

As we delve deeper into this chapter, we'll unpack the critical facets that make leadership not just a role but the backbone of organizational vitality. We'll explore its domino effect on business performance metrics, and examine how robust leadership becomes an organization's strongest asset in navigating global crises. Just as Microsoft transformed its narrative under Nadella, effective leadership can become your organization's most compelling success story.

So before we proceed, perhaps it's worth taking a leaf out of Microsoft's playbook. Nadella's first act as CEO was to gift each of his top executives a copy of "Nonviolent Communication," by Marshall B. Rosenberg, Ph.D., a book that articulates the value of empathy in dialogue—a subtle yet transformative way of inducing self-assessment. Maybe it's time for your self-assessment. Because in this volatile, uncertain, complex, and ambiguous world, understanding the nuances of leadership isn't just strategic; it's existential.

Defining Leadership: The Critical Component of Organizational Success

What truly makes a leader? The answer to this question could span a library of theories, philosophies, and case studies, each highlighting different aspects of leadership. Leadership is as nuanced as the human spirit, as varied as the world's cultures, and as complex as the organizations they spearhead. Yet, we can distill it to its essence, understand its core, and harness its power.

Let's rewind to a crisp, sunny afternoon in Palo Alto,

2007. Steve Jobs, co-founder and then-CEO of Apple Inc., was about to unveil a revolutionary product that would disrupt the telecommunication sector and society as we know it. It was the first iPhone. It wasn't just Jobs's genius as a product developer or a marketer that brought this innovation to life—it was his leadership.

Leadership, as exemplified by Jobs, is not just about positional power. It's about vision—seeing the invisible and making it tangible. It's about identifying opportunities where others see roadblocks, making decisions that others shy away from, and igniting the spark of potential in others to convert vision into reality. This ability to envision and execute is the crux of authentic leadership.

Consider another instance, this time from the world of aviation. On January 15, 2009, US Airways Flight 1549 struck a flock of geese just after takeoff, losing all engine power. Yet, due to the calm, decisive leadership of Captain Chesley "Sully" Sullenberger, the crew managed to perform an emergency landing on the Hudson River, saving all passengers on board. Sullenberger's leadership under duress showcased the critical ability to make swift, effective decisions even in the most high-pressure situations. However, leadership extends beyond crises. It forms the backbone of daily operations within any organization.

Reflect on Sundar Pichai, the CEO of Alphabet Inc. Pichai is not just a leader due to his role; he exemplifies leadership by fostering an environment of collaboration and innovation, turning the search engine giant into a trailblazer across industries. He sets a strategic vision, provides resources, removes obstacles, and then steps back to let his talented team do what they do best.

This is the essence of transformational leadership —inspiring and empowering team members to exceed their potential. This type of leadership sees beyond the transactional nature of tasks and rewards. Instead, it instills a sense of purpose and promotes individual growth, influencing team members to become leaders.

Yet, the picture of leadership is only complete with discussing servant leadership, a concept exemplified by figures like Mother Teresa and Mahatma Gandhi. Despite not having any traditional organizational structure under them, they led millions through their selfless service and relentless pursuit of a vision. Their leadership was about listening, empathy, healing, and community-building, a stark contrast yet equally powerful to the corporate leadership style.

Similar to this, in today's corporate world, leaders such as Satya Nadella, CEO of Microsoft, embody servant leadership. Nadella is known for transforming Microsoft's culture from a 'know-it-all' to a 'learn-it-all' culture. He prioritized empathy, leading to a substantial turnaround for the company regarding financial performance and employee satisfaction.

Therein lies another facet of leadership – its adaptability. A successful leader understands that there's no one-size-fits-all approach. Depending on the situation, a leader may need to take charge, like Sullenberger, during the emergency landing or step back to encourage team innovation, as Pichai does at Google.

Ultimately, leadership is the lifeblood of an organization's success. It's a multidimensional role requiring vision, decisiveness, adaptability, empathy, and a drive for selfless service. But, most importantly, successful leadership is about eliciting these traits in those you lead.

As we probe deeper into the following sections of this chapter, we will dissect these characteristics further, providing a thorough understanding of what leadership entails. This is not a journey; it is a strategic guide. A metamorphosis in leadership thought that will arm you with the knowledge and perspective to drive effective leadership amid unpredictable change.

So, what does leadership mean to you? As you read on, keep this question at the forefront of your mind, and by the end of this chapter, you may find that your answer transforms as you do.

Leadership's Impact on Business Performance

Leadership, the unseen force propelling an organization, is integral to business performance. Like the root system of a mighty oak, leadership serves as the hidden foundation that nourishes an organization, providing stability and allowing for growth. Leaders do more than make decisions: they create an environment that shapes the organization's soul, establishing its tempo, direction, and ethos.

In the bustling corridors of a Fortune 500 company, a group of employees are working late into the night. Their eyes aren't weary, but they are instead alight with passion. Why? It's not because of a looming deadline or the promise of bonuses. It's because their leader has ignited a sense of purpose in them, a shared vision that they believe in and are willing to strive for. Such is the power of effective leadership. It transforms individual effort into collective ambition, sparking an upsurge in productivity and innovation.

Think about the culture within Google, a corporation known for its relaxed work environment, employee autonomy, and innovation. This culture wasn't formed in a day or simply written into a handbook. It was cultivated by the organization's leadership, creating an environment where employees feel trusted and empowered to bring their best. Such a culture attracts and retains talent and fosters creativity, directly impacting business performance.

Now, picture Tesla, a company constantly pushing the boundaries of innovation. This spirit of innovation stems from its leader, Elon Musk, who dares to challenge the status quo and encourages his team to do the same. Its leadership facilitates a culture of innovation, driving performance in a competitive business landscape.

Let's not forget leadership's role in critical decision-making. Imagine a boardroom where a significant decision must be made. With their deep understanding of the organization's workings, the leader balances potential risks and rewards, analyzes all variables, and makes an informed decision. This ability to make wise strategic decisions can significantly influence an organization's performance.

Leadership also manifests itself in an organization's brand image. Recall the turnaround of Microsoft under Satya Nadella's leadership. His emphasis on empathy and a growth mindset not only transformed the internal culture but also reshaped Microsoft's brand image, making it more appealing to customers and partners.

During crises, leadership shines brighter. Picture a global corporation in the throes of a financial downturn. A steadfast leader, armed with resilience and clear communication, navigates through the storm, minimizing damage, keeping the team motivated, and leading the organization towards recovery. It's a testament to the profound impact of leadership on business performance, especially during challenging times.

However, one crucial point remains: the influence of leadership on business performance is more than the sum of individual actions or decisions. It is a testament to a leader's capacity to unite, inspire, and guide an organization towards a shared vision.

Leadership is the pivot around which an organization revolves. It seeps into the organization's fabric, influencing every aspect, from productivity and innovation to culture, decision-making, and brand image. As we delve deeper into the pillars of leadership, we will explore the importance of versatile leadership styles in global crises and the role of self-assessment in refining leadership effectiveness.

In the vast sea of business performance, leadership is the lighthouse, guiding the organization towards success. By harnessing the power of effective leadership, organizations can chart a strategic course, navigate unpredictable change, and achieve extraordinary outcomes.

Leadership's Response to Global Crises

Global crises do not merely pose a threat to leaders; they redefine the very landscape in which leadership operates. A staggering pandemic, economic collapses, conflicts breaching international boundaries - these challenges fling leaders onto an unfamiliar battlefield where previous strategies may falter and proven leadership styles might wane. Amid these unpredictable shifts, leaders emerge as navigators entrusted with steering their organizations through murky waters.

The immediacy of a crisis brings a leader's protective instincts to the forefront. The advent of COVID-19, for instance, transformed leaders into sentinels overnight, charged with ensuring the health and safety of their teams while securing their organizations' survival. Leaders were expected to serve as strategists and as the first line of defense against the waves of instability. Their role transcended traditional boundaries, metamorphosing into beacons providing reassurance and support amid chaos.

To navigate a crisis effectively, leaders must strive to decode its complexities. A conscientious leader does not merely react to a crisis but examines its underbelly. They delve into understanding its inception, its predicted path, and its potential implications on their organization and the wider world. The intricate webs of geopolitical tensions, economic repercussions, societal shifts, and human responses all form part of this complex study. In essence, leaders become dedicated scholars of the crisis.

Armed with this understanding, leaders face the formidable challenge of strategy formulation. In the face of a crisis, leaders must reroute, conjuring innovative paths when traditional routes crumble. Creating new strategies in the throes of a crisis is a daunting task that necessitates strategic acumen, creative problem-solving, astute risk assessment, and a deep-rooted understanding of the organization's strengths and vulnerabilities.

Crises call for a unique balancing act between decisive actions and flexibility. The unpredictable nature of crises demands swift, definitive responses from leaders. Yet, they must also embody the agility to pivot when new developments surface. This dance between prompt action and malleability forms a vital facet of crisis leadership, a nuance that distinguishes static leadership from truly dynamic leadership.

During a crisis, a leader's communication metamorphoses into an invaluable instrument. Leaders are required to communicate with transparency and consistency, providing crucial updates, clarifying their decisions, addressing anxieties, and reinforcing their teams' morale. Amid uncertainty, leaders' communication can provide a semblance of control and clarity, soothing fears and preserving team spirit.

A crisis scenario places a leader's emotional intelligence under the spotlight. Empathy becomes as critical as strategy, with leaders required to resonate with their team's worries, challenges, and emotional turmoil. They must extend support, compassion, and understanding, thus fostering an environment of resilience and camaraderie. This emotional connection becomes an anchor, steadying the organization amidst the storm and fueling its determination to survive.

Leaders' responses to crises aren't limited to ensuring survival; they must also seek growth amid adversity. Paradoxically, crises, despite their disruptive nature, bear the seeds of transformation. Leaders who discern these seeds can harness the crisis as a catalyst for innovation and metamorphosis, propelling their organizations towards a stronger, more adaptive future.

In the darkness of global crises, leaders emerge as luminaries of hope. They imbue confidence, chart the route towards recovery, and light the path for growth. Their actions, choices, and attitudes sculpt the organization's crisis response, shaping its resilience, survival, and eventual evolution.

Leadership Self-Assessment

In our fast-paced and dynamic world, effective leadership is not a destination but a continuous journey of learning and growth. Regardless of the level of expertise or years of experience, there is always room for improvement and evolution. One of the most potent ways to enhance your leadership ability is by regularly conducting a leadership self-assessment. This introspective exercise provides invaluable insights into your strengths, weaknesses, and overall effectiveness as a leader, helping you to understand your impact on your team and organization. Here are eight essential components of a leadership self-assessment to guide your personal and professional development:

1. **Understanding Your Leadership Style:** Recognize your default mode of operation, the principles that guide your decisions, and your reaction to different situations. Do you thrive in change and innovation, or prefer consistency? Are you primarily results-oriented, or do you prioritize the welfare of your team?

2. **Identify Your Strengths:** As a leader, you possess unique strengths that contribute to your effectiveness. It could be your ability to inspire and motivate others or your strategic thinking abilities. Pinpoint these strengths to leverage them more effectively.

3. **Acknowledging Your Weaknesses:** It may be uncomfortable, but identifying areas for improvement is crucial for growth. You might need help with clear communication or decision-making under pressure. Accepting these weaknesses allows you to address them proactively.

4. **Assess the Impact of Your Leadership**

on Your Team: Your leadership style significantly affects your team. Seek feedback to understand their perceptions. Do they feel inspired, motivated, and valued, or do they feel micromanaged and undervalued?

5. **Evaluate Your Adaptability:** As a leader, your ability to adjust to different situations, individuals, and evolving dynamics is essential. Reflect on how well you adapt to changes.

6. **Examine Your Ethical Standards:** Assess the ethics of your decisions. Are you promoting fairness, transparency, and integrity in your actions? Upholding strong ethical standards fosters trust within your team.

7. **Reflect on Your Emotional Intelligence:** How well do you manage your emotions, particularly under stress, and empathize with others? High emotional intelligence promotes effective leadership and improves team outcomes.

8. **Set Goals for Leadership Development:** Following your self-assessment, identify areas you wish to improve and new leadership skills you want to acquire. These goals will guide your growth as a leader.

❋ ❋ ❋

Remember, self-assessment isn't a one-time exercise. It's a continuous process mirroring the ongoing nature of leadership development. By engaging in these assessments, you better understand yourself as a leader and chart a path for ongoing transformation and adaptability.

CHAPTER 2 - AN ARRAY OF RESPONSES: UNDERSTANDING LEADERSHIP STYLES

If you ever wonder what adaptive leadership looks like, think of Indra Nooyi stepping into the PepsiCo CEO role in 2006. At the time, the global snacking and beverage giant faced an existential challenge: adapting to a world increasingly conscious of health and sustainability. The company's leadership style could no longer be a one-note tune; it had to be a symphony of strategies, each tailored for a specific moment and challenge.

Indra Nooyi chose not to go with the flow but to change the current. It could have been easy to leverage PepsiCo's already significant market share in the sugary drinks segment to drive short-term profits. Instead, she looked ahead, envisioning a future where health and wellbeing would be at the forefront of consumer choice. She pushed for diversification, spearheading the acquisition of healthy brands and championing sustainability. These moves necessitated a full spectrum of leadership styles—from authoritative to lead the new vision, to democratic when seeking internal buy-in, to affiliative when managing the change stress among employees.

It's not just the styles she adopted, but the alacrity with which she toggled between them, that showcased the art of adaptive leadership. It's here that we find our entry point into understanding the range of leadership styles. Nooyi's capacity to analyze the strengths and weaknesses of each leadership approach, and to adapt accordingly, led to a transformative era for PepsiCo. They became an organization not only responsive to market shifts but also one that could drive change, setting the agenda for an entire industry.

As we dissect this chapter, we will unveil the spectrum of leadership styles that every leader should be cognizant of, analyzing the pros and cons of each. But we won't stop at theory. We will dive deep into how different leadership styles come into play when the stakes are high—during global challenges that shake the very foundations of an organization. Think of it as your toolkit for adaptive leadership, the mastering of situational styles that can serve as your rudder through the turbulent waters of the 21st century.

So as you turn this page, consider this: What was it that set Nooyi apart? It was her grasp of a simple yet often overlooked truth—that leadership isn't about finding a style and sticking to it come hell or high water. It's about the deft art of adaptation, reading the room, and understanding that what worked yesterday may not work today. Because in a world that's changing faster than ever, adaptability isn't just an asset; it's a necessity.

Unveiling the Spectrum of Leadership Styles

Just as the visible light spectrum reveals a kaleidoscope of colors, the spectrum of leadership styles unfolds a rich array of approaches. Each leadership style represents a unique blend of behaviors, attitudes, and strategies influencing how leaders guide their organizations. Recognizing these styles is akin to understanding different languages—each carries its distinct syntax, semantics, and idioms, all bearing the potential for unique expressions of effective leadership.

Autocratic Leadership

Historically, autocratic leadership was the hallmark of

powerful figures like Alexander the Great, symbolizing complete control. The term stems from Greek, indicating self-rule. This leadership style gained traction in the early 20th century, during an age of strict business hierarchies. This era was influenced by the Scientific Management philosophy of Frederick Winslow Taylor, with companies like Ford exemplifying this approach. Tasks were simplified and employees strictly directed, allowing minimal input.

In modern times, traces of autocratic leadership persist. It's evident in family-run businesses where the head makes all decisions, or in strictly regulated sectors like pharmaceuticals. In high-stakes scenarios, such as surgeries or emergency situations, the precision and swiftness of autocratic leadership can be vital. Its strength lies in clear authority and rapid decision-making, especially beneficial when swift actions are paramount.

Yet, this style has its drawbacks. Over-reliance on a leader can create decision-making bottlenecks and undermine organizational resilience. For instance, a tech startup might stifle innovation if the founder dominates decision-making, or a company might struggle if a micromanaging CEO becomes unavailable suddenly.

Autocratic leadership, while not always wholly dominant, remains a tool in the leadership toolkit. Its efficacy depends on context and application. Today, it's about judicious use, often in combination with other styles, tailored to suit the situation.

Democratic Leadership

Democratic leadership, reminiscent of participative governance, has its origins in the ancient Athenian agora where public decisions were collaboratively made. By the mid-20th century, it became recognized in organizational contexts, largely credited to psychologists like Kurt Lewin. Lewin introduced three leadership styles: autocratic, democratic, and laissez-faire. Here, democratic leadership was defined as one that actively incorporates team input in decision-making. Rensis Likert, in the 1960s, further emphasized its positive effects on job satisfaction and productivity through his 'Linking Pin' model.

Fields such as technology, education, and creative industries cherish this style. They benefit from diverse perspectives, vital for innovation and addressing evolving market demands. The strength of democratic leadership lies in fostering creativity and innovation by embracing inclusivity. For instance, a tech startup might achieve a groundbreaking product by pooling team insights, or a school might see increased teacher commitment when they're part of curriculum design. Such leadership strengthens team dynamics through mutual respect and trust.

However, it's not without challenges. In crises, seeking consensus might delay crucial decisions. There are also situations where team members might lack the expertise to offer meaningful input. Plus, a democratic leader must skillfully handle group discussions and dynamics, balancing guidance with fostering participation.

In essence, democratic leadership thrives on collective decision-making and boosts team engagement and innovation. Recognizing its strengths and challenges ensures its effective application, allowing leaders to reap its benefits while sidestepping potential issues.

Laissez-Faire Leadership

Originating from a French phrase meaning 'let do,' laissez-faire signifies minimal intervention. This concept, often linked to economic debates about governmental roles in the market, was categorized by Kurt Lewin in the 1930s as one of three central leadership styles. Historically, during events like the Industrial Revolution, it was favored in sectors valuing individual creativity, like artisan workshops.

Today, laissez-faire leadership still thrives in domains requiring creativity and expertise, such as research, arts, technology, and academia. Here, professionals often excel with the freedom to innovate without constant oversight. The style resembles a thriving garden, promoting unique growth, innovation, and high job satisfaction among those valuing autonomy. It also encourages personal growth, as individuals own their projects.

However, it has its pitfalls. For instance, a research team might produce scattered results without clear direction. In the absence of proper guidance, inefficiencies and role ambiguities can arise, especially when close supervision or regular feedback is essential.

Laissez-faire leadership can bolster creativity and self-reliance, but demands discerning application. Effective leaders under this style recognize when to guide and when to grant autonomy, ensuring its application suits the situation.

Transformational Leadership

Introduced by James V. Downton and later expanded by James Victor Burns in the 1970s, transformational leadership stands in contrast to transactional leadership. It emphasizes charisma, inspiration, and emotional engagement. Bernard Bass later stressed its intellectual stimulation and individual consideration components.

Historically, transformational leaders like Mahatma Gandhi and Martin Luther King Jr. have emerged in turbulent times, rallying followers towards a unified future vision. Especially crucial in evolving sectors like technology and healthcare, this leadership fosters adaptability and innovation.

Transformational leadership's strengths lie in its ability to boost team performance, engagement, and satisfaction. By connecting individual and collective identities, it promotes personal and professional growth. However, it demands high emotional intelligence from leaders, risking unsustainability. Over-reliance on the leader's charisma can overshadow organizational needs, potentially leading to poor decision-making or stifling team autonomy.

While transformational leadership excels in spurring change and innovation, it necessitates careful management to benefit the organization and its members. This style encourages exceeding perceived limitations and maximizing potential. Due to its significance in the current landscape, chapter 3 delves deeper into this leadership style.

Servant Leadership

First articulated by Robert K. Greenleaf in 1970, the servant leadership principle emphasizes leaders' authentic desire to prioritize followers' growth and needs over their own. Its origins trace back to ancient teachings, exemplified by figures like Mahatma Gandhi and Mother Teresa, who embodied service before self.

This leadership style excels in sectors like healthcare, education, and social work, where service orientation is paramount. Imagine a school principal emphasizing holistic student development over mere test scores. Servant leadership thrives in environments valuing mutual respect, trust, and empathy.

The benefits are manifold: it fosters trust, elevates team morale, boosts collaboration, and enhances employee retention. Consider a CEO actively addressing team concerns, resulting in a harmonious, high-performing culture. Servant leaders also cultivate future leaders by empowering their followers.

However, the emphasis on individual needs might at times overshadow broader organizational goals. A leader might overly focus on personal development, potentially slowing decision-making. There's also a risk of perceived diminished authority or exploitation due to their service-centric approach.

In essence, while servant leadership balances individual needs and organizational objectives, its application promotes engaged and high-performing teams. Its profound impact is explored further in chapter 3 on this pivotal leadership style.

Transactional Leadership

First introduced by sociologist Max Weber in 1947 and later refined by Bernard M. Bass, transactional leadership is rooted in classical management. It emphasizes clear exchanges between leaders and subordinates, with rewards or punishments tied to performance.

This style has historical relevance in settings like the military or factory lines, suitable for sectors like finance, law enforcement, and healthcare, where strict adherence to rules is paramount.

Transactional leadership can be effective in situations demanding rapid, structured responses. For instance, it can streamline patient care during hospital emergencies. Tying rewards to performance can also promote productivity and uphold organizational standards.

Yet, it may curtail creativity and promote short-term thinking. In environments like software development, it might discourage innovative risks. Moreover, its heavy focus on extrinsic motivation can erode intrinsic drive.

While transactional leadership offers structure and efficiency, it may need complementing strategies in today's dynamic business world to nurture innovation and long-term growth.

Charismatic Leadership

Charismatic leadership, as introduced by sociologist Max Weber, hinges on a leader's magnetic appeal and exceptional qualities. Notable examples include Martin Luther King Jr.'s Civil Rights advocacy, Winston Churchill's wartime leadership, and Steve Jobs' innovative vision for Apple. Especially effective in environments needing vision or substantial change, this style can rally teams around a shared goal.

While charismatic leaders excel in motivating and garnering loyalty, especially during challenging times, the style has drawbacks. There's a risk of developing a 'cult of personality,' making teams overly reliant on the leader, potentially stunting their growth. Additionally, such leaders might neglect crucial operational details, engrossed in their larger vision.

In essence, charismatic leadership's success lies in balancing inspirational allure with operational efficiency. It's vital for these leaders to empower their teams, promoting independent decision-making.

Remember, the intent of exploring leadership styles isn't to box leaders into categories but to appreciate the diverse tools available. Recognizing and applying the right leadership style for the context is crucial. It broadens a leader's approach, enhancing adaptability in the evolving organizational landscape.

Leadership Styles and Their Impact on Global Challenges

In the grand tapestry of our global society, the challenges we face are as varied and complex as the threads that weave it. The threads of climate change, pandemics, economic instability, and social inequity weave intricate patterns, creating a picture of a world in flux. Leadership, in this
scenario, is not just a necessity but an imperative, a compass guiding us through these choppy waters. The focus here isn't on a singular approach to leadership but a celebration of diverse leadership styles, each holding its unique strengths in steering the ship amid the storm.

When we examine autocratic leadership, we see its value in circumstances that call for immediate, decisive action. Consider the early days of a pandemic, a moment teetering on the edge of chaos and calm. In this case, an autocratic leader can be the stern hand guiding the ship through the storm, making decisions quickly when every second is precious. Yet, a caveat exists - extended reliance on this style can risk curbing the very innovation and resilience needed to weather long-term challenges. It's akin to constantly trimming a bonsai tree – while it maintains a desired shape, it may hamper its growth potential.

Democratic leadership, conversely, shines brightest when faced with challenges that need collective action, diverse insights, and widespread collaboration. Picture the herculean task of battling climate change, an issue so grand and intricate that it demands wisdom from every corner of our society. In such scenarios, democratic leaders serve as master weavers, integrating diverse strands of knowledge and insight to shape a unified, shared vision. However, while this tapestry of collective wisdom is powerful, the time-intensive process of weaving it might be a disadvantage when rapid responses are needed.

Laissez-faire leadership finds its niche in arenas where unbridled creativity and innovation are paramount, sectors such as technology and healthcare research. Providing team members with the freedom to explore their ideas can lead to groundbreaking solutions to complex global challenges. Yet, like a ship adrift without a course, teams might lose sight of the broader challenge without some degree of structure and direction.

Transformational leadership serves as the catalyst for systemic change. In a world marked by deep-seated inequalities, where social transformation is not just a need but a moral obligation, a transformational leader inspires their team to transcend the status quo and strive towards a better future. Yet, this style necessitates leaders with high emotional intelligence and the stamina to sustain the momentum of their team throughout the long and arduous journey of systemic change.

Servant leadership, which prioritizes the needs of the team and the communities they serve, holds significant potential for addressing social challenges. Such leaders foster a culture of empathy and commitment, especially in nonprofit organizations and public services. However, the balance is crucial here. Servant leaders must ensure their dedication to serving individual needs doesn't eclipse the broader organizational objectives and strategies necessary for effecting change.

Transactional leadership, with its emphasis on consistency and clear expectations, can be an anchor in the turbulent waters of economic instability. Industries with clear-cut roles might find the reward and punishment system of transactional leadership a comforting source of stability amidst the chaos. However, this style carries the risk of stifling adaptability and innovation - elements crucial for successfully navigating economic uncertainties.

Finally, the charismatic leader emerges as a beacon of inspiration and unity in a world often fragmented by geopolitical and cultural divides. Charismatic leaders can galvanize global communities around shared challenges with their magnetic pull. However, while the allure of a charismatic leader can spark change, it's essential to recognize the robust systems and operations that sustain the cause in their absence.

Our journey through the multifaceted world of leadership styles is not designed to box or categorize leaders into predefined slots. Instead, it serves to acknowledge the vast array of tools available in a leader's arsenal. It's crucial to understand that the efficacy of a leadership style doesn't solely rely on the style itself, but rather its apt deployment in the right context. This broad spectrum of leadership styles provides leaders with a diverse toolkit, enabling them to adapt and respond adeptly to various scenarios and obstacles. Comprehending these styles is less about finding a mold to adhere to and more about broadening your spectrum of leadership strategies. This understanding equips you to navigate the dynamic terrain of organizational management with increased finesse and flexibility.

Adaptive Leadership: Mastering the Art of Situational Styles

Leadership is a versatile art. The beauty of this craft lies in its malleability, in its ability to be shaped and reshaped to fit the situation at hand. This section, "Tips & Tools: Adaptive Leadership: Mastering the Art of Situational Styles," invites you into the dynamic world of situational leadership. The tools we provide here are designed not to constrain you within a particular leadership style, but to guide you in recognizing, embracing, and pivoting between styles as situations dictate. It's about learning to wear many hats - a different one for each occasion, each unique set of circumstances that you, as a leader, will inevitably encounter.

Scenarios demonstrating the fluidity of effective leadership:

1. Rapidly Scaling Startup: Leadership may evolve from transformational to democratic as a startup grows. With maturity, a laissez-faire approach may suit some departments, granting autonomy while providing resources.
2. Crisis in a Manufacturing Plant: During crises, managers might transition from transactional to autocratic leadership for swift decision-making. After, returning to transactional style restores normality, with elements of servant leadership aiding team wellbeing.
3. Nonprofit Organization: Servant leadership often suits nonprofits, with democratic styles useful for strategic decisions. Charismatic leadership can inspire at public events.
4. Revitalizing Performance in Crisis: For corporations in recession, a mix of autocratic (swift decisions) and transformational leadership (providing vision and

direction) can help.

* * *

Like a conductor, an effective leader blends styles according to the situation. Leadership styles are tools whose effectiveness depends on context. As leaders face changing dynamics, may they find the right style blend that resonates with their team, aligns with their identity, and steers the organization toward its vision.

PART II: RECOGNIZING AND ADDRESSING LEADERSHIP GAPS

CHAPTER 3 - ADAPTIVE FORCES: TRANSFORMATIONAL AND SERVANT LEADERSHIP

Alan Mulally walked into a calamity when he took the reins at Ford Motor Company in 2006. The company was hurtling toward a $12.6 billion loss for the year. Any sensible person might have asked why he would leave his secure position as the executive vice president at Boeing to board a sinking ship. But Mulally wasn't just any leader; he was an adaptive force, a rare blend of transformational and servant leadership styles.

At first glance, these two approaches might appear contradictory. Transformational leaders often focus on vision, innovation, and setting new directions, while servant leaders emphasize empathy, team dynamics, and a ground-up approach to problem-solving. Mulally made it clear that these styles aren't mutually exclusive; they are two sides of the same coin.

He began by laying down a transformative vision for Ford—a plan he called "One Ford." It was a roadmap to streamline processes, unify the fragmented divisions, and concentrate on fewer models but with higher quality. A powerful vision indeed, but what made it stick was the servant leadership qualities he exhibited. Mulally listened—to employees, to stakeholders, to customers. He set up a culture where everyone's voice mattered, from the factory floor to the executive suite. He was known for his "Business Plan Reviews," weekly meetings where transparency was the norm, not the exception. Here, bad news was welcomed as an opportunity to solve problems collectively.

Throughout this chapter, we'll explore the characteristics that mark transformational and servant leaders. We'll delve into the scientific and psychological underpinnings of each and look at how they can serve as catalysts for change, particularly in periods of crisis. Then, we'll study how the hybrid approach—a marriage of transformational and servant leadership—can be more than just the sum of its parts. Think of it as your toolkit for becoming a multi-dimensional leader, with real-world advice on how to cultivate the most relevant traits for today's ever-changing landscape.

As you read on, consider the lessons from Mulally's tenure at Ford. The story isn't just about avoiding bankruptcy; it's about how Ford became a symbol of resilience and innovation. And at the heart of this transformation was a leader who understood that real power lies in the ability to adapt one's leadership style to the needs of the hour. In a volatile, uncertain, complex, and ambiguous world, this adaptability is not a 'nice-to-have,' but a critical asset.

Transformational Leadership as an Adaptive Force

In the ever-evolving landscape of business and organization, there stands a beacon, resilient and resolute. It's not a new management fad or technological marvel; it's the very essence of transformational leadership. This leadership is akin to the roots of a tree, burrowing deep into the core of an organization, instilling growth, renewal, and unwavering strength.

Maria, a senior executive in a tech firm, grappling with dwindling morale and productivity. Instead of resorting to a status quo response, she poses a question: "How can we harness the existing energy and potential of our team to rewrite our narrative?" This question, simple yet profound, is the very premise of transformational leadership. It's not about altering the essence but elevating it.

Imagine for a moment the world of sports. A fledgling football team, always in the shadows of its more illustrious competitors, finds itself under the guidance of a new coach, Alex. Rather than dismantling the team and starting anew, Alex spends time understanding each player's strengths and dreams. He cultivates an environment where players are inspired to exceed their perceived limits, where their growth becomes the team's growth. This real-world scenario isn't just about sports; it's a masterclass in transformational leadership.

Yet, one might ask, isn't adaptability a given in any leadership model? What sets transformational leadership apart is not the act of adapting, but the purpose behind it. It's adaptive not out of reaction but out of vision. Transformational leaders don't just respond to change; they anticipate and shape it, weaving a tapestry where every thread, every individual, forms a cohesive, vibrant image.

Now, recall the fable of the wind and the sun, vying to make a traveler shed his cloak. While the wind's forceful gusts only made the traveler clutch his cloak tighter, the sun's gentle warmth made him willingly take it off. Transformational leadership is much like the sun. Instead of coercion, it thrives on inspiration. It's not about telling people where to go but making them yearn to get there.

However, it's crucial to understand that transformational leadership isn't a one-size-fits-all solution. It demands vulnerability. Leaders must be willing to challenge their assumptions, to lay bare their ambitions and fears, and in doing so, create an atmosphere of mutual trust and respect.

On the bustling floor of a renowned hospital, Dr. Lisa faced a dilemma. The hospital, once a pioneer in medical innovations, had become complacent. Lisa could have implemented stricter rules or incentives, but she chose a different path. She began weekly sessions, sharing her vision of the hospital's potential, her dream of it being not just a place to heal but a beacon of hope. In doing so, she ignited a spark in her team, pushing them not out of obligation but out of shared purpose.

In organizations across the globe, there lies a latent force, often untapped: human potential. Transformational leadership recognizes this force. It understands that every individual, given the right environment, can transcend their limitations, evolving into an agent of profound change.

A skeptic might raise an eyebrow: "Is transformational leadership just about charisma?" To that, one could argue that it goes beyond charm or eloquence. It's about authenticity. Employees and team members, in their heart of hearts, recognize genuine intent. When a leader exudes a sincere desire for collective growth, it resonates, creating ripples of positive change.

Peel back the layers, and at its core, transformational leadership is a dance of change and constancy. While it encourages growth, innovation, and adaptability, it also cherishes the foundational values of an organization, ensuring that in the pursuit of the new, the essence remains untainted.

It's also worth noting that transformational leadership is not a destination but a continuous process. It demands reflection, recalibration, and most importantly, the humility to acknowledge when one is off course. In a dynamic world, the true prowess of a transformational leader lies in recognizing that while change is inevitable, how one steers it makes all the difference.

Transformational leadership as an adaptive force offers more than just a pathway to success; it offers a vision of what could be. It challenges leaders to ask not just "How can we adapt?" but "How can we inspire?" In the maelstrom of unpredictable change, this leadership doesn't just provide a strategy; it provides a compass, guiding organizations toward horizons they once only dreamt of.

The Role of Servant Leadership as a Catalyst for Change

The heart of an organization pulses not from its boardroom, but from its people. Amidst the tapestries of leadership narratives, one stands stark in its humility and impact: Servant Leadership. Picture the mosaic of a bustling marketplace, each vendor dependent on the other, yet led by a singular purpose. The most effective vendor isn't the loudest or the most opulent but the one who listens, aids, and guides others. That, in essence, is servant leadership.

Consider Tyson, the CEO of a prominent manufacturing company. He began his career on the factory floor, understanding the nuances of every machine, listening to the concerns of every worker. When he ascended to leadership, he didn't leave behind those memories. Instead, Tyson used them as a cornerstone for his leadership approach, always prioritizing the needs of his employees, ensuring that they had the tools and environment necessary to excel.

Let's shift gears and delve into a seemingly unrelated realm: education. In the halls of an inner-city school, Principal Grace faced dwindling student engagement. Rather than mandate stricter regulations or punish teachers, she flipped the script. She initiated one-on-one meetings with teachers, asking them: "What do you need to succeed?" This question, stemming from genuine concern, changed the school's trajectory. Test scores improved, but more crucially, so did morale and collaboration.

The underpinning ethos of servant leadership is a delicate intertwining of empowerment and accountability. It's not about relinquishing power but redistributing it, ensuring that every team member feels both valued and responsible. This redistribution isn't just symbolic; it translates to tangible organizational growth.

Dive into the annals of business literature, and one might posit that leaders should be fierce, assertive, even dominating. But in the modern, interconnected world, where collaboration trumps competition, the spotlight shines brightly on servant leaders. They understand that an organization's strength lies not in its ability to dictate but to elevate.

Servant leadership is not about being servile. It's about service. This nuance is vital. It's not a passive act of waiting for directives but an active commitment to understanding and addressing the needs of others. A leader's influence isn't gauged by their capacity to command but by their ability to inspire and nurture.

Now, imagine an orchestra. The conductor stands tall, wielding a baton, guiding every note. But what if the conductor took the time to understand each musician, their strengths, aspirations, and fears? The music would no longer be just harmonious; it would be transformative. This orchestra paints a vivid portrait of servant leadership in action.

Amidst tales of organizational success, there's a whisper, sometimes more audible, of toxic cultures, burnout, and attrition. In such settings, the introduction of servant leadership doesn't just lead to incremental changes; it catalyzes a cultural metamorphosis. When leaders transition from 'me' to 'we', it fosters a climate of mutual respect and shared purpose.

Yet, embracing servant leadership isn't an effortless switch. It requires leaders to confront their vulnerabilities, challenge their ego, and most significantly, to listen. It demands a willingness to shift from the familiar corridors of top-down mandates to the uncharted terrains of bottom-up insights.

Consider a renowned software company, once hailed for its innovations, but now grappling with stagnation. The newly appointed CEO, Li, could have implemented a slew of new strategies or projects. Instead, she initiated 'listening tours' across departments, absorbing feedback, understanding challenges, and crafting solutions in collaboration with her team. The result? A reinvigorated company, with employees deeply invested in its success.

History brims with examples of leaders who were not just powerful but also revered. Their secret wasn't just strategy or vision but empathy. They were servant leaders, who understood that their true prowess lay not in leading from the front but in elevating those around them.

There's a misconception that servant leadership might dampen ambition or competitiveness. On the contrary, it magnifies it. When every individual feels seen, heard, and valued, it ignites a collective ambition, steering the organization toward unparalleled heights.

Servant leadership, as a catalyst for change, is not just a leadership style; it's a leadership ethos. In an era defined by rapid change and unpredictability, this ethos doesn't just offer a way to navigate the tumult but to thrive within it. Servant leadership provides not just a blueprint but a moral compass, ensuring that in the pursuit of organizational success, the human spirit remains invigorated and intact.

Merging Transformational and Servant Leadership: A Hybrid Approach

In the vast landscape of leadership models, two emerge with prominence: transformational leadership, with its fierce focus on vision and inspiration, and servant leadership, rooted in empathy and service. While they may seem like disparate philosophies, imagine the power harnessed when they merge. It's akin to the marriage of fire and water, each element amplifying the other's potency.

Start by visualizing a modern tech campus, sprawling and pulsating with innovation. Nidley, a division lead, isn't just passionate about cutting-edge solutions; she's equally invested in ensuring every coder and designer feels valued and heard. Under her leadership, her team doesn't just meet targets; they redefine them. Nidley embodies the hybrid of transformational and servant leadership.

Understanding this merger begins by acknowledging the strengths of each style. Transformational leaders inspire, driving change with charisma and vision. They're the torchbearers, illuminating paths hitherto unseen. Conversely, servant leaders, with their attentive ear and nurturing spirit, ensure that no one treads this path alone or unequipped.

Now, let's pivot to healthcare. In a bustling metropolitan hospital, Dr. Raj helms a unit dedicated to pioneering surgical techniques. He's a visionary, constantly pushing boundaries. But post-surgery, he's known to sit beside patients, understanding their anxieties and ensuring their comfort. It's this duality that makes Dr. Raj not just respected, but beloved.

At the confluence of these leadership styles lies a dynamic equilibrium. On one hand, there's a relentless pursuit of excellence and on the other, a grounded commitment to the well-being of each team member. This equilibrium isn't static; it's fluid, adapting to the unique needs of situations and individuals.

Reflect on the world of sports. Maya, a basketball coach, is known for her game strategies, always ten steps ahead of her opponents. But off the court, she's seen mentoring players, addressing personal challenges, and fostering a culture of mutual respect. It's this blend that has turned her team into consistent champions.

The hybrid approach also addresses a vital question: What happens after the vision is set? Transformational leaders might set the direction, but without the servant leadership ethos, the journey might become isolating. It's one thing to know where you're headed; it's another to ensure everyone arrives together and enriched.

Consider the narrative of a thriving eco-resort in Bali. Its founder, Liam, envisioned a haven that was sustainable and luxurious. But instead of imposing this vision, he involved every local artisan and worker, understanding their insights, and weaving them into the resort's fabric. Today, it stands not as Liam's dream, but a collective realization.

However, merging these leadership styles isn't about creating a homogenized blend. It's about recognizing when to stoke the fires of inspiration and when to provide a listening ear. It's about oscillating between being the guiding star and the anchor.

Delve into the realm of non-profits. Aisha leads an organization dedicated to urban farming in marginalized communities. She not only paints a picture of self-sustaining neighborhoods but actively collaborates with residents, ensuring they have the skills and resources to realize this vision. Her leadership isn't just effective; it's transformative.

Organizations today grapple with complexities unheard of a decade ago. The challenges are multifaceted, and a singular leadership style might not suffice. In this intricate dance, the hybrid approach offers a rhythm that's both dynamic and grounded.

Let's contextualize with a multinational corporation, navigating the turbulent waters of global politics and digital disruptions. Its CEO, Enrique, paints a compelling vision of the company's future. But he's equally present in town-hall meetings, addressing concerns and co-creating solutions. Under his stewardship, the company doesn't just weather storms; it learns to dance in the rain.

In the grand tapestry of leadership, the threads of transformational and servant leadership might seem distinct. But when woven together, they create a fabric that's resilient, vibrant, and inclusive. It's this fabric that organizations need as they chart courses through the unpredictable seas of change.

In essence, the hybrid approach isn't about compromise; it's about amplification. It's about magnifying strengths and bolstering weaknesses. It's not about diluting vision or empathy but creating a leadership paradigm that's holistic and adaptive.

One truth emerges with clarity: leadership in the modern era isn't about fitting into boxes or labels. It's about crafting a unique, potent blend that serves both the mission and the people. And in this endeavor, the merger of transformational and servant leadership offers not just a model but a compass, ensuring that change is not only effective but also deeply human.

Cultivating Transformational and Servant Leadership Traits

Leadership, at its core, is a tapestry woven with varied threads of character, skills, and experiences. In a rapidly evolving world, this tapestry needs to reflect vibrant patterns of transformational and servant leadership, all against the backdrop of harnessing diversity. These are not just qualities to be admired from afar; they are actionable traits that every leader can – and should – cultivate within themselves. As we delve into this realm, remember leadership isn't about standing out, but rather standing up for values, people, and visions.

1. Authentic Listening: The Heartbeat of Engagement
Imagine Carlos, the head of a tech startup, who holds monthly sessions named 'Heartbeats'. Here, team members share not just project updates, but personal experiences, fostering a space of trust. To harness diversity, leaders must genuinely listen, valuing every voice, and ensuring their team knows they've been heard.

2. Radical Empathy: Walking in Others' Shoes
Lisa, a manager in a multinational, recently encountered an employee struggling with personal issues affecting performance. Instead of a stern warning, she arranged for flexible working hours, showcasing empathy. When leaders demonstrate such understanding, they don't just solve problems; they nurture potential.

3. Visionary Inclusivity: Broadening the Horizon
Think of Amrita, a young entrepreneur, who launched a product line inspired by input from diverse team members, from finance experts to interns. A transformational leader invites all perspectives, ensuring that the organization's vision is not just grand, but also grounded in varied realities.

4. Empowerment: The Seedbed of Potential

A local bakery, under the stewardship of David, soared in popularity when he empowered his diverse team to contribute unique recipes from their cultural backgrounds. Leaders must recognize and amplify the diverse strengths within their teams, offering opportunities for every member to shine.

5. Nurturing Growth: Cultivate, Don't Command

Sophie, leading a digital marketing team, doesn't just assign tasks; she pairs experienced members with new recruits for mentorship. Servant leaders prioritize the growth of their team members, understanding that the organization's success is deeply intertwined with individual development.

6. Courageous Conversations: Building Bridges, Not Walls

James, a CEO, once addressed an unintentional oversight in a campaign that was culturally insensitive. Instead of defensiveness, he facilitated a workshop on cultural understanding. Addressing the elephant in the room, especially around diversity issues, strengthens trust and rapport.

7. Feedback as a Gift: The Dual Lane Highway

Remember Elena, a director, who not only provides feedback but also actively seeks it after every presentation? Creating a culture where feedback flows both ways ensures that diverse perspectives are continually shaping and refining the leadership approach.

8. Celebrate Diversity: Beyond Tokenism to True Value

Consider Hassan's textile firm, which celebrates international festivals, valuing the varied backgrounds of his team. By integrating diverse celebrations into organizational culture, leaders can foster a sense of belonging and appreciation.

9. Continuous Learning: The Expanding Repository

A tech giant recently introduced a 'Global Perspectives' module, initiated by their leader, Zoe. Committed leaders invest in learning and training resources that highlight the importance of diverse viewpoints, preparing their teams for inclusive thinking.

10. Flexibility: The Pulse of Modern Leadership

An NGO, led by Mia, introduced remote working much before it was a global trend, respecting personal dynamics of her diverse team. By being adaptable in leadership strategies and work arrangements, leaders ensure that the diverse needs of their team members are addressed.

* * *

To truly weave diversity into the leadership tapestry, it's imperative to move beyond just acknowledging differences. It's about actively integrating these differences into the very fabric of organizational culture and leadership styles. And as this fabric is woven, it's these actionable tips – authentic listening, radical empathy, visionary inclusivity, and more – that act as the vibrant threads, creating a leadership masterpiece that's both inclusive and effective.

CHAPTER 4 - SPOTLIGHT ON WEAKNESSES: IDENTIFYING LEADERSHIP DEFICIENCIES

When Sarah Thompson took the helm at NexaTech in 2010, the technology landscape was buzzing with innovation and opportunity. NexaTech was already a well-established player, pioneering in cloud computing and big data solutions. By 2018, however, the company's fortunes had changed dramatically. Stock prices plummeted, key talent left in droves, and competitors had raced ahead, leaving NexaTech struggling to catch up. This wasn't a story of market volatility or an unforeseeable Black Swan event. This was a tale of leadership deficiencies that left an entire organization vulnerable.

Sarah had always been known for her grand visions and ambitious five-year plans. Yet, as time revealed, her leadership style was riddled with gaps. For one, she struggled with the tactical aspects of strategy. She could inspire her team with uplifting speeches, but when it came to execution, her lofty ideas often failed to materialize into concrete results. Even as red flags began appearing—falling quarterly revenues, skyrocketing employee turnover—Sarah was not adept at facing these challenges head-on.

In this chapter, we'll use NexaTech's journey as a backdrop to explore the various types of leadership deficiencies that can hamper an organization. We'll dissect common pitfalls, like a lack of strategic clarity, ineffectual communication, and an inability to adapt during crises. And yes, we'll discuss the consequences, which extend far beyond just numbers on a balance sheet. Leadership deficiencies affect team morale, innovation, and ultimately, an organization's long-term viability.

By the end of this chapter, you'll be equipped with practical tools to identify and tackle your own leadership gaps. After all, the first step in solving any problem is recognizing there is one. The NexaTech story serves as a cautionary tale, reminding us that the risks of leadership deficiencies are all too real and can strike at the very heart of an organization's identity.

In our fast-paced, ever-changing business landscape, understanding your weaknesses as a leader isn't just a matter of personal growth—it's a business necessity. As you navigate this chapter, consider it a roadmap for steering clear of the pitfalls that befell NexaTech, ensuring that your organization remains resilient, competitive, and above all, led with wisdom and insight.

Unearthing Common Leadership Gaps

Within every leader, there lies a hidden geography, a landscape filled with towering strengths and cavernous weaknesses. Unseen, these weaknesses can subtly undermine a leader's effectiveness. The first step towards addressing these gaps is to unearth them, shedding light on the shadowy recesses of our leadership abilities.

When the Harvard Business Review analyzed thousands of 360-degree reviews, they discovered that one of the most common leadership gaps was failing to provide appropriate feedback. It seems so simple on the surface, but leaders often struggle to deliver constructive feedback in a way that encourages growth and learning. Consider the case of Fiona, a senior executive at a Fortune 500 company. Her team was high-performing and motivated, but they consistently reported feeling 'in the dark' about their performance. Fiona believed she was protecting them from criticism, but her silence instead bred uncertainty and stagnation.

Just as crucial as providing feedback is the ability to receive it. Leaders often fall into the trap of becoming too insulated from criticism, engendering a culture where feedback is seen as disloyalty. This lack of openness stunts personal growth and inhibits the organization's potential. Take Robert, a CEO of a thriving tech startup. He was admired for his vision but was often seen as 'untouchable'. This gap led to a slow but steady erosion of trust within the organization, ultimately stunting its growth.

Another common gap lies in the failure to develop others. The best leaders aren't just skilled in their own right; they're also committed to nurturing the skills of those around them. Consider Jennifer, a sales manager who was known for her remarkable sales figures. However, her team struggled to meet their targets. Jennifer was so focused on her own achievements that she neglected to mentor her team members, a gap that left the team struggling and demotivated.

A significant gap seen even in seasoned leaders is the inability to balance assertiveness with empathy. Leaders often swing too far one way, either bulldozing over others with their assertiveness or, on the flip side, being overly empathetic to the point of indecisiveness. Think of Patrick, a project leader known for driving results. However, his aggressive approach often led to high turnover in his team. Balancing assertiveness and empathy is a delicate act, but mastering it can greatly enhance a leader's effectiveness.

In the unrelenting drive for results, leaders often overlook the importance of building relationships. Leading isn't just about achieving goals; it's also about connecting with people on a personal level. Leaders who fail to form genuine connections find themselves at the helm of disengaged teams. Take Laura, a CFO who was exceedingly competent in her role. Despite her capabilities, Laura struggled to inspire her team, largely because she neglected to build meaningful relationships with them.

Lastly, a subtle but impactful gap is the lack of strategic thinking. Too often, leaders get mired in the daily operations and lose sight of the bigger picture. This myopic view can lead to missed opportunities and a lack of innovation. Consider David, the head of a production unit in a manufacturing company. His fixation on daily output prevented him from noticing a growing market trend that could have positioned his company as an industry pioneer.

These examples are mere glimpses into the complex terrain of leadership gaps. The common thread running through them is a neglect of the human element of leadership. It's a stark reminder that leading isn't merely about driving results but also about guiding, nurturing, and connecting with others. While the task of unearthing these gaps may be daunting, it is the first crucial step in the transformation of an effective leader. For it is in acknowledging our weaknesses that we can begin to chart a path towards strength and resilience.

Evaluating the Impact of Leadership Deficiencies on Organizations

Like a ripple in a pond, leadership deficiencies can spread far and wide within an organization, subtly yet pervasively influencing its culture, performance, and overall health. But how do we measure the extent of this impact? Let's delve into the compelling stories of organizations and leaders that illustrate the profound consequences of these gaps.

Begin with an ambitious tech startup, Nexalto Tech, poised to disrupt the industry with its innovative solutions. At the helm was Marcus, a brilliant visionary with a notable weakness: he struggled with giving and receiving feedback. As Nexalto Tech grew, a culture of silence took root. Without constructive criticism, the team's growth stagnated. Their innovative spark dimmed, and the once promising startup found itself struggling to keep up with industry advancements.

Meanwhile, consider the story of PharmEX, a pharmaceutical giant, whose CEO, Robert, was known for his assertiveness. His go-getter attitude had catapulted the company to new heights. However, his leadership style left little room for empathy, leading to a high employee turnover rate. The exodus of talent led to a decrease in productivity and a noticeable drop in morale among the remaining employees.

Now let's turn our attention to Cr8 Finance, a powerhouse in the financial industry. Jennifer, a high-performing executive, was renowned for her sales prowess. Yet, her failure to develop others resulted in a weak sales team. Despite her stellar individual performance, the overall sales figures were uninspiring. Her leadership gap cast a long shadow over the team's potential.

For Collin, a project leader in a thriving marketing firm, results were all that mattered. His relentless drive, however, manifested as an aggressive approach, creating a stressful environment for his team. Over time, the project team's performance declined, leading to missed deadlines and lost clients, significantly impacting the firm's reputation and bottom line.

At a popular e-commerce company, Laura, the CFO, was highly competent but failed to build relationships with her team. The result? An uninspiring work environment marked by disengaged employees. Productivity dropped, and so did the company's financial performance. Laura's leadership gap had a direct impact on the organization's bottom line.

On the manufacturing front, David led a successful production unit but was so fixated on daily output that he failed to strategize effectively. His unit missed out on a lucrative market trend, resulting in lost opportunities and a significant reduction in potential revenue. His leadership gap was a costly misstep for the company.

Through these stories, it becomes abundantly clear

that leadership deficiencies significantly affect organizations, reverberating through every level. A lack of feedback can smother innovation, while an absence of empathy can lead to talent drain. Neglecting to develop others can stunt team performance, and an aggressive approach can diminish productivity. A failure to build relationships can dampen employee engagement, while a lack of strategic thinking can result in missed opportunities.

Each story underscores the undeniable truth that leadership deficiencies are not just individual shortcomings. Instead, they reverberate throughout the organization, influencing its culture, its performance, and ultimately its success. These stories serve as a powerful reminder that leaders are the architects of their organizations' fate. It is incumbent upon them to bridge these leadership gaps, not just for their own growth but for the vitality and resilience of the organizations they lead.

Just as an experienced sailor knows to correct course at the first sign of deviation, an effective leader must be ever vigilant, ready to address these gaps before they widen into insurmountable chasms. The task may seem daunting, but the rewards are immense. A leader who can chart this course with determination and skill can shape not only their own fate but that of their entire organization. After all, leadership isn't just about leading; it's about transforming — oneself, one's team, and ultimately one's organization.

As we journey through these pages, let's strive to shine a light on our leadership gaps and begin the transformative process of bridging them. The first step is acknowledging these deficiencies. Only then can we navigate the path towards effective leadership and guide our organizations into a future marked by success and resilience.

Leadership Deficiencies and Crisis Response

Crises are inevitable. When they strike, their shockwaves can shake organizations to their core, exposing vulnerabilities that might otherwise remain unnoticed. It is at this critical juncture where the mettle of a leader is truly tested, and deficiencies, if present, are thrown into sharp relief. As we explore the impact of leadership deficiencies on crisis response, we'll illuminate this intricate relationship through compelling narratives that underline its significance.

Consider the case of a major hospital network facing a sudden outbreak of a deadly virus. With patient numbers soaring and resources stretched thin, the CEO, Dr. Stanley, faced a grave crisis. Known for his analytical acumen, Stanley was quick to devise an action plan. However, his lack of empathy made his communication seem cold and detached, causing alarm and distress among his staff, leading to errors in patient care and low morale in the workforce.

Then there's the story of an environmental NGO, caught in a funding scandal that threatened its reputation. Angela, the organization's leader, renowned for her charisma and visionary ideas, found herself navigating turbulent waters. Her charisma, while inspiring in good times, was not enough to allay stakeholders' concerns in a crisis. Her inability to clearly articulate a path forward and lack of transparency deepened the crisis, leading to a significant loss in donor support.

Let's also consider a tech firm that suffered a massive data breach. Kendall, the CTO, was technically proficient but struggled with communication. His inability to articulate the scope of the breach and the steps taken to rectify it, created a panic among clients. Consequently, the firm suffered massive client losses, causing a significant hit to their revenue.

In the heartland of America, severe flooding devastated a small town. Mayor Collins was popular for his jovial nature and community outreach. Yet, when disaster struck, his lack of strategic planning was laid bare. His failure to coordinate effective relief efforts amplified the crisis, leading to immense hardship for the town's residents and long-term damage to his leadership.

Then, there is the airline industry giant, Sky2 Airlines, which suffered a terrible accident. CEO Douglas, known for his strong decision-making skills, quickly enacted safety checks across the fleet. However, his autocratic style and failure to seek inputs from his team led to overlooking crucial safety considerations, resulting in another incident, damaging the company's reputation and passenger trust further.

Each of these stories brings to light the potential danger of leadership deficiencies in crisis response. Dr. Stanley's lack of empathy amplified distress during an already stressful crisis. At Angela's charisma couldn't shield her organization from the repercussions of a financial scandal, as her lack of clarity and transparency only deepened mistrust. Kendall's communication deficiencies stoked panic and lost business following a data breach. Mayor Collins' lack of strategic planning at the small town escalated the crisis caused by flooding. Finally, the autocratic style of Douglas resulted in overlooking critical details, further endangering the company and its customers.

Leadership deficiencies don't merely remain as individual limitations. In times of crisis, they can unravel an organization, exacerbating the situation, and undermining the recovery process. The ability to respond to crises effectively is a testament to the quality of leadership. When leadership is deficient, crises management becomes a Herculean task, often with dire consequences.

What makes these stories truly compelling is not just their narrative of failure but the opportunity for learning they present. They underscore the significance of understanding our own leadership gaps, particularly when it comes to crisis management. For it is often in the heat of crisis, under the harshest of spotlights, where these gaps become most apparent, and their effects most profound.

Crises are an unavoidable part of organizational life. How leaders respond to these crises, particularly those with leadership gaps, can significantly influence the course of their organization's destiny. Through the lens of real-world crises, we have seen the profound impact of these leadership deficiencies. As we continue, we will learn how we can bridge these gaps, making our organizations not only more resilient in the face of crisis but also more robust in their journey towards growth and success.

Leadership Gap Analysis

One of the surest ways to drive growth is not by focusing on strengths, but rather by identifying and addressing gaps. Leadership, like any other discipline, has areas of strength and areas of weakness. Spotting leadership deficiencies can be challenging, particularly for those immersed in the helm of affairs. A meticulously executed leadership gap analysis can be an invaluable instrument for identifying these blind spots and for formulating a strategic course of action. With that in mind, let's uncover the tools and tips that can guide leaders in conducting an effective Leadership Gap Analysis.

1. Understanding Your Leadership Competencies:
The initial step in conducting a leadership gap analysis is understanding your leadership competencies. You might be adept at making quick decisions, or perhaps your strength lies in the area of team building. Recognize these strengths and write them down. Reflect on the instances that illustrate these competencies, like that successful project you led or that crisis you averted.

2. Identifying Key Leadership Behaviors:
Leadership is not just about competencies, but behaviors too. How you interact with your team, communicate your vision, and handle criticism are all elements of leadership behavior. Jot down these behaviors, and pay close attention to those that have been particularly effective.

3. Requesting 360-Degree Feedback:
One of the most insightful ways to uncover your leadership gaps is through 360-degree feedback. Invite your colleagues,

superiors, and subordinates to provide feedback on your leadership style, decision-making abilities, and interpersonal skills. This kind of comprehensive input can give you a more holistic view of your leadership style, complete with its strengths and deficiencies.

4. Analyzing Leadership Deficiencies:

Once you've compiled your leadership competencies, behaviors, and feedback, analyze them to identify your deficiencies. You may realize that you struggle with delegating tasks, or perhaps your strategic planning needs fine-tuning. Pinpoint these areas of improvement and make a commitment to work on them.

5. Setting Leadership Development Goals:

With your leadership deficiencies in sight, it's time to set leadership development goals. These goals should be SMART: Specific, Measurable, Achievable, Relevant, and Time-bound. For instance, if you've identified that you struggle with delegating, you might set a goal to delegate at least one task per week to a team member.

6. Creating an Action Plan:

A goal without a plan is just a wish. Once you've set your leadership development goals, create an action plan to achieve them. If your goal is to improve your strategic planning, your action plan might include reading strategy-focused books or attending strategic planning workshops.

7. Regularly Re-evaluating and Adapting:

Leadership is dynamic, and so should be your approach to improvement. Regularly re-evaluate your leadership style, skills, and behaviors. Adapt your goals and action plans as necessary, taking into account your progress, new challenges, and changes within your organization.

❊ ❊ ❊

Leadership deficiencies, while they may seem daunting, are

not insurmountable obstacles. They are stepping stones on the path to more effective leadership. And in identifying and addressing these gaps, you're not just improving as a leader; you're charting a more successful and resilient course for your organization. Remember, in leadership, as in life, it's not our weaknesses that define us, but how we respond to them. So, pick up that pen, roll up your sleeves, and let's get to work on bridging those gaps.

CHAPTER 5 - COACHING TOWARDS CHANGE: IMPROVING LEADERSHIP THROUGH GUIDANCE

In the vast landscape of leadership responsibility, coaching emerges as a guiding light, enhancing leadership effectiveness. At its core, leadership coaching is a symbiotic partnership. Picture a seasoned mentor guiding an eager apprentice: one imparts wisdom while the other absorbs, questions, and adapts. This partnership molds leaders, sharpening their acumen to navigate organizational challenges.

Yet, how does coaching truly benefit leaders? Consider a gifted violinist, her finesse enhanced by a conductor's insight. Similarly, even adept leaders can amplify their capabilities under a coach's guidance. This chapter demystifies this process, highlighting its influence across teams and organizations.

Today's business terrain is ever evolving, where sudden upheavals test a leader's mettle. In such turbulent times, coaching becomes indispensable. A coach, akin to a seasoned sailor in a storm, provides leaders the strategies and support to weather crises. We'll further explore how adept coaching can turn challenges into opportunities for growth.

Leadership Coaching: Process and Importance

Delving into the realm of leadership coaching, we embark upon the fascinating process that transforms the potential within an individual into the profound ability to inspire, guide, and motivate others. The essence of leadership coaching lies in its duality - it is both a science, a structured process steered by established techniques, and an art, a delicate dance that adapts to the rhythm of each unique individual. This section opens up this intriguing world, illuminating the process and highlighting its importance in leadership development.

As a humming, metropolitan city pulses with life, so does an organization pulse with its employees, each playing a crucial role in maintaining the rhythm. Now imagine, a city mayor working alongside a seasoned consultant - a partnership designed to optimize the city's operations, improve the quality of life for its residents, and make it a paragon of urban development. Similarly, leadership coaching creates a symbiotic relationship between a leader and a coach, weaving a bond based on mutual respect, trust, and a shared goal - optimizing the leader's effectiveness.

The process of leadership coaching can be likened to a carefully plotted route on a nautical chart. It begins with an assessment of the leader's current state, akin to identifying the ship's location. This assessment encompasses an exploration of the leader's strengths, weaknesses, leadership style, and the challenges they face. It's a moment of reflection, like a mirror held up to the leader, offering a candid view of their current leadership landscape.

Then, with the leader's active involvement, the coach identifies the desired state - the destination. This is a future vision of the leader's capabilities and effectiveness, a glimpse into what could be. This vision is both aspirational and grounded in reality, a balance that makes it a compelling and achievable goal. The destination isn't merely a point on a map; it's a symbol of the leader's potential and the positive impact they can have on their organization.

The next phase is charting the course. The coach and leader, now partners in this expedition, collaboratively develop a personalized leadership development plan. This strategic blueprint outlines the steps necessary to traverse the path from the current state to the desired state. This process is akin to plotting a course on a nautical chart, with clearly marked waypoints representing short-term goals and the final destination symbolizing the long-term objective.

Just as a ship's voyage isn't devoid of challenges - storms, shifting currents, unexpected obstacles - the path to leadership development is laden with hurdles. Here, the coach assumes the role of a guiding light, helping the leader navigate through these challenges. By providing feedback, support, and encouragement, the coach helps the leader stay on course, reinforcing their commitment to their goals.

Coaching sessions serve as the fuel propelling the ship towards its destination. These regular interactions, be they face-to-face or virtual, provide a platform for discussion, feedback, reflection, and learning. They're a checkpoint to monitor progress, address concerns, refine strategies, and celebrate achievements. They're a recurring reminder of the leader's commitment to their growth, a testament to their dedication to becoming more effective leaders.

If we were to distill the essence of leadership coaching into one word, it would be transformation. The entire process is geared towards enabling the leader to evolve, to harness their potential, and to transform into an influential figure who can drive their organization towards success. The importance of leadership coaching, therefore, lies in its transformative power - the ability to metamorphose potential into proficiency.

Leadership coaching isn't a magic wand that conjures overnight results. It's a process that requires time, effort, patience, and perseverance. However, the fruits of this labor are bountiful. Effective leaders, honed through coaching, become catalysts for positive change in their organizations. They foster a culture of motivation, productivity, and innovation, creating ripples that can propel the organization towards growth and success.

The significance of leadership coaching extends beyond the individual leader. A well-coached leader acts as a role model, inspiring others in the organization to embrace learning and development. They foster an environment that values continuous improvement, nurturing future leaders, and promoting a culture of shared success.

So, as we dive deeper into the world of leadership coaching, we'll encounter real-world scenarios that illustrate the process and its impact. We'll uncover the nuances of the coaching relationship, delve into the details of coaching sessions, and examine the transformative effect of leadership coaching. Through these insights, we'll understand why leadership coaching isn't merely a desirable element of leadership development; it's an indispensable tool that empowers leaders to steer their organizations confidently towards their vision.

By bringing the process of leadership coaching to life and underscoring its importance, this section lays the foundation for the subsequent discussions. As we unravel the threads of leadership coaching, we'll discover its multifaceted role in enhancing leadership effectiveness and managing crises, thereby painting a comprehensive picture of this pivotal tool in leadership development.

Through it all, remember this: leadership coaching isn't about changing who you are; it's about enabling you to become the best version of yourself. It's about guiding you to harness your strengths, address your weaknesses, and develop skills that will make you an effective leader. It's a strategic guide, a companion, and a catalyst that fuels your metamorphosis into an influential leader capable of driving your organization towards its vision. It's a process that does more than just improve your leadership skills; it reinvents your entire approach to leading, setting the stage for continuous growth and impactful transformations.

Just like how a skillful gardener prunes a tree to encourage its growth, a coach gently removes the barriers that may be limiting a leader's growth, enabling them to reach their full potential. They help leaders to make informed decisions, encourage new perspectives, and support the growth of emotional intelligence. They act as catalysts, accelerating the transformation process from within.

The essence of leadership coaching is deeply rooted in communication - a continuous dialogue that facilitates understanding, promotes clarity, and propels actions. Think of it as an ongoing conversation that turns the spotlight on what is, what can be, and how to bridge the gap. This dialogue is not a monologue; it's a two-way interaction that respects the leader's views, encourages their input, and values their perspective.

Through the process of coaching, leaders can develop greater self-awareness, understanding their emotions, and how they impact their actions and decisions. With increased self-awareness, leaders can manage their emotions better, paving the way for enhanced emotional intelligence. This emotional intelligence, in turn, contributes to better interpersonal relationships, improved decision-making, and a positive organizational culture.

As the coaching process unfolds, leaders may discover latent talents, hidden strengths, and untapped potentials they didn't realize they had. This process of discovery and self-realization often leads to an increased sense of confidence, greater motivation, and an enhanced sense of purpose, acting as a key driver of their leadership effectiveness.

Coaching isn't a sign of weakness or an admission of incompetence. Instead, it's a symbol of a leader's commitment to their growth, a testament to their dedication to becoming the best they can be. It's a courageous step towards self-improvement, a bold leap towards realizing their leadership potential.

On a broader scale, leadership coaching benefits the organization as a whole. By optimizing the effectiveness of its leaders, an organization can enhance productivity, improve morale, and foster a culture of continuous improvement. As the leaders grow, so does the organization, reaping the rewards of their leaders' enhanced capabilities.

As we delve deeper into the intricacies of leadership coaching in the following sections, we'll witness its transformative power, discover its pivotal role in crisis management, and explore practical tools that facilitate this process. Through this exploration, we'll realize that leadership coaching isn't just a process; it's an experience that enriches the leader, enhances their capabilities, and empowers them to steer their organization towards success.

Coaching is a compass, pointing leaders towards their goals. It's a guidebook, offering strategies for navigating leadership challenges. It's a torch, illuminating the path towards leadership excellence. More importantly, it's a catalyst that sparks the metamorphosis of an individual into an effective leader, driving the organization towards its vision amidst unpredictable change.

Remember this: Leadership coaching is not a destination; it's a process. It's a continuous journey of learning, growth, and transformation. And in this journey, every step you take brings you closer to becoming the leader you aspire to be. As we navigate the unpredictable seas of change, leadership coaching is the steadfast lighthouse guiding us towards our desired destination.

How Coaching Enhances Leadership Effectiveness

Let's take a moment to step back and visualize leadership as a ship sailing across the vast ocean of organizational management. The leader is the captain of this ship, guiding it through calm waters and tumultuous storms alike. Now, how does coaching fit into this metaphor? Imagine coaching as the compass and the lighthouse that guide the captain - the compass providing the direction and the lighthouse offering illumination amid obscurity. Leadership coaching, hence, is a crucial beacon that aids leaders in navigating their path towards success.

Delving into the nuances of how coaching enhances leadership effectiveness, we begin by acknowledging the powerful impact of self-awareness. Self-awareness is the foundation upon which effective leadership is built. Through coaching, leaders gain invaluable insights into their behaviors, understanding how their actions influence others and the organization at large. This awareness brings clarity, enabling leaders to make informed decisions that align with their values and those of the organization.

Consider the case of a senior executive who was widely known for her technical expertise but faced challenges when interacting with her team. Through coaching, she realized that her approach, though effective for problem-solving, was inadvertently creating a culture of dependency. This awareness empowered her to adjust her leadership style, fostering a more collaborative environment that encouraged independence and innovation within her team.

Another crucial area where coaching can significantly enhance leadership effectiveness is in the development of emotional intelligence. Emotional intelligence, an essential trait of successful leaders, comprises self-regulation, motivation, empathy, and social skills. Coaching provides leaders with the necessary tools to manage their emotions, understand others' feelings, and navigate interpersonal relationships successfully.

Take the example of a CEO who had the brilliant strategic mind to steer the company to new heights but struggled with empathy. His interactions were often perceived as cold and unapproachable, impacting morale and productivity. Through coaching, he was able to understand and value the importance of empathy in leadership, leading to improved relationships with his employees and a significant increase in overall employee satisfaction and productivity.

Coaching can also prove invaluable in enhancing leaders' communication skills. Clear, consistent, and open communication is the backbone of effective leadership. Coaches can help leaders refine their communication style, ensuring their message is clear, concise, and coherent. Effective communication fosters a sense of trust, boosts morale, and ensures everyone is aligned towards a common goal.

Consider a leader who, despite having excellent strategic planning skills, was often misunderstood due to his complex communication style. Through coaching, he learned to communicate his ideas more simply and clearly. The result was improved team cohesion, better execution of strategies, and overall organizational growth.

Leadership coaching further enhances effectiveness by promoting a growth mindset – the belief that talents and abilities can be developed through hard work, effective strategies, and input from others. Coaches facilitate this shift in mindset, encouraging leaders to view challenges as opportunities for growth, thereby fostering resilience and adaptability.

Reflect upon a leader who viewed failures as career-ending roadblocks. Through the transformative process of coaching, he was able to adopt a growth mindset, viewing setbacks as steppingstones to success. This shift enabled him to bounce back from failures quicker, fostering a culture of resilience within his team.

Moreover, coaching assists leaders in developing a clear vision and mission, offering strategic guidance to help translate these into actionable goals. A clear, compelling vision inspires and motivates teams, acting as the fuel that drives organizational growth. By facilitating the development of this vision, coaching directly contributes to enhancing leadership effectiveness.

Coaching also equips leaders with tools and techniques to manage stress and avoid burnout. In the high-pressure environment that leaders often find themselves in, the ability to manage stress is crucial. Through coaching, leaders learn techniques to maintain balance, stay focused, and remain productive even under intense pressure.

The power of coaching extends to the development of strategic thinking skills. Coaches facilitate the cultivation of this skill, enabling leaders to anticipate, envision, maintain flexibility, and work with others to initiate changes that will create a viable future for the organization.

Coaching is an empowering process that strengthens a leader's ability to effectively guide their teams and organization. It's a transformative tool that cuts through the obscurity, guiding leaders to the shores of success. From enhancing self-awareness to fostering a growth mindset, from refining communication to stress management, the positive impacts of coaching are manifold and multidimensional. Indeed, coaching is the lighthouse that illuminates the path to effective leadership.

The Role of Leadership Coaching in a Crisis Context

The specter of a crisis is not an uncommon visitor to the realm of leadership. A financial downturn, a public relations scandal, a global pandemic, or an unexpected competitor entering the market are just a few examples of the crises that leaders often find themselves facing. Amid such turbulent times, the role of leadership coaching gains a whole new level of significance.

During a crisis, emotions run high, and uncertainty can breed fear. Leaders are expected to remain steadfast, guiding their teams with confidence. This is where leadership coaching steps in, acting as the North Star guiding leaders through the murkiness of crises. Coaches provide leaders with the tools and strategies needed to maintain composure, stay resilient, and keep their teams focused and motivated.

Let's consider the case of a tech start-up grappling with a serious data breach that threatened its reputation and customer trust. The CEO, a brilliant mind in technology, found himself in uncharted territory. His leadership coach, however, helped him navigate this crisis. Together, they worked on maintaining transparency, devising a remedial plan, and communicating effectively with stakeholders. The CEO was able to turn the crisis into a demonstration of the company's resilience and commitment to its customers, thereby salvaging the company's reputation.

During a crisis, leaders may also be required to make difficult decisions under pressure. This could range from financial cutbacks to strategic shifts, and each decision carries potential implications for the organization and its people. Leadership coaching can support leaders in making these tough calls. Coaches can provide a sounding board, helping leaders evaluate their options and understand the potential impacts of their decisions.

For instance, consider a manufacturing firm hit hard by an economic downturn. Faced with decreasing sales and mounting costs, the leader was forced to consider downsizing. His leadership coach helped him navigate this painful decision, ensuring he considered all alternatives and approached the process with empathy and transparency. The result was a necessary yet compassionate action that preserved the company's integrity and the remaining team's morale.

Leadership coaching can also be invaluable in helping leaders manage their own emotions during a crisis. Coaches can provide strategies to handle stress, prevent burnout, and stay resilient. These self- skills are essential for leaders who need to project stability and inspire confidence in their teams during challenging times.

Consider a leader who was tasked with steering her organization through a public relations scandal. The stress of the crisis was taking a toll on her mental health, affecting her leadership performance. Through coaching, she learned to manage her stress and remain resilient. This enabled her to guide her team more effectively and navigate the organization through the crisis.

Leadership coaching also plays a vital role in helping leaders communicate effectively during a crisis. Clear, timely, and transparent communication is crucial during a crisis, and coaches can assist leaders in honing management these skills. From deciding what information should be shared to ensuring that messages are delivered in an empathetic and understanding manner, leadership coaching can ensure that leaders communicate effectively during crises.

The benefits of leadership coaching in a crisis context are manifold. From providing emotional support to offering strategic guidance, from sharpening communication skills to fostering resilience, leadership coaching is a powerful ally for leaders during turbulent times.

As we navigate the unpredictable seas of change, let us remember that no ship is expected to brave a storm without a compass and a lighthouse. In the stormy seas of crisis, leadership coaching is that compass and lighthouse, guiding leaders safely to shore.

Leadership Coaching Plan Template

As we delve deeper into the labyrinth of leadership coaching, it becomes evident that strategic planning is a cornerstone of its effectiveness. A leadership coaching plan is the blueprint of your coaching journey, a powerful tool that guides both the coach and the coachee toward their desired outcomes. It enables you to chart a clear course, measure progress, and adapt as necessary.

Now, let us turn our attention to constructing this vital tool - the Leadership Coaching Plan Template. This guiding framework must be fluid, adaptable, and considerate of the unique needs and goals of each leader. With that in mind, here are some core components that a dynamic and effective plan should include:

1. Clarify Coaching Goals: Start with the end in mind. What does the leader hope to achieve through coaching? These goals can be diverse, ranging from enhancing communication skills to learning how to navigate a crisis. Remember, these objectives should be SMART – Specific, Measurable, Achievable, Relevant, and Time-bound.

2. Assess Current State: What are the leader's strengths and weaknesses? An honest assessment of where they stand currently provides a solid foundation for the coaching journey. Tools such as 360-degree feedback can be instrumental here.

3. Identify Skill Gaps: This step involves aligning the leader's current state with their coaching goals. What skills does the leader need to develop or strengthen to achieve these objectives?

4. Map Out an Action Plan: This is where the rubber meets the road. The action plan should detail the specific steps the leader will take to close the identified skill gaps. It might involve reading certain books, attending workshops, or practicing new behaviors in the workplace.

5. Establish a Schedule: Consistency is key in coaching. Determine how often the coach and the leader will meet and the duration of these sessions. Also, plan time for the leader to reflect on their progress and practice new skills.

6. Define Success Metrics: How will the leader know they are making progress? Defining clear metrics of success is crucial for maintaining motivation and gauging effectiveness.

7. Include a Feedback Mechanism: Continuous feedback is the lifeblood of coaching. Both the coach and the leader should regularly share their thoughts on how the coaching process is progressing and make adjustments as necessary.

8. Plan for Roadblocks: Anticipate potential challenges that might impede the leader's progress and plan how to address them. This makes the plan resilient and adaptable.

9. Document Lessons Learned: Regularly capture insights and lessons learned during the coaching process. This promotes continuous learning and provides valuable material for reflection.

10. Review and Revise: The coaching plan is a living document. Regularly review and revise it to ensure it stays aligned with the leader's evolving goals and circumstances.

* * *

Armed with these tips, you are now ready to embark on the journey of creating your own Leadership Coaching Plan. May this template serve as a dependable compass, guiding you toward the rich, untapped potentials of your leadership capabilities. Remember, the secret to successful coaching lies in strategic planning, continuous feedback, and an unwavering commitment to growth and learning.

PART III: CULTIVATING A ROBUST LEADERSHIP CULTURE

CHAPTER 6 - BUILDING A LEADERSHIP CULTURE: EMPHASIZING LEARNING AND DEVELOPMENT

In the heart of Silicon Valley, not too long ago, a tech startup was on the brink of a critical shift. With a commendable product and an enthusiastic team, they seemed to have all the ingredients for success. Yet, their growth graph began to stagnate. Angela, the company's COO, had a hypothesis. They had exceptional minds at the helm, but the culture wasn't enabling leadership at every tier. It's a scenario we've seen play out in various organizations, revealing a universal truth: the difference between thriving and merely surviving lies in the essence of a leadership-first culture.

Ask any thriving organization about their secret sauce, and amidst the cacophony of different answers, a common theme will emerge. These companies, whether they realize it or not, have integrated leadership into their very DNA. They don't just prioritize top-tier leadership; they democratize it. Every employee, regardless of rank or role, is given the tools, trust, and training to be a leader in their domain. In essence, they build a culture where taking initiative isn't just encouraged; it's expected. When leadership isn't just a role but a culture, that's when magic happens.

Now, envision a leader who doesn't rest on past laurels,

who is ever-eager, perpetually hungry for knowledge. This is the *learning leader*. Someone like Satya Nadella, who, when taking over as Microsoft's CEO, emphasized a "learn-it-all" mindset over a "know-it-all" one. The results? A reinvigorated company culture and unprecedented growth. These leaders, perpetually inquisitive, recognize that the world shifts daily. They adapt, not by relying on old successes but by continuously integrating new knowledge, being ever-responsive to the changing tides of their industries.

There's an undeniable harmony between leadership and learning. Like a well-orchestrated duet, when one rises, the other invariably follows. It's not a mere coincidence. When learning and leadership dance in tandem, there's an alchemical reaction, spawning innovation, resilience, and growth. Angela, with her keen insight, tapped into this. She didn't just train her team in the latest tech; she empowered them with leadership workshops, peer mentoring, and opportunities to lead. The outcome? A company that wasn't just working on products but was reinventing the game.

Before we embark on dissecting the strategies, the insights, and the practical tools that will aid you in weaving learning and leadership into your organization's fabric, remember Angela's startup. Reflect upon their metamorphosis. This chapter serves as more than a guide—it's a mirror, a challenge. As you progress, ask yourself: Is leadership the exception or the rule in your culture? Are you merely training employees, or are you cultivating leaders? This transformation, this metamorphosis, is within reach. The tools are at your fingertips, waiting to be wielded.

The Importance of a Leadership-First Culture

In the neon-lit streets of Tokyo, there exists a small restaurant, its entry masked by delicate noren curtains. Diners, ranging from elite businessmen to local students, patiently wait for a seat. The eatery's appeal isn't just its delectable sushi but its head chef, Hiroshi. Observing Hiroshi work is like watching a maestro conduct an orchestra. Every slice, every roll has intent. But more impressive is the way Hiroshi empowers his apprentices, allowing them to take the lead in crafting specials, ensuring they represent the restaurant's ethos. The result? An eatery that thrives, even without its maestro present. This, in essence, is the mark of a *leadership-first culture.*

Many corporations amass success based on the genius of a single leader or a close-knit group at the helm. But what happens when that genius is no longer there? The lights fade, and the momentum wanes. The antidote, it seems, isn't a single person's brilliance but a culture where leadership permeates through every rank and file.

Let's divert our gaze from the sushi masters to a tech conglomerate we're all familiar with: Apple. Post-Steve Jobs, many questioned its future. But here's the thing: Jobs had instilled a culture where leadership wasn't reserved for corner offices. It became a part of Apple's DNA, allowing the company not only to survive his loss but to innovate and expand. It's an instructive tale about the sustainability of a leadership-first culture.

At the heart of such cultures lies trust—a belief that every employee, when given the right tools and direction, can lead. It's a deviation from the old-school model of 'command and control'. Instead, it's about empowering, guiding, and sometimes stepping back, allowing employees to take the reins. Leadership, after all, isn't about dominance; it's about influence.

Consider a middle school in Copenhagen, where every student is handed a significant project each year. They're tasked with identifying problems in their community and devising actionable solutions. Notably, there's minimal teacher intervention. Come year-end, the results are staggering. From innovative recycling initiatives to community support programs, these young minds are leading. It raises a poignant question: If middle-schoolers can be leaders, why do we limit leadership in our organizations to a select few?

Resisting the lure of the traditional hierarchical model demands courage. It's about embracing vulnerability, acknowledging that the collective intelligence of a diverse group often trumps the insights of one. It's reminiscent of a renowned jazz ensemble. While there's a bandleader, every musician takes their turn to lead, their improvisations driving the performance. The music soars, not because of one but the collective.

In corporations, this approach materializes as decentralized decision-making, cross-functional teams, or open forums where ideas are welcomed, irrespective of hierarchy. The outcomes? Enhanced innovation, agility, and a workforce that's invested, seeing themselves not just as cogs but integral parts of the organization's future.

Yet, it's essential to differentiate between promoting leadership and anarchy. A leadership-first culture isn't about eliminating guidance. It's about fostering an environment where individuals feel secure enough to voice opinions, take initiative, and yes, sometimes fail. It's not the absence of direction but the proliferation of many directional voices.

One may wonder about the real-world implications of such a cultural shift. Look no further than companies like Pixar or Google. Their consistent ability to push the envelope is rooted in their culture, where leadership is ubiquitous, not isolated.

Embedding this culture requires intentional efforts. It's not about grand gestures but consistent, everyday practices. It's the CEO who, during a meeting, pauses to ask a new intern for their perspective. It's the team lead who encourages members to drive projects, providing support from the shadows.

But, why bother? Why upend tried and tested structures for this idealistic leadership model? The answer is simple yet profound: because the future is unpredictable. In a rapidly evolving world, the organizations that thrive will be those that can adapt, innovate, and pivot. And that agility comes from leadership at all levels, not just the top.

As we wrap this section, picture again Hiroshi's restaurant. Imagine a world where every employee, irrespective of title, feels the weight and privilege of that leadership mantle. Then, understand this isn't a distant dream. It's a tangible reality, waiting to be sculpted, one empowered individual at a time.

The Learning Leader: Key to Continuous Development

Imagine a quaint town in southern Italy, where the community gathers every Sunday to watch elderly men play chess in the local piazza. One of these men, Antonio, is a legend of sorts. He's never lost a game, yet every move is met with thoughtful contemplation, as if he's still learning. Antonio's strategy? He never plays the same game twice. Instead, he constantly adapts, learns from every move his opponent makes, and always seeks to evolve his strategies. The board, to Antonio, is more than just a battleground; it's a classroom.

Leadership, much like Antonio's chess games, demands this relentless pursuit of learning. However, the modern business landscape doesn't allow the luxury of time that Antonio enjoys on his lazy Sundays. Decisions must be made quickly, and stakes are often high. But therein lies the paradox. The faster-paced our world becomes, the more crucial it is for leaders to embrace learning as an essential tool.

Consider the story of Sarah, a CEO of a burgeoning tech startup. In her initial days, she relied heavily on her technical know-how to drive her company. But as the business grew, Sarah realized that her expertise, while valuable, was not enough. New challenges arose, ones that her engineering background didn't prepare her for. Instead of resisting, Sarah began setting aside dedicated hours every week solely for learning—be it about human psychology, team dynamics, or market trends. Her commitment bore fruit, and her startup transformed from a novice player to an industry trailblazer.

The essence of a *learning leader* isn't about knowing all the answers. Instead, it's about the humility to acknowledge what one doesn't know, coupled with the insatiable curiosity to find out. It's about trading the comfort of the familiar for the uncertainty of the new, understanding that growth is often birthed from discomfort.

But how does this translate in real terms? Think of industries that have seen rapid changes in the past decade —publishing, music, retail. Leaders who clung to the "this is how we've always done it" mantra soon found themselves overshadowed by those willing to learn, adapt, and innovate. The pages of corporate history are littered with companies that failed to evolve, not because they lacked resources, but because they lacked the vision to learn.

Yet, the question arises: How can leaders cultivate this learning mindset? The first step is embracing vulnerability. It requires leaders to admit, "I don't know," without fearing judgment. It's a trait often seen in the best classrooms, where teachers encourage questions, celebrate mistakes as learning opportunities, and model a growth mindset.

In the corporate realm, a learning leader might foster an environment where team members are encouraged to share articles, attend workshops, or even take short sabbaticals to pursue passion projects. These aren't just perks but strategic investments in the company's intellectual capital.

Furthermore, continuous development doesn't solely revolve around acquiring new knowledge. It's also about unlearning. Sometimes, the most potent insights come from letting go of outdated beliefs or methods, much like a sculptor chiseling away excess stone to reveal the masterpiece beneath.

There's a potent case study in Nokia, once the titan of the mobile world. Despite their technical prowess, they became ensnared in their legacy thinking. On the other hand, companies like Samsung, which prioritized learning and agility, quickly adapted to the smartphone revolution, redefining the industry's landscape.

But it's not enough for leaders to be learners in isolation. The real magic happens when this ethos permeates the entire organization. When every team member, from interns to executives, adopts a learning mindset, organizations become more resilient, innovative, and agile.

For leaders, the goal isn't to be the most knowledgeable person in the room but to foster a culture where everyone's knowledge grows collectively. It's about asking the right questions rather than having all the answers. It's about celebrating the process of discovery, much like Antonio revels in every chess game, win or lose.

The learning leader isn't just a title but a philosophy. In a world of constant flux, the leaders who will shape the future will be those who view leadership not as a destination but as a continuous path of growth and discovery.

Fusing Learning and Leadership: A Symbiotic Relationship

It was a crisp morning in San Francisco, and the fog had not yet lifted from the Golden Gate Bridge. In a cozy café downtown, a group of Silicon Valley's brightest were engrossed in discussion. Amidst them was Tonya, a mid-level manager at a tech giant. She leaned forward, her eyes sparkling with intensity, as she shared an anecdote about a recent project. To the casual observer, this might have appeared to be a regular meeting. But to those in the know, this was the legendary 'Innovator's Breakfast Club', an informal gathering where leaders met not to network, but to learn from each other's experiences.

Leadership, for all its glamor, isn't about being in the spotlight. At its heart, it's about lighting the way for others. Leaders are trailblazers, yes, but they're also attentive students, always on the lookout for lessons to internalize and impart. And where does this learning come from? Often, from the most unexpected places.

Take, for instance, the world of classical music. Renowned conductor Benjamin Zander once remarked that his best performances weren't those where he led with authority, but those where he listened intently to his orchestra, learning from each note, each pause, each crescendo. This insight wasn't just about music; it was a leadership lesson in disguise. Like a conductor, a leader must learn to listen, to harmonize diverse voices into a cohesive whole.

But why is this fusion of learning and leadership so vital? Simply put, because the world is changing at an unprecedented pace. Traditional models of doing business, once thought infallible, are now being questioned. Look at the rise of remote work, a trend that few could have predicted a decade ago. Leaders who approached this shift as an opportunity to learn—by studying best practices, gathering feedback, and iterating—were the ones who thrived.

It's not just about adapting to change, though. The melding of learning and leadership is about envisioning possibilities. When leaders wear the hat of learners, they see potential where others see problems. They ask 'What if?' and 'Why not?', questions that often pave the way for innovation.

Consider the story of Dianna, a CEO of a healthcare startup. When the pandemic hit, her company, which focused on elective surgeries, faced potential bankruptcy. Instead of panicking, Dianna chose to learn. She immersed herself in global health trends, spoke to frontline workers, and within weeks, pivoted her business to telehealth, turning a crisis into an opportunity.

This union of learning and leadership also fosters resilience. Leaders, contrary to popular belief, don't have all the answers. But those committed to continuous learning develop a reservoir of knowledge and perspectives, equipping them to navigate the murky waters of uncertainty with confidence.

Now, let's shift our lens to organizational culture. When leaders champion learning, it trickles down. Teams begin to see challenges as puzzles to be solved rather than roadblocks. A culture of curiosity emerges, where each setback is viewed as a lesson, each success as a stepping stone.

But how does one cultivate this symbiotic relationship? It begins with humility. Leaders must set their egos aside and embrace the beginner's mindset, recognizing that there's always something new to discover. It's about seeking feedback actively, even when it stings, understanding that growth often lies in discomfort.

Equally essential is creating spaces for collaborative learning. Think of it as a larger version of the 'Innovator's Breakfast Club'. Monthly roundtables, cross-departmental workshops, or even casual coffee chats can be arenas where ideas cross-pollinate, and leaders learn from the collective wisdom of their teams.

While leadership often finds itself glamorized in grand gestures and bold decisions, its true essence is far subtler. It's in the leader's capacity to learn, adapt, and grow. In this dance between leadership and learning, both partners are crucial. One sets the direction, while the other ensures the journey is rich, informed, and ever-evolving. As leaders, the challenge isn't just to lead but to learn while leading, understanding that in this fusion lies the secret to enduring success.

Cultivating a Culture of Learning and Leadership

1. **Reverse Mentorship:** Create a platform where junior employees mentor senior leaders. This not only bridges generational gaps but allows leaders to stay in touch with the ground realities. *Imagine a fresh graduate teaching the CEO about the latest digital marketing trends, and in return, learning about strategic decision-making.*

2. **Knowledge Exchange Days:** Once a month, have a day where team members share insights or skills they've acquired outside their job roles. It becomes a breeding ground for innovation. *Consider the graphic designer who learns about*

financial modeling and collaborates with the finance team to create visually engaging annual reports.

3. Foster Psychological Safety: Leaders should encourage open dialogue, where every team member feels safe to voice their opinions, ask questions, or admit mistakes. In such an environment, learning is organic, and leadership skills are honed in real-time.

4. Personal Development Funds: Allocate a budget for each employee's personal development. It could be used for courses, seminars, or books. When people learn, they naturally want to lead and apply their newfound knowledge.

5. Set Learning Goals: Alongside performance goals, encourage team members to set quarterly learning objectives. These objectives can be tied to their roles or entirely outside their current purview, fostering holistic growth.

6. Lunch & Learn Sessions: Initiate casual sessions where team members discuss books they're reading, podcasts they're listening to, or interesting articles. It's informal, yet the ripple effects on leadership thinking can be profound.

7. Recognize & Reward: Just as top performers are highlighted, have a 'Learner of the Month' or similar recognition. When learning is celebrated, it sends a clear message about its importance in the organizational culture.

8. Feedback Loops: Implement a system where feedback isn't top-down but multi-directional. Everyone learns, everyone grows, and leadership becomes a shared responsibility.

9. Collaborative Projects: Occasionally, mix teams up for certain projects. A diverse group brings varied perspectives, leading to richer outcomes and mutual learning.

10. Leadership Book Clubs: A classic yet effective tool. Choose books that challenge traditional leadership norms, promoting discussion, reflection, and application.

* * *

By nurturing both learning and leadership, organizations don't just survive; they thrive, adapt, and innovate. The world of business is ever-evolving, and standing still is akin to moving backward. The real magic happens when leaders are learners, and every learner has the potential to lead. Like Clara's bookstore, the fusion of these elements can create an atmosphere where every challenge is an opportunity, and every individual, a beacon of potential.

CHAPTER 7 - LEADING BY NUMBERS: QUANTIFYING LEADERSHIP IMPACT

Leadership transcends charismatic speeches and assertive decisions; it's also about the tangible, measurable outcomes that attest to its efficacy. While the essence of leadership is rooted in human connection, numbers offer a concrete reflection of a leader's influence and effectiveness.

Take the case of a Silicon Valley tech start-up. Guided by a dynamic CEO, the firm initially flourishes. But as it expands, challenges emerge—rising employee turnover and missed deadlines, amongst others. Despite the CEO's motivational addresses, the numbers convey a contrasting narrative, raising questions about the actual impact of leadership.

This underscores the necessity to evaluate leadership through measurable outcomes. Beyond charisma, the tangible metrics—such as employee retention, project accomplishments, and financial growth—paint a comprehensive picture of leadership's influence. They act as objective touchstones, ensuring leadership impact is not just emotionally resonant but also quantifiably demonstrable.

To discern leadership's true influence, we'll delve into diverse metrics like employee engagement levels and customer feedback. These indicators offer insights into leadership's multifaceted efficacy, serving as a navigational tool in the vast sea of quantifiable data.

Metrics further evolve in crisis situations. For instance, if our start-up faces delays in product development, does it indicate flawed leadership? Or do we turn our focus to metrics like team morale and crisis management efficiency, which shine a light on the shifting nuances of leadership during challenges?

We'll equip you with tools and strategies to effectively track and interpret leadership metrics, emphasizing the balance between numerical data and the underlying human factors. Remember, these numbers aren't mere digits—they are a reflection of your leadership journey.

In essence, this chapter is not about boiling leadership down to numbers but understanding the symbiotic relationship between actions, outcomes, and their quantifiable indicators.

The Significance of Measuring Leadership Effectiveness

There's a phrase that carries weight in business circles, "What gets measured gets managed." In its simplicity, it speaks volumes about the importance of quantifying performance - especially leadership effectiveness. The merit of this statement will be our focus, as we delve into the significance of measuring leadership effectiveness.

The stage is set with a software giant that's taking the industry by storm. At the helm is an astute CEO, applauded for her electrifying presentations and engaging meetings. When asked about their CEO, employees speak highly of her. Investors tip their hats to her strategic foresight. On face value, her leadership appears stellar. However, without any empirical measures, it's akin to valuing a house based on curb appeal without ever stepping foot inside.

To accurately assess this house - or in this case, leadership - we need to go beyond the surface. We must scrutinize its foundation, its structure. How resilient is it? How does it weather the storms? Similarly, when analyzing leadership, we need metrics that tell us not only about the charm but also about the structural integrity that upholds the charm.

Consider employee morale, engagement, and retention rates. These are the invisible "beams" that constitute the foundation of our hypothetical house. If morale is high, engagement strong, and turnover is minimal, we're looking at a well-structured, effectively led organization. On the flip side, low morale, disengagement, and high turnover often indicate structural problems within leadership.

Consider another story: a world-renowned non-profit has been making significant strides in environmental conservation. The leader is a charismatic figure who has won global recognition. However, the organization is plagued by a high attrition rate among its staff. Regardless of the leader's outward appeal, there seems to be internal discord. Here, the high attrition rate becomes a crucial measure of leadership effectiveness. It signals that something in the leadership structure needs amending.

The significance of measuring leadership effectiveness is further magnified when you consider its impact on an organization's financial health. Research conducted by the Center for Creative Leadership found that companies that perform better financially often have more effective leadership. The link between an organization's financial health and effective leadership is stark, and the numbers bear this out.

The process of measuring leadership effectiveness allows us to pinpoint areas of strength and highlight areas that need improvement. It sets clear expectations for our leaders, provides them with constructive feedback, and, crucially, holds them accountable. These metrics, these figures, give us a roadmap to navigate the vast landscape of leadership improvement.

Consider a third narrative: a school principal known for his innovative approach to teaching. His students' grades are impressive, but the teachers are burning out. While the leadership seems effective at a glance, the high burnout rate among teachers suggests a need for balance. By measuring leadership effectiveness, we not only reveal the bright spots but also expose the shadows that might need attention.

In essence, the process of measuring leadership effectiveness is far from a luxury—it's a necessity. It's the compass that navigates the waters of leadership improvement, the tool that uncovers hidden strengths and unearths potential weaknesses. This allows us to pivot from a subjective evaluation of leadership—rooted in charisma and appeal—to an objective one, anchored in tangible results and quantifiable data.

After all, effective leadership is not just about seeming competent—it's about demonstrating competence in a measurable, sustainable manner. Therefore, by measuring leadership effectiveness, we're not merely observing the surface—we're scrutinizing the very framework that upholds the edifice of effective leadership.

Methods for Evaluating Leadership Success

If we were to compare the process of evaluating leadership success to painting a picture, it would not be a simple pencil sketch. Instead, it would be a multi-layered oil painting, rich with depth, complexity, and nuance.

Imagine an enterprise that has been in the business for decades. The CEO, a second-generation family member, is known for his ability to foster an environment of innovation. But how do we determine the success of his leadership? One option is to look at the company's stock price or sales growth. It's akin to judging the painting based on its first few strokes, quick and easy, but lacking depth.

The first method to consider is the 360-degree feedback approach. Picture the CEO as the center of a circle. Feedback flows from all sides—subordinates, peers, superiors, and even external stakeholders like customers and partners. Just like the multiple hues in an oil painting, each piece of feedback offers a unique perspective. It goes beyond the apparent, revealing the CEO's impact on every stakeholder. This method offers a holistic view, one that is hard to dismiss as subjective or biased.

Let's add another layer to our painting with the method of engagement surveys. An engaged employee is one who is committed, passionate, and motivated—qualities that reflect effective leadership. When the engagement scores are high, we can infer that the leadership is connecting, inspiring, and motivating their teams. But when they're low, it indicates a disconnection somewhere along the leadership chain.

Next, we delve into the method of employee retention rates. The ability to retain talent is a testament to the strength of leadership. If a company has a revolving door of employees, it may indicate a disconnect between the leaders and the led. However, if the company is a magnet for talent, holding onto its skilled workers like a ship anchored in a storm, we can glean that its leadership is effectively navigating the choppy seas of team dynamics.

Our painting takes on more vibrancy with leadership development programs and their assessments. These programs are like mirrors that leaders can look into, reflecting their strengths, weaknesses, and potential areas of growth. Through pre and post assessments, we can measure the evolution of a leader's skill set, thus evaluating the success of their leadership.

The method of customer satisfaction surveys adds another layer. Leaders, after all, do not operate in a vacuum. Their decisions, their strategies, their vision, all have an impact on the customer experience. High levels of customer satisfaction often signal effective leadership at play.

The succession planning readiness method then provides another dimension to our painting. Effective leaders are not just concerned with the now; they're focused on the future. They ensure a pipeline of potential successors, nurturing talent for the sustainability of the organization. Therefore, the robustness of succession planning can be a telltale sign of successful leadership.

Lastly, we add the method of financial performance. While it isn't the only yardstick for leadership success, it certainly cannot be dismissed. After all, the health of an organization's bottom line is a direct reflection of the strategic decisions made by its leaders.

Thus, the canvas of evaluating leadership success is complex, layered, and multi-dimensional. It is not a monochromatic sketch, but a richly textured oil painting that reveals its depth and brilliance upon closer inspection. This complexity is necessary, for it mirrors the intricate nature of leadership itself. A single metric or method is no more sufficient to measure leadership success than a single brushstroke is to complete a masterpiece.

Assessing Leadership During and After a Crisis

Picture a city on the brink of a storm. The weather forecast warns of potential chaos, and the air carries a palpable tension. As the leader, you are the city's mayor, tasked with steering your citizens through the impending storm safely. How you perform in the face of this crisis will be a litmus test of your leadership.

Now, we understand that crises aren't confined to city borders or weather forecasts. For businesses, crises can manifest as financial downturns, scandals, sudden market changes, or even a global pandemic. Leaders, like mayors on the eve of a storm, are tasked with navigating these rough seas. The effectiveness of their leadership can often only be truly gauged during and after a crisis.

Assessing leadership during a crisis is like measuring the mayor's actions as the storm hits. It's about evaluating decisions made under pressure, the ability to instill calm and confidence, and to maintain or even boost morale. It's a testimony to their resilience, adaptability, and agility.

To illustrate this point, let's consider a scenario. Suppose a global retail giant, let's call it RetailComp, is hit by a severe supply chain disruption due to a global pandemic. The CEO, known for her dynamic leadership, faces her biggest test yet. The assessment of her leadership begins as soon as the crisis hits.

During the crisis, she pivots swiftly, strategizing with her team, exploring new suppliers, expediting digital transformation to boost online sales, and communicating transparently with stakeholders. Here, her leadership is being evaluated based on her crisis response strategy, team collaboration, and communication effectiveness.

Now, let's move on to the phase after the crisis. The storm has passed, but the cityscape is changed. The leader, like the mayor, now grapples with the aftermath. They face the task of recovery, restoration, and rebuilding. The real measure of leadership success here lies in how well they facilitate this recovery and learn from the crisis.

Going back to RetailComp, post-crisis, the CEO focuses on assessing the impact, learning from the disruption, and planning to mitigate future risks. She invests in strengthening the supply chain, improving digital infrastructure, and enhancing employee well-being programs, acknowledging the toll the crisis took on her team.

The evaluation of her leadership now focuses on how effectively she spearheads the recovery, learns from the crisis, and implements changes to fortify against future upheavals. It's about assessing her ability to turn crisis-induced disruption into an opportunity for learning and growth.

It is important to remember, however, that these assessments are not isolated. They form part of the wider leadership evaluation process, linking back to methods discussed previously, such as 360-degree feedback, engagement surveys, or financial performance. The goal is to form a holistic view of the leader's effectiveness, integrating crisis response into the broader leadership picture.

This is not just about assessing leadership during and after a crisis; it's about reassessing our understanding of leadership itself. Crises shake up the status quo, challenging leaders in ways that daily operations don't. How they respond can reveal aspects of their leadership that may remain unseen in calmer waters.

For instance, the crisis might reveal a leader's innovative streak, as they come up with novel solutions under pressure. Or it might showcase their empathetic side, as they prioritize their team's well-being amidst the turmoil. Thus, a crisis can serve as a mirror, reflecting the leader's true capabilities.

Assessing leadership during and after a crisis is a vital part of measuring leadership success. It complements traditional evaluation methods, offering unique insights into a leader's ability to navigate change, maintain resilience, and spearhead recovery. Just as the storm tests the mettle of the city and its mayor, a crisis examines the strength, resilience, and adaptability of a leader, revealing the full spectrum of their effectiveness.

Leadership Success Metrics

As we navigate the ocean of leadership, our compass is as crucial as our ship. This compass is the metrics we employ to gauge leadership success. But, similar to a physical compass, the needle must point towards a precise direction—towards accurate and relevant indicators of success. So, how do we identify these indicators? What are the most crucial metrics to consider when evaluating leadership success? Here are five key metrics, each one a vital point on our leadership success compass:

1. Engaged Employees: Our first stop is employee engagement. It is a powerful indicator of leadership effectiveness. Employees who are deeply involved and enthusiastic about their work and their workplace signal that leaders are succeeding in creating an environment conducive to engagement. Organizations like Gallup offer employee engagement surveys that allow leaders to measure this crucial metric.

2. Reduced Employee Turnover: When the ship sails smoothly, fewer people jump overboard. In other words, if leadership is effective, fewer employees will leave the organization. A low employee turnover rate can, therefore, be an important gauge of leadership success. When leaders create a supportive work culture, provide growth opportunities, and make employees feel valued, they will want to stay.

3. Achievement of Strategic Objectives: Leaders are captains steering their organizations towards their strategic goals. The achievement of these objectives is a crucial metric for leadership success. How well are leaders translating strategy into action? Have they led their teams in reaching the set targets? Achieving strategic objectives implies that leaders are effectively guiding their organizations on the path to success.

4. Leaders Developed: A leader's success can be measured not only by what they achieve but also by the leaders they help develop. The number of individuals who have grown, learned, and taken on leadership roles under their mentorship is a strong indication of their leadership success. After all, one of the most impactful legacies a leader can leave is a line of competent, confident leaders ready to carry on their work.

5. Feedback from Multisource Reviews: Finally, 360-degree feedback is a robust and comprehensive metric of leadership success. It encompasses the viewpoints of superiors, peers, subordinates, and sometimes even customers. This feedback provides a well-rounded assessment of a leader's performance, as it includes perspectives from all those affected by their leadership.

❈ ❈ ❈

These metrics are the magnetic forces that guide our leadership success compass. But remember, not all metrics carry equal weight in all situations. Leaders must discern which metrics are most pertinent to their context and objectives. For example, RetailComp's CEO's success was assessed by crisis response, recovery actions, supply chain strengthening, and employee well-being programs, emphasizing employee engagement, strategic objectives, and leadership development. Leadership success is a nuanced process, demanding the right metrics, flexibility, and context understanding. It's a compass guiding organizations through both calm and stormy seas.

CHAPTER 8 - LEADING CHANGE: ENSURING ENDURING LEADERSHIP PROGRESS

In our exploration of leadership, we've underscored the essence of change and relentless enhancement. Our pivotal focus now turns to: How do we cement these enhancements, preventing them from fading amidst organizational inertia?

Change, particularly in leadership, isn't a fleeting moment; it's an enduring journey. Leaders, influential as they are, create ripple effects throughout an organization. Think of a corporation embedding sustainability at its core; such endeavors extend beyond financial metrics, reshaping long-term societal and environmental norms.

Recognizing the need for persistent change is vital. Equally critical is grasping the mechanics of ensuring its longevity. Reflect on a tech startup adopting a flat leadership model; its innovative approach wasn't a transient phase but a continuously nurtured philosophy, demanding dedicated strategies and intrinsic comprehension of human dynamics.

In our interconnected world, reshaped by globalization, sustaining leadership adjustments amidst global shifts becomes an intricate dance. Consider a multinational's leader adapting to evolving geopolitical and market dynamics, all while ensuring internal organizational changes remain robust.

In our final segment, Leadership Sustainability

Assessment, we translate theories into practice. Leadership, more than charisma, is a quantifiable discipline. We present a pragmatic tool to continually appraise and fine-tune your leadership longevity. Imagine a seasoned sailor, always recalibrating the ship's path, reacting to the sea's whims – that's the essence of resilient leadership.

This chapter empowers you to not only champion change but also guarantee its enduring impact. Our journey is not merely about reaching leadership pinnacles but firmly establishing oneself there. Prepare for a demanding ascent, but remember, the panorama from the summit is unparalleled.

The Need to Sustain Leadership Changes

Let's peel back the layers on the necessity of sustaining leadership changes. Imagine an orchestra that starts playing a symphony with exquisite precision, only to fizzle out after a few bars, slipping back into discordance. That's what leadership changes without sustenance feel like - a promise unfulfilled, a melody unfinished. The sound bites of change that reverberate within the organization's walls need a consistent rhythm, a steady pulse that fuels the momentum of transformation.

Every leader has a role in the symphony of change. Leadership changes, once initiated, need nurturing and attention to take root and grow. Reflect on the evolution of Walmart under the leadership of CEO Doug McMillon. McMillon embarked on an ambitious journey to make Walmart a more sustainable and socially responsible company. But he understood that the initiation of these changes was just the first step. Ensuring the new values were deeply ingrained required commitment and consistency, not just from him, but from everyone in the organization.

Leadership changes are a tool to sculpt the culture of an organization. But a chisel and hammer in the hands of a sculptor are not enough to bring the statue to life; it's the persistent chipping away, the continuous refinement, that breathes life into the marble. Look at Microsoft's cultural shift under the leadership of Satya Nadella. He moved away from a culture of "know-it-all" to a "learn-it-all" mentality. The consistent reinforcement of this mindset, over time, has resulted in a resilient learning culture that has driven the company's growth and innovation.

Innovation and change are siblings born of the same parent: leadership. However, they're not identical twins. Innovation is the spark, the bright idea, the fleeting inspiration. Change is the long game, the strategy, the follow-through. It's like the development of the iPod under the leadership of Steve Jobs. The innovation was the concept of a thousand songs in your pocket. The change was the persistent improvements and iterations, refining the design, enhancing the user interface, introducing the click wheel, and syncing with the newly created iTunes.

Leadership changes touch the very core of an organization's DNA, altering how it thinks, acts, and interacts with the world. Reflect on the transformation of Xerox under the leadership of Anne Mulcahy. She took the helm when the company was on the brink of bankruptcy. The changes she initiated, from restructuring debt to focusing on high-profit areas, were not a one-time rescue act. They were sustained efforts that fundamentally altered the company's direction, paving the way for a remarkable turnaround.

Sustained leadership changes communicate a clear and consistent message, reinforcing the credibility of the leader and the organization. For instance, consider the transformation at IBM under the stewardship of Ginni Rometty. Her persistent focus on AI and cloud-based services wasn't merely a change of products, it was a testament to the company's adaptability and resilience, attributes that elevated IBM's credibility in the eyes of stakeholders.

Leadership changes, when sustained, build an undercurrent of trust within the organization. When changes are not just announced but are seen to be consistently pursued, it sends a message of commitment to the team. Reflect on the impact of Paul Polman's tenure at Unilever. His long-standing commitment to sustainable practices created a sense of trust and unity among employees, fostering a shared belief in the company's mission.

But there's also an external dimension to sustaining leadership changes. In our interconnected world, every organization exists within a network of relationships—with customers, suppliers, shareholders, and society at large. Leadership changes, when sustained, shape how the organization is perceived within this network. Consider the impact of Elon Musk's sustainability initiatives at Tesla. His unwavering commitment to renewable energy has not only helped reshape the automobile industry but has also positioned Tesla as a trusted and respected brand among consumers, investors, and environmentalists alike.

There's a nuanced interplay between change and stability in the realm of leadership. Change without stability can lead to chaos, but stability without change can breed stagnation. Sustaining leadership changes strikes the right balance, creating an atmosphere of dynamic stability. It's the tightrope that leaders must walk, with the weight of their organizations on their shoulders.

In the broader scheme of things, sustaining leadership changes is about leaving a legacy. Leaders come and go, but the changes they initiate and sustain live on, shaping the organization's destiny long after their tenure. Think about Jack Welch's impact at General Electric. His relentless focus on operational efficiency and employee productivity didn't just boost GE's bottom line during his tenure; it set the stage for the company's operational strategy for years to come.

Ultimately, the need to sustain leadership changes hinges on a simple, irrefutable fact: Change is not a destination; it's an ongoing process. A leader's task isn't just to initiate change but to embed it in the organization's marrow, making it a part of its identity, its story, its rhythm. And that is the heartbeat of sustained leadership change. It's a symphony, not a solo, a marathon, not a sprint. In this persistent rhythm, you'll find the music of transformation, a melody that reverberates through the corridors of time, echoing the tale of true leadership.

Strategies for Ensuring Lasting Leadership Improvements

When we delve into the world of leadership, sustaining improvements is akin to an accomplished dancer maintaining the perfect balance during an intricate performance. It's a delicate art. Yet, there are strategies that help ensure that leadership improvements continue to grace the stage long after the curtain rises.

Let's consider the first strategy as the establishment of a clear vision. Just as a lighthouse guides a ship safely to the harbor, a clear and consistent vision steers an organization towards its goals. Alan Mulally, former CEO of Ford, is a prime example. When he took the helm, Ford was losing billions and was on the brink of bankruptcy. Mulally not only turned Ford around, but he also ensured that the turnaround lasted. He did so by setting a clear vision – "One Ford" – a mantra that galvanized the entire organization, breaking down internal silos and fostering a culture of collaboration that outlasted his tenure.

A second strategy pivots around the concept of communication. Much like the strings of a marionette, effective communication connects the leader to the team, orchestrating a harmonious performance. When Mary Barra took over General Motors, amidst a crisis of safety recalls, she faced the daunting task of restoring trust. Her strategy? Regular and transparent communication. By openly addressing the issues, setting clear expectations, and consistently updating her team on the progress, she turned the crisis into an opportunity for organizational learning and improvement.

A third strategy revolves around the investment in people. In the realm of leadership, people are not just assets; they're the architects of sustained change. When Satya Nadella stepped into the role of CEO at Microsoft, he embarked on a bold mission to shift the company's culture. His secret weapon? Investing in people. Through initiatives like growth mindset training, he empowered his team to become change agents, fostering a learning culture that continues to drive Microsoft's success.

Another strategy to ponder upon is the integration of change into the organizational fabric. Change cannot be an isolated event; it must be woven into the very fabric of the organization. Consider Howard Schultz's return to Starbucks in 2008. Facing dwindling sales and a diluted brand, he set out to restore the company's focus on customer experience and coffee quality. His strategy involved integrating these changes into the company's operations, from closing stores for barista training to restructuring the supply chain. The result? A revived Starbucks that continues to thrive.

Fostering a culture of accountability is another strategy leaders can use to ensure lasting improvements. Accountability is the glue that holds commitment to results. When Virginia Rometty assumed the leadership role at IBM, she initiated a shift towards cloud computing and AI. To sustain this strategic shift, she fostered a culture of accountability where everyone, from executives to frontline employees, were responsible for contributing to the new strategic direction.

A sixth strategy revolves around agility, the ability to adapt and respond to change. In today's world of rapid and relentless change, agility isn't just an advantage; it's a necessity. Take the case of Adobe's transition from selling packaged software to providing cloud-based services under Shantanu Narayen. This pivot required Adobe to be agile, to learn new skills, adopt new business models, and let go of old practices. It was this agility that allowed Adobe's transformation to take root and flourish.

Next in line is a commitment to continuous learning. Leadership improvements aren't a one-and-done deal; they're an iterative process, a cycle of learning, implementing, evaluating, and learning again. When A.G. Lafley led Procter & Gamble, he fostered an environment where continuous learning was the norm. This culture of learning helped sustain improvements across product innovation, customer understanding, and brand-building.

Moreover, celebrating wins, both big and small, also contributes to sustaining leadership improvements. Celebrations not only recognize achievements but also reinforce the behaviors that led to those achievements. At PepsiCo, under the leadership of Indra Nooyi, the practice of sending 'thank you' notes to employees' families was a small but significant way of celebrating and reinforcing the company's values.

In addition, creating safe spaces for feedback and open conversations can ensure the durability of leadership improvements. When employees feel safe to voice their opinions and concerns, leaders receive crucial insights for improvement. At Pixar, Ed Catmull cultivated an environment where everyone, irrespective of their role, could give and receive feedback. This culture of open dialogue helped sustain Pixar's creative excellence over the years.

Last but not least, leaders can sustain improvements by role-modeling the changes they wish to see. When leaders walk the talk, they not only set an example but also create a powerful ripple effect. Consider Richard Branson, who has consistently modeled the entrepreneurial spirit and customer-first approach that define Virgin's brand, inspiring employees across diverse Virgin companies to do the same.

Sustaining leadership improvements isn't a sprint; it's more of a relay race where the baton of change is passed from leader to team, from today to tomorrow, from intention to action. It's a team sport, and victory lies not just in crossing the finish line, but in how the race is run. Because, in the grand theater of leadership, it's not just the opening act that matters; it's the entire performance. It's not about hitting the right notes once; it's about making beautiful music, consistently and harmoniously. After all, that's what leadership is about, isn't it? A symphony of sustained changes, a composition of continuous improvements, a ballet of balance between the old and the new, the tried and the novel.

Sustaining Leadership Improvements Amidst Global Changes

As leaders, we find ourselves standing on the shores of a vast ocean, the waves of global change crashing relentlessly. Yet, we need to sustain our leadership improvements amidst these choppy waters. It's like navigating a ship through a storm, without the luxury of calm seas, ever.

One might ponder why this is crucial. Picture the global pandemic that swept across the globe in 2020. Leadership during this time was not just about steering organizations through crisis but also about maintaining the strides made in leadership development. In fact, crises often serve as the litmus test for sustained leadership improvements, exposing the strength of their anchors.

To anchor leadership improvements amidst global changes, consider the case of Unilever under the leadership of Paul Polman. The world was barely recovering from the financial crisis of 2008 when Polman took the helm. Amidst this global change, he launched the Unilever Sustainable Living Plan, intertwining the company's growth with a positive social impact. This audacious vision remained steadfast amidst the shifting global landscape, an anchor rooted in the stormy seas of change.

Similarly, consider the leadership of Brian Chesky at Airbnb. The travel industry was hit hard by the pandemic. However, Chesky made hard decisions, including restructuring the company and focusing on local travel. Despite the drastic changes, he sustained his commitment to the company's core values, demonstrating that even in a crisis, leadership improvements can be sustained.

Then there's the story of the technology giant, Microsoft, under the leadership of Satya Nadella. In the face of rapidly changing technological landscapes and fierce competition, Nadella shifted Microsoft's focus to cloud computing. This wasn't a mere strategic shift; it was a cultural transformation that prioritized learning and innovation. This strategic and cultural transformation, despite the global changes, demonstrates a leader's ability to sustain improvements.

Leaders who manage to sustain improvements amidst global changes share a common trait: resilience. Consider Mary Barra, CEO of General Motors, who, during the 2014 safety crisis, proved that resilience is key in maintaining improvements during challenging times. Despite the crisis, she stayed committed to transforming GM's culture into one that valued safety and quality above all else.

Another key trait is adaptability. It's about adjusting the sails according to the winds of change. Consider the leadership of Sundar Pichai at Google. Amidst the dynamic changes in the tech industry, Pichai continues to adapt and lead Google towards new frontiers such as AI and cloud computing, all the while maintaining improvements in transparency, openness, and employee wellbeing.

Yet, sustaining leadership improvements isn't only about adaptation; it's about anticipation. Leaders who anticipate global changes can prepare their organizations to navigate them. When Reed Hastings, CEO of Netflix, anticipated the shift towards streaming services, he began Netflix's transition from DVD rentals to online streaming. He was steering the ship not just based on the current winds, but the ones that were forecasted.

A leader's ability to maintain a steady hand on the

helm, no matter how rough the sea, is also pivotal. Bob Iger's leadership of Disney during the 2008 economic crisis and the shift to digital media is a case in point. Iger's steady leadership ensured that Disney's culture of creativity and innovation thrived, even amidst tumultuous changes.

Moreover, it's about anchoring improvements in a strong organizational culture. This culture serves as the North Star, guiding leadership behavior amidst the changing tides. Adobe's transition from selling packaged software to providing cloud-based services under Shantanu Narayen provides an example. Narayen sustained improvements in Adobe's customer-centric culture amidst these significant changes.

Another vital aspect is engaging the collective intelligence of the organization. Just as multiple oars steer a boat faster, collective intelligence accelerates the process of sustaining improvements. At Inditex, parent company of Zara, the practice of fast-fashion was rooted in engaging collective intelligence - from designers to store managers - enabling them to navigate shifts in consumer behavior and trends.

In addition, leaders need to build and nurture trust. In a world of constant change, trust is the adhesive that binds an organization. Doug McMillon's leadership of Walmart offers a lesson. Amidst global changes like the rise of e-commerce, McMillon has maintained improvements in employee engagement and digital transformation, built on a foundation of trust and transparency.

Sustaining leadership improvements also requires the courage to take calculated risks. Leaders need to be willing to venture into uncharted waters. Elon Musk's leadership of SpaceX illustrates this. Despite the inherent risks and unpredictable changes in space technology, Musk has sustained improvements in SpaceX's innovative culture.

Lastly, there's a need for unwavering commitment. Amidst the shifting sands of global changes, this commitment serves as the bedrock on which leadership improvements stand. Howard Schultz's return to Starbucks in 2008, during a period of economic crisis and internal challenges, showcases the power of unwavering commitment in sustaining leadership improvements.

Sustaining leadership improvements amidst global changes is not an easy feat. It's like trying to paint a masterpiece while riding a roller coaster. Yet, as leaders, that's exactly what we're called upon to do. Not just to paint, but to create a masterpiece. Not despite the roller coaster ride, but because of it. After all, isn't that the essence of leadership? An art that flourishes amidst chaos, a beacon that shines brighter in the storm, a symphony that echoes louder amidst the cacophony of change.

Leadership Sustainability Assessment

When it comes to preserving the vitality of leadership improvements, having a robust toolkit is just as essential as the intention to change. The assessment tools and tips below are akin to navigational instruments, helping leaders measure their progress, identify areas for improvement, and realign their course when necessary. They serve as our compass, sextant, and map on this voyage of leadership sustainability.

1. **Resilience Index:** Just as engineers test a structure's resilience to withstand various forces, leaders need to gauge their resilience in the face of global changes. Measuring factors such as adaptability, optimism, and determination can provide insights into a leader's ability to maintain leadership improvements amidst adversity. Think of Paul Polman at Unilever, who demonstrated extraordinary resilience during the global financial crisis.

2. **Culture Audit:** A strong organizational culture is a key pillar for sustaining leadership improvements. Periodic culture audits can help leaders understand how well their culture aligns with their leadership improvements. Adobe's transition to cloud-based services under Shantanu Narayen, rooted in a

customer-centric culture, illustrates this principle.

3. Collective Intelligence Quotient: Much like an IQ measures individual intelligence, a collective intelligence quotient measures an organization's ability to pool and utilize the collective wisdom of its members. Inditex, Zara's parent company, serves as an excellent example of harnessing collective intelligence.

4. Trust Barometer: Trust is the bedrock of leadership sustainability. A trust barometer can be useful for leaders to assess the level of trust within their organization and develop strategies to build upon it. Doug McMillon's leadership at Walmart, underpinned by a foundation of trust and transparency, is a testament to this.

5. Anticipation Scorecard: Leaders need to anticipate global changes and prepare their organizations to navigate them. An anticipation scorecard, which measures a leader's ability to foresee and plan for future changes, can be a valuable tool. Netflix's transition to online streaming, led by Reed Hastings, reflects the value of anticipation.

6. Adaptability Assessment: This tool can help leaders evaluate how well they adjust their strategies based on the evolving global landscape. Sundar Pichai's leadership at Google, marked by constant adaptation to the dynamic changes in the tech industry, illustrates this principle.

7. Risk Tolerance Gauge: Leadership often involves taking calculated risks. A risk tolerance gauge can help leaders determine their comfort level with risk-taking, an essential aspect of sustaining improvements amidst unpredictable changes. SpaceX under Elon Musk provides a stellar example.

8. Commitment Scale: An unwavering commitment is crucial for sustaining leadership improvements. A commitment scale can help leaders assess the depth of their dedication to leadership improvements. Howard Schultz's return to Starbucks during a challenging period showcases the power of unwavering commitment.

9. Steadiness Meter: A steadiness meter helps leaders evaluate their ability to maintain a steady course amidst changing circumstances. Bob Iger's steady leadership during a period of crisis and transition at Disney serves as a compelling case study.

10. Organizational Feedback System: Finally, feedback from team members is invaluable in assessing leadership sustainability. An open, transparent feedback system allows leaders to understand the effectiveness of their improvements from those they lead.

❋ ❋ ❋

In essence, these tools and tips serve as a mirror, reflecting both the strengths and areas for development in our quest to sustain leadership improvements. They are not mere instruments, but catalysts that can ignite a cycle of continuous improvement, enabling us to harness the winds of global change and sail towards a horizon of sustained leadership success. After all, leadership is not a destination, but a continuous voyage of growth and evolution. A voyage that we, as leaders, have the privilege and responsibility to embark upon, charting the course for ourselves and those we lead.

PART IV: LEADERSHIP IN A CHANGING WORLD

CHAPTER 9 - LEADING IN THE AI ERA

Artificial Intelligence (AI) has ushered us into a defining moment in human history, reshaping leadership at the intersection of human intellect and machine prowess. Much as the Industrial Revolution redefined leadership norms, AI prompts a reimagining of contemporary leadership strategies. In this era, leaders are not mere observers but key players sculpting the AI narrative.

Like an orchestra conductor, today's leaders must synchronize human intuition with AI precision. This integration demands more than just AI knowledge; it necessitates an adaptable mindset. Leaders must view AI as an ally, enhancing capabilities and offering actionable insights, while preserving the invaluable human essence of leadership.

However, this integration isn't about rendering humans obsolete. While AI can offer data and patterns, interpreting these within an organizational context remains a human prerogative. This delicate equilibrium between AI and human acumen defines the new leadership paradigm.

Global crises, like recent pandemics, underscore AI's role in aiding leaders during tumultuous times. Harnessing AI during such events demands strategic foresight and an understanding of AI's strengths and limitations. To assist in this journey, we offer practical tools, including a checklist, ensuring your leadership remains AI-aligned yet human-centric.

In the AI era, leaders require a revamped toolkit and mindset, seeing AI not as a cure-all but as a powerful augmenter of human skills.

AI and Leadership: The Emerging Dynamics

As we edge deeper into the age of AI, we are witnessing an epochal shift in leadership dynamics. This change is not merely about adding AI to the leadership toolbox; it's about reshaping the very fabric of leadership, stretching its contours, and finding new definitions of what it means to lead. We're no longer playing checkers on a two-dimensional board; we're engaged in a complex game of three-dimensional chess where the pieces are evolving even as we strategize our moves.

Consider the case of a multinational corporation deploying AI to manage inventory and logistics. The AI system's predictive abilities reduced stock wastage by 20% and improved delivery times by 30%. The leader of this corporation didn't just utilize AI but also had to manage the ramifications of this technology on their workforce, a task that required immense tact and insight.

Traditionally, leadership has been human-centered, anchored in relationships, and driven by empathy. The arrival of AI as a co-worker in the leadership space challenges this dynamic. Leaders are now managing hybrid teams of humans and AI, and this requires a distinct approach. Navigating this new terrain requires leaders who can straddle the world of algorithms and the world of human emotions, harmonizing the two to yield an efficient and empathetic workplace.

Leadership, in essence, is the art of influencing others towards a common goal. With AI in the picture, the act of influence extends beyond humans. Consider an AI that assists in decision-making. Its recommendations are based on complex algorithms that process vast amounts of data. The leader's role here is to understand and interpret these recommendations, influence their integration, and manage the resulting outcomes.

In an AI-driven workplace, leaders will find themselves at the intersection of technology and humanity. For instance, an AI might recommend laying off a percentage of the workforce for cost efficiency, but a leader must weigh this against the human cost, the impact on morale, and the organization's values. This is the emerging dynamic where a leader must act as the bridge between cold data and warm human realities.

Yet, amidst these challenges, AI also presents a valuable opportunity. By taking over routine tasks, AI frees leaders to focus on what they do best - envisioning the bigger picture, cultivating a culture, and building relationships. Leaders can now invest more time in their teams, empowering them, understanding their needs, and fostering a collaborative environment.

The impact of AI on leadership dynamics extends to how leaders learn and grow. With AI providing data-backed insights into their performance, leaders have a unique opportunity to enhance their self-awareness. By interpreting data about their decision-making patterns, communication style, and team interactions, leaders can identify their strengths and areas of improvement.

As leaders, we cannot underestimate the importance of learning to 'speak AI'. This does not imply becoming data scientists but understanding the basics of AI technology. It's like learning a new language to communicate with a colleague from a different country. The language of AI includes understanding data, algorithms, and machine learning. The more fluently a leader speaks this language, the more effectively they can harness AI's potential.

Despite AI's growing influence, the core tenets of effective leadership - integrity, empathy, vision - remain unchanged. The shift lies in how these principles are applied in the context of AI. This balance between the timeless and the timely is a key dynamic in AI-impacted leadership.

Embodying this balance requires a new breed of leaders, ones who can embrace ambiguity, learn continuously, and lead with curiosity and humility.

Just like the steam engine transformed leadership during the Industrial Revolution, AI is reshaping leadership in the Information Age. However, unlike the steam engine, AI isn't just a tool; it's a team member, a consultant, a mirror reflecting our leadership styles. This multi-faceted role of AI is creating an intricate new dance of leadership, where the steps are evolving even as we learn them.

AI is a powerful tide reshaping the shores of leadership, but leaders are not driftwood carried by this tide. They are the sailors who can chart the course of this change. They are the architects who can shape the AI-impacted leadership landscape. The challenge and the opportunity lie in understanding these emerging dynamics and transforming them into effective strategies.

As we conclude this exploration, let's remember that AI doesn't diminish the role of a leader; it amplifies it. With AI as an ally, leaders can redefine the frontiers of their influence, extending it from the boardroom to the server room. As leaders in the age of AI, we are standing on the brink of an exciting new era, an era that beckons us not just to adapt but to evolve, to metamorphose.

Navigating these emerging dynamics may feel like navigating a labyrinth. But remember, every labyrinth has a thread that leads to its heart. In our context, that thread is the understanding that while AI is changing the 'how' of leadership, the 'why' remains deeply human - to create a shared vision, to empower teams, and to make a meaningful impact. As we step into this AI-influenced world, let's hold on to this thread, using it to guide our strategies, our decisions, and our growth.

Leadership Adaptability to AI

Adaptability has always been a leadership imperative, but in the age of AI, it takes on a unique complexity. The adaptability we're talking about here isn't merely about learning new skills; it's about reshaping mindsets, embracing ambiguity, and navigating the intricacies of the human-machine relationship. It's a dance of change, where the rhythm is set by the relentless beat of technology and the choreography involves integrating AI into our leadership ethos.

Let's consider a real-life example, the transformation of a traditional retail brand that embarked on the journey of integrating AI into its operations. The company introduced AI-powered chatbots to handle customer service, a move that freed up human employees to focus on strategic tasks. But this change wasn't without its challenges. The leadership had to manage the apprehension among the staff, train them to work with AI, and create a culture that valued AI not as a threat but as a partner.

A key aspect of leadership adaptability to AI is the ability to unlearn. Leaders are often accustomed to linear problem-solving and decision-making. But with AI in the mix, the decision-making landscape becomes multidimensional. For example, AI might offer insights based on data that contradict a leader's intuition. A leader's adaptability lies in their willingness to unlearn their instinctive decision-making approach and embrace a data-driven one.

Adapting to AI is also about creating an organizational culture that is not intimidated by AI but sees it as an opportunity. This demands leaders who are not just change agents but also translators, decoding the language of AI for their teams, and demystifying the change it brings. Leaders must create an environment where curiosity about AI is encouraged, where failure in the face of new tech is seen not as a setback but as a steppingstone to innovation.

Leadership adaptability to AI is also about acknowledging and managing the ethical implications of AI.

With AI's ability to collect and analyze vast amounts of data, issues of privacy and consent take center stage. An adaptable leader must navigate these tricky terrains, ensuring that the use of AI aligns with the organization's ethical standards and societal norms.

Consider the hypothetical scenario of a leader relying on AI for recruitment. The AI tool, based on past data, might exclude certain demographics from the recruitment process. An adaptable leader would recognize this bias, challenge the AI's decision, and ensure an inclusive recruitment process. Adaptability, in this case, manifests as the ability to question AI, to ensure it's a tool for equity and not bias.

A critical facet of leadership adaptability to AI is emotional intelligence. As leaders manage hybrid teams of humans and AI, they must display empathy towards their human team members. The anxiety and uncertainty that AI might induce in the team cannot be underestimated. An adaptable leader is one who acknowledges this emotional landscape, offering reassurance and clarity in the face of AI-induced change.

Yet, amid these challenges, AI also presents an exciting opportunity for leadership growth. With AI taking over routine tasks, leaders have the time and mental bandwidth to focus on strategic thinking, team building, and culture creation. Adapting to AI, then, is also about seizing these opportunities for growth and innovation.

But how does one cultivate this adaptability? One strategy is to embrace a learning mindset. Leaders must stay updated with AI trends, understand its implications, and continually evolve their leadership style. This might involve formal learning programs, self-education, or collaborative learning where leaders and teams learn together.

The adaptability to AI is also about building resilience. In the face of rapid AI developments, there will be failures, setbacks, and unforeseen challenges. Leaders must have the resilience to navigate these roadblocks and the ability to foster a similar resilience in their teams.

Adapting to AI is not a one-time exercise but an ongoing process, a rhythm that leaders need to integrate into their leadership dance. As AI evolves, so should leadership. This fluidity, this willingness to grow and evolve, is at the heart of leadership adaptability to AI.

L of algorithms and empathy. It's a dance where the steps are not fixed but evolve with the music of AI. It might seem like a complex dance, but with adaptability as our guide, we can not only learn the steps but also add our unique flair to it. As we step onto this dance floor, let's remember that while AI changes the rhythm, the music of leadership – its purpose, its vision, its human-centricity – remains the same. Adapting to AI isn't about losing our leadership essence to technology; it's about amplifying this essence with the power of AI.

AI and Leadership During Global Crises

The challenge of navigating a global crisis, whether it's a pandemic, an economic downturn, or a climate disaster, becomes magnified when it is combined with the ever-evolving landscape of artificial intelligence. These two dimensions of change — one spontaneous and unpredictable, the other systematic yet uncertain — create a leadership challenge that is unparalleled. Yet, they also offer opportunities for innovative solutions that are transformative in nature.

Consider the global healthcare industry during the onset of the COVID-19 pandemic. The abrupt and overwhelming demand for healthcare services tested the capacities of global healthcare systems. In this challenging scenario, AI offered a lifeline. AI-powered robots were deployed to disinfect hospital wards, telemedicine platforms leveraged AI to offer online consultations, and AI algorithms were used to speed up vaccine research.

However, the seamless integration of AI during a crisis

is no easy task. It requires leaders who can swiftly adapt, make informed decisions, and guide their teams through uncharted territories. These leaders must balance the tension between the pressing urgency of the crisis and the careful deliberation required to implement AI effectively. The task is daunting, but the leaders who navigate it successfully often rewrite the rulebooks of crisis leadership.

A key role that leaders play in this context is acting as a bridge between AI and their teams. During a crisis, the stress and fear of the unknown can magnify the apprehensions around AI. Here, leaders must step in as translators, making AI relatable and accessible to their teams. By doing so, they not only foster a positive AI culture but also accelerate the adoption of AI solutions during the crisis.

Leadership during crises also involves tapping into the predictive capabilities of AI. Data-driven insights can help leaders anticipate the trajectory of the crisis and strategize accordingly. A case in point is Taiwan's successful handling of the COVID-19 pandemic, where AI-driven data analytics played a critical role in shaping the country's swift and effective response.

Yet, using AI during crises isn't without its ethical dilemmas. With crisis often comes the urgency to bypass usual protocols, which might include essential ethical considerations around AI usage. Leaders are then tasked with the delicate balance of harnessing the power of AI while ensuring ethical standards are not compromised. It's a tightrope walk that tests a leader's integrity and judgment.

Emotional intelligence, a critical leadership quality, takes on a new meaning in the context of AI during crises. Leaders not only need to empathize with their team's emotional responses to the crisis but also understand their reactions to AI-driven changes. The leaders who can acknowledge this dual emotional landscape, offering reassurance and clarity, can foster a resilient and adaptable team culture.

Leadership in the age of AI during global crises is also about forging partnerships. The magnitude of crises often requires collaborations that extend beyond the boundaries of one organization. Here, leaders must leverage AI to build data-sharing alliances, foster collaborative problem-solving, and create solutions that are impactful on a global scale.

The ability to lead during global crises powered by AI is also about resilience. The road to crisis resolution, paved with AI, is filled with roadblocks – technical glitches, resistance to AI, ethical dilemmas. Leaders must navigate these roadblocks with resilience and determination, modeling a similar resilience for their teams.

Leaders must also be prepared for the long-term implications of using AI during crises. The crisis might be temporary, but the AI changes implemented can have lasting effects on the organization and its culture. Anticipating these changes, preparing the team for them, and integrating these changes into the organization's strategic narrative is a crucial aspect of crisis leadership.

The final, and perhaps most crucial, piece of this leadership puzzle is maintaining a human-centric approach. Amid the chaos of a crisis and the excitement of AI, leaders must never lose sight of the human element. Decisions should be made not just based on data but also on the basis of compassion, empathy, and societal good.

Leading during global crises in the age of AI is about navigating the confluence of AI and crisis with agility, foresight, and compassion. It's about harnessing the power of AI to solve, to innovate, and to transform, while keeping the human at the heart of leadership. It might seem like an insurmountable challenge, but with the right leadership mindset, it can become an opportunity to redefine the boundaries of crisis leadership.

As we gear up to lead in this unique landscape, let's remember that while the terrain is unfamiliar and the challenges are many, our leadership compass — guided by purpose, integrity, and empathy — remains our most reliable tool. In the dance of leadership amidst AI and crises, this compass is our rhythm, our anchor, and our guide.

Leadership in AI Checklist

The realm of leadership in an AI-dominant world is as challenging as it is exciting. Leaders have to navigate a unique blend of technological advancement and ethical quandaries, all while remaining true to their fundamental leadership traits. Navigating this world requires a distinct set of tools and strategies. Let's delve into some tips and a checklist that can guide leaders as they shape their approach towards leadership in the age of AI.

1. **Foster AI Literacy:** Knowledge empowers action. It's important to develop a fundamental understanding of AI, its capabilities, and its limitations. This includes understanding the language of AI, its various applications, and its potential ethical implications.

2. **Cultivate a Data-Driven Mindset:** In the age of AI, data is the lifeblood of decision-making. Encourage your team to utilize data when making decisions and setting strategies. This doesn't mean neglecting intuition, but rather integrating data insights into your intuitive processes.

3. **Develop an AI Ethics Framework:** Create a set of guidelines that outline the ethical use of AI in your organization. This should include data privacy, transparency, and accountability principles. Remember, ethical considerations should never be an afterthought in AI implementation.

4. **Embrace Change Management:** The integration of AI into your organizational operations will inevitably bring change. Be proactive about managing this change by communicating clearly, providing necessary training, and addressing any concerns that arise.

5. **Harness AI for Crisis Management:** Understand and utilize the potential of AI in crisis management. From predictive

analytics to automate response mechanisms, AI can provide invaluable tools during crises.

6. Be a Translator: Part of your role as a leader is to make AI accessible to your team. Break down complex AI concepts into understandable language, and highlight how these technologies can support individual roles and the wider organization.

7. Maintain a Human-Centric Focus: Despite the centrality of technology, never lose sight of the human element. Empathy, emotional intelligence, and a commitment to your team's wellbeing should always form the core of your leadership strategy.

8. Leverage AI for Collaborative Alliances: Use AI to strengthen collaborations and partnerships. Shared data and integrated AI platforms can lead to more powerful problem-solving and strategic planning.

9. Plan for the Long-Term: AI is not a quick fix, but a long-term commitment. When implementing AI, consider how it aligns with your strategic goals and the long-term vision of your organization.

10. Celebrate Wins, Learn from Losses: As with any change, there will be successes and failures with AI. Celebrate the wins to foster a positive culture around AI. Similarly, don't shy away from the losses. Use them as opportunities for learning and growth.

❋ ❋ ❋

As leaders navigate the tumultuous seas of AI, this checklist serves not as an exhaustive map, but as a compass – offering direction but still requiring the leader's intuition, insight, and judgment to reach the destination. The balance between technological mastery and human touch, data-driven strategy, and ethical integrity, will define the effective leader in the age of AI.

CHAPTER 10 - THE TIMELESS TRAITS OF LEADERSHIP

While the world of leadership frequently sees shifting trends, certain traits endure across ages, industries, and cultures. These qualities define the evergreen leader, consistently shining through their ability to motivate, guide, and impact, regardless of evolving circumstances.

Imagine a CEO in New York fostering trust through open dialogue and a school principal in Kenya embodying service and humility. Despite the stark differences in their environments, both demonstrate enduring leadership traits that spark loyalty, drive, and achievement.

Evergreen leaders are architects of their surroundings, with qualities that don't fade under strain or adversity. Instead, they bloom—maturing with each challenge, gaining strength with every experience. From boardrooms to playing fields and academic arenas, foundational leadership attributes like trust, vision, empathy, resilience, and adaptability remain universally revered.

Take the story of a mayor, whose composed demeanor during a disaster and faith in community cohesion inspired a town to rise above a crisis. Such leadership isn't merely situational but is deeply ingrained within.

But what makes these traits so innate in some? Is it natural or can it be nurtured? As our world speeds up, driven by technology and connectivity, does age-old leadership still matter?

Modern leadership, amidst rapid innovations, requires adaptability. However, timeless leaders maneuver these changes by integrating age-old wisdom with fresh insights, filtering lasting leadership essence from transient trends.

In chaotic times, timeless leaders shine, blending core principles with evolving realities. They don't resist change but leverage it. Acting as steadfast anchors in a volatile world, this chapter delves into the essence of timeless leadership, offering strategies for cultivating such traits and providing a tool to assess and refine your leadership journey.

The Qualities of a Timeless Leader

Like a grand oak standing tall in a forest of ever-changing foliage, timeless leaders possess certain distinctive qualities. These qualities persist through every season of leadership, unaltered by shifting trends or the passing of time. Let's consider each of these qualities, painting them vividly through real-world scenarios, illustrating their undeniable value.

Integrity forms the heartwood of the timeless leader. Consider the actions of the CEO of a successful manufacturing company. When the discovery of a potential product flaw put millions at stake, she chose transparency over obfuscation. It would have been easy to gloss over the problem, to hide it under mountains of corporate double-speak. Instead, she faced it head-on, informing consumers and stakeholders, absorbing financial losses, and earning a reputation for honesty that far outvalued the short-term monetary loss. Integrity, as they say, is doing the right thing, even when no one is watching.

Then, there is **empathy**, the ability to understand and share the feelings of others. This was aptly demonstrated by a team leader at a tech startup, who despite pressing deadlines, noticed a decline in one of his coder's performance. Rather than chastising the employee, he took the time to engage in a personal conversation, discovering that the coder was going through a challenging personal situation. The leader's empathetic response, offering flexibility and emotional support, not only boosted the employee's morale but also fostered a deeper sense of loyalty within the team.

Resilience shines as a vital quality. This becomes evident when we recall a non-profit director who, during an economic downturn, faced significant funding cuts. Many doubted whether the organization could survive, but the leader remained undeterred. Through resourceful problem-solving, the mobilization of volunteer support, and creative fundraising, she steered her organization through the storm. Her resilience, in the face of potential catastrophe, helped her team to keep faith and continue their valuable work.

The gift of **vision** is another essential trait. A prime example is a renowned architect who was known not just for designing buildings but for envisioning communities. His projects did not stop at blueprints and construction but extended to how spaces would be used, how people would interact, and how communities would form over time. His profound vision led to spaces that were cherished for decades, standing as testaments to thoughtful, visionary design.

Now consider **adaptability**, a trait more crucial than ever in our fast-paced world. A once successful retail giant faced declining sales with the rise of e-commerce. It would have been easy for the leader to insist on traditional methods, yet he showed a willingness to change. He rapidly integrated an online sales platform, revamped the supply chain, and embraced digital marketing. Through his adaptability, he salvaged his business, sustaining it for the next generation.

Humility is often undervalued in a world that champions charisma and certainty. However, it was the humble hospital administrator who, realizing her knowledge of emerging medical technologies was lacking, sought advice from her younger, less experienced team members. She did not let hierarchy or ego impede her learning. Her humility earned her the respect of her team and helped keep the hospital at the forefront of patient care.

Lastly, let's reflect on **commitment**. This was exemplified by a mayor who, despite political pressures and wavering popularity, remained steadfast in his pursuit of sustainable policies for his city. He faced criticism and pushback, but his unwavering commitment eventually resulted in a greener, healthier urban environment that will benefit generations to come.

These qualities are by no means exhaustive, and certainly, there exist other valuable traits within the makeup of timeless leaders. However, these stand out as particularly enduring and universal. Integrity, empathy, resilience, vision, adaptability, humility, and commitment - they form the foundation of timeless leadership, a foundation that remains robust regardless of the vagaries of the world around them. They are not just traits but principles, not just qualities but commitments. They are the lifeblood of the evergreen leader, the pulse that keeps them standing tall, season after season, year after year, change after change.

Strategies to Develop Timeless Leadership Traits

One might wonder if these timeless leadership traits we've identified are inborn or if they can be developed. It's a familiar question, reminiscent of the age-old debate of nature versus nurture. And while it's true that some may naturally incline towards these traits, let us reassure you - these qualities can indeed be honed and nurtured within you. What we need, then, are strategies, practical steps that enable us to cultivate these timeless leadership traits.

To foster **integrity**, it's crucial to remember the old adage: practice what you preach. This was demonstrated by a CEO of a fast-growing FinTech firm who promised transparency to his stakeholders. He ensured his actions echoed his words, whether it was sharing the company's financial health, business strategies, or even acknowledging mistakes. It was this consistent practice of his principles that led to a culture of trust within the organization. For those aspiring to build integrity, reflect on your values, and seek out actions that align with those values, even when it might be easier or more profitable to do otherwise.

Cultivating **empathy** might start by stepping into someone else's shoes. The principal of a prestigious high school demonstrated this when he took the time to shadow students and teachers, experiencing their daily routines and challenges first-hand. This immersive experience gave him a fresh perspective and allowed him to lead with deeper understanding and empathy. A potential strategy here? Make a regular habit of seeking out and understanding diverse perspectives within your organization.

For **resilience**, consider the strategy employed by a successful sales manager who had to grapple with a series of setbacks. Instead of dwelling on the negatives, she made it a point to learn from each failure. She analyzed her shortcomings, gained new insights, and then bounced back with renewed strength. For leaders aiming to build resilience, it is key to view setbacks as opportunities for growth rather than as insurmountable obstacles.

Developing a **vision** might start with asking the right questions. An entrepreneur seeking to open a chain of environmentally friendly cafes began by asking, "What impact do I want to have in ten years?" This set the stage for her bold vision of a sustainable, community-oriented brand that was more than just a place to grab a cup of coffee. For those seeking to develop vision, invest time in long-term, big-picture thinking, and don't be afraid to challenge the status quo.

To be **adaptable** in leadership, a continuous learning mindset is crucial. Take the story of a factory supervisor who embraced emerging industrial automation technologies instead of resisting change. He self-initiated learning, took courses, and gradually became an in-house expert, helping his team transition smoothly into the new production methods. The lesson here? Stay curious about emerging trends, technologies, and ideas in your field.

Developing **humility** in leadership can begin with recognizing and acknowledging the contributions of others. A university department head, despite her extensive expertise, regularly solicited ideas and inputs from her staff and students. This not only fostered an atmosphere of mutual respect but also led to innovative ideas that enriched the department. A useful strategy for leaders would be to regularly seek and value inputs from all members of their teams, regardless of hierarchy.

Finally, cultivating **commitment** might involve setting a clear purpose and sticking to it. The founder of a social enterprise demonstrated this when he persisted with his mission to alleviate poverty in his community, even when profits were meager. He stayed true to his purpose, and his unwavering commitment eventually led to greater support and success for his enterprise. If commitment is your goal, define your purpose, your 'why,' and let it guide your actions and decisions.

It's important to remember that these strategies are not prescriptive. There isn't one path to cultivating timeless leadership traits; the process is as individual as the leaders themselves. The key lies in reflection and conscious action. It involves understanding yourself, acknowledging where you need to grow, and then taking tangible steps towards that growth. As with any worthwhile endeavor, cultivating these timeless traits requires time, patience, and consistency. But rest assured, the results, in the form of strong, effective, and revered leadership, are truly worth the effort.

Timeless Leadership in a Rapidly Changing World

In a world marked by constant change, how do timeless leadership traits maintain their relevance? Can concepts like integrity, empathy, and resilience keep pace with the dizzying speed of innovation and change? Let's draw a parallel from nature - the evergreen tree, a symbol of endurance, which stays green through all seasons. It adjusts its internal processes to survive winter's cold, summer's heat, and everything in between, yet, its essential nature remains unaltered. Similarly, timeless leaders, while responsive to change, hold fast to their foundational traits, which are their roots.

Take **integrity** for instance. As business models evolve and ethical boundaries are tested, integrity shines as a beacon. In the era of misinformation and deep fakes, a CEO of a reputable news organization faced a choice: chase viral sensation with sensationalized news or uphold journalistic integrity. He chose the latter, reinforcing the fact that while mediums may change, the essential demand for truth and transparency remains.

With the advent of artificial intelligence, **empathy** takes on new dimensions. In a healthcare startup that uses AI for preliminary diagnoses, the CEO faced backlash when patients felt reduced to mere data points. Acknowledging this, she ensured that all AI interactions were followed up with human contact - a simple strategy, but one that balanced innovation with the enduring need for human connection and empathy.

In an uncertain economy, **resilience** becomes crucial. The COO of a company manufacturing solar panels showcased this trait when a sudden change in tariff regulations threatened their bottom line. Instead of retreating, he adjusted the company's strategy, exploring new markets and negotiating better terms with suppliers. The crisis became an opportunity, all due to a resilient approach towards change.

A timeless leader's **vision** becomes the compass in navigating change. Consider an NGO focusing on education. With digital learning becoming the new normal, their traditional model faced obsolescence. However, their visionary leader recalibrated their approach, harnessing the power of technology to reach more underprivileged children.

The medium changed, but their vision of inclusive education remained consistent.

In a rapidly evolving marketplace, **adaptability** is indispensable. The leader of a traditional publishing house showcased this when e-books disrupted the market. She chose to adapt, integrating digital formats, online distribution, and even exploring audio books. By being adaptable, she turned a potential existential threat into a new opportunity.

Even in an age of individualism and personal branding, **humility** stands tall. The founder of a successful software company, after an initial public offering (IPO) that made him a billionaire, kept his modest office and continued to have lunch in the company cafeteria. His humility reminded everyone that it was collective effort, not personal glory, that made their success possible.

Finally, **commitment**. In a fast-fashion era, a clothing brand leader made a commitment to sustainable practices, which often meant higher costs and lower margins. Despite pressures, the leader stuck to his commitment, steadily building a brand known for its ethics as much as its products.

These stories bring to light an important revelation: the traits that define timeless leadership are not relics of the past, incompatible with a high-speed, high-tech world. Quite the contrary, they are the anchors that prevent us from being swept away in the current of constant change.

This is not to suggest that leaders should resist change. Adapting to new technologies, market trends, and societal shifts is essential. But in this flux, these timeless traits remain constant, not because they are rigid, but because they are universally valued.

The rapid pace of change can make the world seem increasingly complex and unstable. Yet, it is within this very instability that timeless leadership shines. It reminds us that amidst all the variables, some things hold true. And it is these qualities that people seek in their leaders, now more than ever.

In our race to the future, we must not lose sight of

these enduring leadership traits. Like the evergreen, they are our constant, standing tall through all seasons, providing guidance, stability, and hope. They form the bridge between what has always mattered and what the future holds, a testament to their enduring relevance in a rapidly changing world.

Timeless Leadership Self-Assessment

The concept of self-assessment is not new; it's an age-old tool that paves the way for self-discovery and improvement. Self-assessment is the personal equivalent of a business audit. For leaders aiming to embody timeless traits, such a personal audit becomes essential. The insights gained can assist in identifying strengths and spotlight areas for further development. In this section, we provide a comprehensive self-assessment guide to help leaders evaluate their alignment with these timeless leadership traits. It's about understanding where you stand and envisioning where you aspire to be.

1. **Assessing Integrity**: Are you consistent in your values, both in public and private? How do you handle situations that test your ethics? Think about the difficult choices you've made and their alignment with your moral compass.

2. **Evaluating Empathy**: How well do you understand and respond to the feelings and needs of your team? Reflect on feedback, both formal and informal, you've received regarding your emotional intelligence.

3. **Gauging Resilience**: How have you reacted to setbacks or challenges? Consider situations where you've demonstrated resilience and think about the mechanisms that helped you bounce back.

4. **Determining Vision**: Are you able to effectively communicate a compelling vision for your team or organization? Reflect on whether your vision inspires others to strive towards a common goal.

5. **Checking Adaptability**: How do you handle change

or uncertainty? Take into account instances where you've had to adapt your plans or strategies due to unforeseen circumstances.

6. Analyzing Humility: Do you acknowledge your mistakes and share credit for successes? Think about how you respond to achievements, your own and those of your team.

7. Reviewing Commitment: How deep is your commitment to your role, team, and organization? Reflect on times when your commitment was tested and how you responded.

❋ ❋ ❋

This self-assessment is not a one-and-done process. Just as businesses regularly audit their performance, so should leaders periodically review these traits within themselves. This encourages continuous growth and helps ensure their leadership remains evergreen, relevant, and impactful amidst an ever-changing landscape.

Remember, this is not about judging yourself harshly or striving for perfection. No leader, no matter how exceptional, will score perfectly in all these areas. This is about identifying patterns, acknowledging the gaps, and understanding your unique leadership style.You may find that you naturally excel in certain areas while others require more effort. That's perfectly fine. Leadership is not about perfection; it's about authenticity. It's about the courage to look inward, recognize areas for improvement, and commit to personal growth. After all, isn't that what an evergreen leader, always learning and growing, does?

PART V: INTERPERSONAL DYNAMICS OF LEADERSHIP

CHAPTER 11 - LEADERSHIP'S EMOTIONAL CORE: EMOTIONAL INTELLIGENCE

In an era dominated by data-centric decisions and analytics, the role of emotional intelligence in leadership often goes overlooked. Yet, this trait differentiates routine management from truly effective leadership.

Emotional intelligence isn't mere sentimentality; it's a sophisticated balance of self-awareness, self-regulation, motivation, empathy, and social skills. Consider a CEO, aware of her emotional triggers, who leads calmly under stress, aligns her team with shared visions, understands diverse perspectives, and cultivates positive relationships. Such leaders not only champion with intellect but also resonate emotionally.

Take, for instance, a tech company disrupted by rival innovation. While strategy is pivotal, understanding the emotional fallout—fears, anxieties, insecurities—is equally crucial. An emotionally astute leader identifies and addresses these feelings, fostering resilience and unity during challenging times.

Emotional intelligence's role in crisis management cannot be overstated. Beyond strategical insights, tapping into the human emotional response can unify teams, fostering collaboration and sustaining morale amidst adversity.

So, how does one enhance emotional intelligence? It's

more than just online tests and generic advice—it's a journey of introspection, awareness, and continuous effort. As we progress, we'll share tools and guidance to support this journey. Enhancing emotional intelligence is about personal growth that culminates in stronger leadership and a thriving organizational culture. Dive into this chapter with an open perspective to harness the transformative potential of emotional intelligence in leadership.

Understanding Emotional Intelligence: Definitions and Dimensions

Let's peel back the layers of emotional intelligence (EI) to truly understand its essence. Emotional intelligence, at its core, is the ability to recognize, understand, and manage our own emotions, and recognize, understand, and influence the emotions of others. But isn't that the definition of empathy, you might ask? Well, it's a common misconception. Empathy is a part of emotional intelligence, but EI encompasses more.

A closer look reveals emotional intelligence as a four-dimensional construct: self-awareness, self-management, social awareness, and relationship management. Understanding these dimensions creates a mental blueprint for leaders looking to cultivate their emotional intelligence. Each dimension holds a different key to unlocking the potential within.

Consider self-awareness. It's not just knowing that you're irritated because your morning coffee was lukewarm or elated because your team won a match. It goes deeper, asking why. Why did lukewarm coffee irritate you so? Is it a symbol of a day starting less than perfectly? Why does your team's victory matter so much to you? Is it a reflection of your craving for triumph in other areas of your life?

Take the case of Sara, a high-performing team leader at a renowned software company. She found herself increasingly frustrated with her team's performance. Her first instinct was to blame her team. After all, their output was what directly affected her. However, through cultivating self-awareness, she realized that her irritation stemmed from the pressure she was feeling from upper management. Recognizing this, she was able to address the root cause rather than misdirecting her frustration towards her team.

Self-management, the second dimension of EI, takes self-awareness to the next level. It's not just about understanding your emotions, but also about managing them. Picture an angry response to an email critique that, upon reflection, you regret. Self-management would allow you to feel that anger but choose a more constructive response. It's akin to being at the steering wheel of your emotional vehicle rather than in the passenger seat.

Think about Jackson, a project manager, who felt challenged by one of his team members during a meeting. His initial response was to shut down the conversation and assert his authority. But, practicing self-management, he took a moment to breathe, channel his feelings, and then thanked the team member for his input and promised to revisit the issue later.

Social awareness, or empathy, is the third dimension. It's not merely understanding what someone else is going through but feeling it with them. It allows leaders to respond to the emotional needs of their team members effectively.

Consider the story of Tianna, a CEO who noticed that one of her department heads, usually an energetic and motivated individual, had been seeming down. Instead of reprimanding him for a lack of enthusiasm or ignoring it as a personal problem, she reached out, offering an open conversation. It turned out he was going through a difficult divorce. Anna's empathetic response helped strengthen their professional relationship and enabled him to navigate his personal situation without feeling alienated at work.

The final dimension is relationship management, leveraging your understanding of your own and others' emotions to manage interactions and build strong relationships. It's about creating an environment where others feel understood and valued.

Take Alex, a middle manager, who was always able to defuse tense situations within his team. He had an intuitive understanding of how people felt and knew what to say to soothe and reassure them. This ability to manage relationships fostered a positive team environment and led to higher performance.

Understanding emotional intelligence's dimensions opens a leader's eyes to a new perspective. It's not just about task lists, strategic plans, and productivity reports. It's about emotions, those intangible factors that can ignite or extinguish motivation, build or break teams, and make an organization thrive or falter. As we continue our exploration of emotional intelligence, let's remember these dimensions, for they are the foundation of a new kind of leadership – leadership that resonates and inspires.

The Role of Emotional Intelligence in Effective Leadership

Leadership, while undoubtedly requiring tactical acumen and strategic foresight, is more profoundly a human endeavor. At its heart lies the complex, fascinating world of emotions. So, what role does emotional intelligence play in effective leadership? In essence, emotional intelligence is the thread that weaves through the very fabric of leadership.

The interplay between emotional intelligence and leadership becomes apparent when one considers the role of a leader. To lead is to influence, motivate, and inspire others towards a common goal. And how can one influence, motivate, or inspire without an understanding of emotions?

Consider self-awareness, the first dimension of emotional intelligence. In a leader, self-awareness is like a navigational compass. It gives a leader an understanding of their emotional landscape, their strengths and weaknesses, their motivations and fears. Picture the story of Tensi, a CFO of a tech startup. Her strength was her detailed, analytical mindset. However, her tendency to focus on details sometimes bogged her down in meetings. Once she became aware of this, she was able to use her strength more judiciously, thereby making meetings more efficient and effective.

Self-management, the next dimension of emotional intelligence, enables a leader to make decisions in a rational, thoughtful manner, rather than reacting impulsively. It doesn't negate emotions; instead, it helps in managing them for a better outcome. As an illustration, take the example of Rohan, a senior manager in a logistics company, known for his short temper. When Rohan began to practice self-management, he noticed a significant improvement in his team's morale and productivity. Not only was he able to manage his reactions better, but his team felt more comfortable approaching him with ideas and concerns, fostering a more inclusive and innovative environment.

The third dimension, social awareness, allows leaders to recognize and respond to the emotional climate of their team or organization. It's akin to having an emotional barometer that measures the ebb and flow of group dynamics. Imagine Sandra, a school principal, who sensed a growing feeling of frustration among her teachers towards the new curriculum. Instead of ignoring these feelings or reprimanding the teachers, she held open forums to understand their concerns better and address them, demonstrating her empathy and commitment to her staff.

The final dimension, relationship management, is like the glue that binds a team together. It helps leaders in fostering a positive atmosphere, resolving conflicts, and building strong, mutually respectful relationships. For instance, recall the tale of Alton, a team leader at a call center. Alton was known for his ability to resolve disputes and encourage cooperation within his diverse team. His secret? A keen understanding of the emotions at play and a knack for managing relationships effectively.

But is emotional intelligence just a tool for managing people? Or does it have a more profound impact on leadership? To answer this, we need to delve a little deeper. When a leader exhibits high emotional intelligence, they don't just create a harmonious work environment. They model behavior that encourages others to develop their own emotional intelligence.

Consider this: Maria, a team leader, is known for her calm demeanor, even in stressful situations. Her team, seeing her as a role model, begins to mirror her behavior. Over time, the entire team learns to manage stress better, improving not only their work-life balance but also their productivity.

Emotional intelligence is also instrumental in building trust, a crucial ingredient of leadership. Leaders with high emotional intelligence are often perceived as more authentic and trustworthy because they show understanding and empathy towards others. This authenticity fosters trust and loyalty, strengthening the bond between leaders and their followers.

The role of emotional intelligence in leadership is akin to that of a conductor in an orchestra. Just as the conductor brings together different instruments to create a harmonious symphony, a leader uses emotional intelligence to bring together diverse team members and guide them towards a common goal.

Emotional intelligence also shapes a leader's decision-making process. Emotionally intelligent leaders consider not only the logical aspects of a decision but also the emotional aspects. They understand the emotional implications of their decisions and use this understanding to make choices that benefit the organization while also respecting and considering the emotions of their followers.

In a world of rapid change and uncertainty, emotionally intelligent leadership can be a beacon of stability and hope. Emotionally intelligent leaders can sense the emotional undercurrents of change and respond effectively, providing guidance and support to their team members.

The role of emotional intelligence in effective leadership is multi-faceted and profound. It's not merely an add-on, but rather an essential ingredient of effective leadership. As we move forward in our discussion, let's remember the role emotional intelligence plays in shaping the contours of leadership, for it is the soul of the leader's journey.

How Emotional Intelligence Shapes Crisis Leadership

When an organization encounters a crisis, it's like a sudden storm erupting in the ocean, making the sailing ship tumble and sway with its violent winds. A good leader is akin to an experienced captain who navigates the ship amidst the tempest, keeping the crew composed and the vessel afloat. And just like that captain, a leader's emotional intelligence becomes their guiding star in the darkest of times.

Take the story of Eliza, CEO of a prominent healthcare organization, when they were hit by a sudden and unexpected public relations crisis. The situation was tense, with the potential to tarnish the organization's reputation severely. Eliza had a choice to react impulsively or respond thoughtfully. Choosing the latter, she harnessed her self-management skills, staying calm and focused, demonstrating to her team that panic wouldn't be their course of action. Her emotional stability had a ripple effect, providing the team with a sense of reassurance and direction amidst the crisis.

While calmness in crisis is essential, a leader must also be adept at sensing the emotions swirling within the organization. This is where social awareness comes into play. Think of the story of Joshua, a plant manager whose facility was hit by a strike due to sudden policy changes. Instead of taking a defensive stance, Joshua used his emotional intelligence to understand the underlying emotions behind the strike. This understanding helped him address the grievances of his workers effectively, mitigating the impact of the crisis.

A crisis often brings with it a tidal wave of emotions: fear, anxiety, anger, and uncertainty. How a leader manages these emotions can make the difference between escalating the crisis or navigating through it successfully. It's here that self-awareness becomes a leader's best ally. Remember the case of Anaya, a school superintendent, who was dealing with a district-wide controversy. Anaya's self-awareness allowed her to recognize her initial defensive reaction. Instead of letting that reaction dictate her actions, she paused, reflecting on the emotions driving her reaction. This self-reflection enabled her to respond to the controversy in a balanced and fair way.

An emotionally intelligent leader doesn't just manage their own emotions during a crisis; they also play a critical role in managing the emotions of their followers. When a crisis hits, team members look to their leader for guidance and reassurance. The leader's ability to manage relationships effectively becomes a stabilizing factor during turbulent times.

Consider the story of Laurence, a project manager in a software company. When a major project hit a roadblock, the team was on the edge, fearing project failure and potential job losses. Laurence, using his relationship management skills, brought the team together, acknowledging their fears while also encouraging collaboration to find a solution. His approach not only reduced the team's anxiety but also promoted a problem-solving mindset, eventually leading to the successful completion of the project.

The impact of emotional intelligence on crisis leadership can be profound. During a crisis, people are often on an emotional rollercoaster. A leader with high emotional intelligence can empathize with their followers, validating their emotions, and providing much-needed emotional support. This validation can help to lower anxiety levels, improve morale, and foster a sense of unity and resilience among team members.

Beyond emotional support, emotional intelligence can

also play a vital role in strategic decision making during a crisis. Emotionally intelligent leaders can balance the rational and emotional aspects of decision-making, taking into account not only the strategic implications of their decisions but also the emotional impact on their followers. This balanced approach can lead to more effective crisis management, reducing the potential negative impact on the organization and its stakeholders.

Emotional intelligence can also help leaders communicate effectively during a crisis. A crisis can lead to information overload, with rumors and misinformation often adding to the confusion. Emotionally intelligent leaders understand this and are adept at clear, concise, and empathetic communication. They are aware that what they say, how they say it, and when they say it can significantly influence the emotional climate within the organization.

In addition, emotional intelligence helps leaders to build and maintain trust during a crisis. Leaders with high emotional intelligence are often perceived as authentic and empathetic, traits that foster trust. When a crisis hits, this reservoir of trust can be a critical asset, helping to ensure that followers believe in their leader's decisions and actions, even in the face of uncertainty.

Leaders with high emotional intelligence also foster resilience, both in themselves and in their followers. They understand that a crisis can trigger a wide range of emotions in individuals, from fear and anxiety to anger and disillusionment. By acknowledging these emotions, providing emotional support, and promoting positive coping strategies, emotionally intelligent leaders can help to build resilience, enabling their followers to recover from the crisis and move forward.

In a world that is increasingly unpredictable, the role of emotional intelligence in crisis leadership has never been more important. The ability to understand and manage emotions, both one's own and those of others, can provide a beacon of light in the midst of a storm. As leaders, we need to recognize this and strive to cultivate our emotional intelligence, for it is not just an asset, but a lifeline in times of crisis.

As we conclude this discussion, let's remember that while a crisis can be a test of leadership, it can also be an opportunity. An opportunity to demonstrate compassion, resilience, and unity. An opportunity to shine amidst the storm. And emotional intelligence, the very lifeblood that pumps through the heart of leadership, is the incandescent beacon that guides us through these opportunities, paving the way for a stronger, more resilient organization.

Crises inevitably unmask the true character of an organization, and the leader's emotional intelligence is the cloak that shields this character from descending into chaos. Just as a heart pumps blood to the rest of the body, providing life and vitality, the emotionally intelligent leader pumps hope, calm, and clear-headed decisiveness into the life of their organization. The storm may be fierce, but with emotional intelligence, we can not only weather it but also emerge stronger and more united.

An organization's strength lies not in its immunity to crises but in its ability to navigate them. Just as a lighthouse guides ships safely to the shore amidst turbulent seas, emotional intelligence guides an organization safely through crises. It acts as a compass, helping the organization find its bearings when the storm of a crisis threatens to throw it off course. It allows the leaders to not only "see" the storm but to understand it, to understand its impact on the organization and its people, and to chart a course that steers the organization towards safety and resilience.

However, it is important to remember that emotional intelligence is not a static trait; it's a dynamic skill that can be cultivated and developed. It's an evolving toolkit that leaders can and should constantly refine. And this evolution becomes most visible, most critical, during a crisis. As the storm rages, the toolkit expands, giving leaders the resources they need to guide their organizations and people through the storm, ensuring their collective survival and growth.

The application of emotional intelligence during crises is not just about surviving the storm. It's about learning from it, about growing stronger because of it. It's about turning the ship towards the wind, using the gusts to power forward rather than be pushed backward. And it's emotional intelligence that provides the leader with the insight to know when to hold steady, when to change course, and when to advance.

Emotional intelligence is what separates a good leader from a great one, particularly during a crisis. It's the ability to understand and manage one's emotions and those of others. It's the ability to maintain a calm and collected demeanor when everything seems to be falling apart. It's the ability to demonstrate empathy and compassion when they're most needed. And above all, it's the ability to inspire trust, resilience, and hope in the midst of uncertainty and fear.

In a crisis, an emotionally intelligent leader is like the sun after a storm: warming, comforting, and life-giving. They are a beacon of hope that guides their organization out of the storm and into calmer waters. But this doesn't happen by chance; it happens by choice. It happens when leaders choose to cultivate their emotional intelligence, when they choose to use this intelligence to navigate through crises, and when they choose to lead with their heart, as well as their mind.

Leadership in crisis is like walking a tightrope: on one side, there is chaos, and on the other, there is calm. Emotional intelligence is the balancing pole that helps leaders maintain their equilibrium, allowing them to walk this tightrope with grace, composure, and effectiveness. It's not about avoiding the storm; it's about learning to dance in the rain.

Indeed, the role of emotional intelligence in crisis leadership is like a conductor in an orchestra. When the symphony of an organization descends into a cacophony due to a crisis, the emotionally intelligent leader, like a conductor, brings back harmony. They know when to hold back the violins of fear, when to cue in the cellos of empathy, and when to let the trumpets of hope play their triumphant tune.

Emotional intelligence, in crisis leadership, is not just a desirable trait; it's an indispensable one. It's the compass that guides the ship of leadership through the stormy seas of a crisis. It's the heart of effective leadership, pumping life, hope, and resilience into the organization, allowing it to not just weather the storm, but to grow stronger and more unified because of it. It's not just about surviving the storm; it's about learning to dance in the rain. Because, after all, the greater the storm, the brighter the rainbow.

Emotional Intelligence Self-Assessment

The cornerstone of any great leader's toolbox is the ability to engage with and refine one's emotional intelligence. It is the lens through which we decipher the world and its emotional complexities. But how do you know where you stand in this essential leadership trait? Fear not, for we have crafted a set of tools and tips that can provide a gauge for your current level of emotional intelligence and offer suggestions for its enhancement. As with a garden, it requires a steady hand and a patient heart to cultivate, but the harvest is rewarding.

1. Self-awareness Self-assessment: Pay close attention to your reactions, particularly during stressful situations. Note how you respond to conflict, criticism, or high-pressure situations. Are your reactions overly emotional or disproportionately subdued? This self-reflection can serve as an initial measure of your emotional awareness.

2. Journaling: Make it a daily practice to document your emotions and reactions. This process can help you identify patterns, triggers, and blind spots, and it can provide an opportunity to examine and manage your emotions in a more controlled environment.

3. Emotional Intelligence Test: Utilize an Emotional

Intelligence (EI) test or assessment tool. These evaluations are designed to measure your ability to perceive, control, evaluate, and express emotions. You can use the results to create a tailored plan for improvement.

4. Seek Feedback: Actively solicit feedback from those around you - your team, your peers, your mentors. How do they perceive your emotional responses? Their insight can provide you with a different perspective, revealing potential areas for improvement that you might not have recognized.

5. Mindfulness and Meditation: Both are proven methods to improve emotional control and awareness. Just as you might exercise to improve physical strength, consider these practices as a workout for your emotional muscle.

6. Active Listening: Actively engage with others, showing genuine interest in their thoughts and feelings. This practice can improve your ability to empathize with others, a key component of emotional intelligence.

7. Empathy Practice: Deliberately place yourself in scenarios where empathy is required. This might involve volunteering at a local charity, mentoring a colleague, or even reading a book from a perspective very different from your own.

8. Emotional Intelligence Training or Coaching: If you're serious about improving your emotional intelligence, consider enrolling in a formal training program or hiring a coach who specializes in this area.

9. Read about Emotional Intelligence: There are many books, articles, and studies available that delve into the subject. A deeper understanding of the theory and science behind emotional intelligence can aid in your application of it.

10. Continual Learning: Emotional intelligence, like all aspects of leadership, is a continual learning process. Regularly reassess your emotional intelligence and adjust your development strategies as needed.

❋ ❋ ❋

Cultivating emotional intelligence is an ongoing process, a delicate dance between self-reflection, external feedback, and intentional practice. It's the steady hand on the tiller during the storm, the calm voice that commands respect, and the empathetic ear that engenders trust. Remember, the aim is not perfection, but progress. As the saying goes, "a smooth sea never made a skilled sailor." In the end, it's your commitment to honing your emotional intelligence that will distinguish you as a truly effective leader.

CHAPTER 12 - COMMUNICATION WITH IMPACT: THE LEADER AS AN EFFECTIVE COMMUNICATOR

The age-old art of communication stands as a cornerstone in leadership. It is more than a mere exchange of words; it's a nuanced blend of verbal and non-verbal signals, tone, and active listening. Much like a conductor's pivotal role in an orchestra, a leader's communication steers the direction, harmony, and effectiveness of a team.

Consider a Fortune 500 company nearing collapse, not due to a scarcity of resources or ideas, but a communication breakdown. This disruption led to a disjointed vision and a dejected workforce. Conversely, the tale of a tech startup illustrates how refining communication can turn tides; though technically skilled, the CEO's lack of communicative finesse nearly led to the company's downfall until they sought expertise in communication.

Challenges in communication are multifaceted, varying across leaders and their teams' unique contexts. The nuances in addressing seasoned oil rig workers in Texas differ from those in the tech-savvy environments of Silicon Valley. Moreover, crises, such as natural disasters or global pandemics, underscore the paramount importance of clear, empathetic communication. It isn't just about the message's content, but the manner of its delivery. Recall the airline executive post a tragic accident: his demeanor and clear conveyance offered solace during trying times.

As we delve further, we'll provide actionable strategies to refine your communication toolkit. The key takeaway? Great leaders aren't merely speakers; they communicate meaningfully. Throughout this chapter, you'll find a tailored checklist to guide your communication journey, acting as a compass to lead you towards resonant and effective dialogue.

Ultimately, leadership communication isn't about vocal dominance but ensuring everyone feels acknowledged and appreciated. As you delve into this chapter, remain receptive and eager to sculpt your distinct, impactful communication narrative.

The Importance of Communication in Leadership

The magic of communication in leadership is often underplayed, yet its significance is as compelling as the beating heart in the human body. Think of the importance of communication like a humble rivet that holds the massive Golden Gate Bridge together; it may appear minuscule, but its role in keeping the colossal structure steady is undeniable. Now, let's take a voyage through its importance, harnessing tales from the business world and beyond to elucidate the essence of effective communication.

To comprehend the profundity of communication's role, we'll start with a story. The CEO of a multinational corporation was faced with plummeting stock prices. Rather than silencing the internal noise and shrouding the situation in secrecy, she held a company-wide town hall. Transparently, she shared the challenges they were facing, offered a strategic plan, and showed empathy towards her anxious employees. Her actions resulted in an inspired workforce, ready to collaboratively overcome the company's hurdles. This story underlines the power of open and honest communication in fortifying leadership.

In the theatre of leadership, communication doesn't

only command center stage during crises. Its importance is sewn into the fabric of day-to-day operations, shaping the culture and performance of organizations. Look at Google, a company famed for its innovative spirit and productivity. Its leadership communication is built on a culture of openness, encouraging its 'Googlers' to question, to challenge, and to ideate. This powerful communication philosophy engenders a creative engine that has driven some of the most revolutionary products of our era.

Yet, the importance of communication doesn't end with fueling innovation and managing crises. It is also the key that unlocks the door to effective decision-making. The legendary Apollo 13 mission serves as a compelling testament to this. With lives at stake and a spacecraft malfunctioning 200,000 miles away from Earth, effective communication was the lifeline that facilitated collaborative decision-making, enabling the safe return of the astronauts.

Peeling back another layer, we see that communication serves as the linchpin for fostering relationships within a team. It breaks down walls, builds bridges, and creates an environment of trust and mutual respect. Think of the revered basketball coach, Phil Jackson, whose open and empathetic communication style helped mold disparate athletes into a cohesive team, leading to an enviable tally of NBA championships.

Communication in leadership also plays an invaluable role in managing change, a constant in today's turbulent business environment. When Satya Nadella took the reins of Microsoft, he had to steer the tech giant through significant strategic shifts. Through clear, consistent, and inspiring communication, Nadella was able to rally the troops towards a new vision, transforming Microsoft's performance and perception in the process.

Moreover, the importance of communication is elevated when we consider its role in shaping a leader's personal brand. Effective communication helps leaders articulate their vision, values, and personality, leaving indelible impressions in the minds of their followers. Remember how Elon Musk's audacious communication style has helped him build a personal brand synonymous with innovation and risk-taking?

Let's not forget that communication is a two-way street. Effective leaders don't just talk; they listen. Active listening is a potent tool in a leader's communication arsenal, building trust, gaining insights, and promoting openness within teams. We can look to the leadership of Indra Nooyi, the former CEO of PepsiCo, whose keen listening skills have been praised as a cornerstone of her effective leadership style.

While understanding the importance of communication is vital, it is equally crucial to recognize the potential pitfalls of poor communication. The infamous collapse of Enron, steeped in a culture of misinformation and secrecy, stands as a stark reminder of the devastation that miscommunication can unleash.

Yet, amidst the potential perils of poor communication, lies the promise of growth and learning. Communication missteps should not be feared, but embraced as opportunities for improvement. We might look at the initial public relations mishaps of Facebook and its CEO, Mark Zuckerberg, and how they evolved over time, paving the way for a more transparent and responsive communication approach.

As leaders, mastering communication is not an optional extra; it's a fundamental requisite. Whether it's navigating change, inspiring innovation, fostering relationships, or managing crises, effective communication acts as a guiding light, illuminating the path to impactful leadership.

We conclude this section with an important observation. A leader's communication should not be viewed as a monolith, but rather as a mosaic, each piece contributing to the overall image. Every conversation, every email, every town hall meeting - they all matter. Each interaction is a thread, and when woven together, they create the tapestry of a leader's influence.

In the end, the importance of communication in leadership can be summarized in a single, poignant truth: A leader without effective communication is like a ship without a compass, destined to lose its way in the vast ocean of leadership. As we delve deeper into the subsequent sections, remember that communication isn't just about the words we say; it's about the echoes they leave behind.

Common Challenges and Strategies in Leadership

Effective leadership communication isn't a smooth sail; it's more akin to navigating a ship through the treacherous, ever-changing waters of the sea. In this section, we dive into the common challenges leaders face while communicating and the strategic responses to overcome these hurdles.

One of the primary challenges leaders face is a phenomenon known as the "curse of knowledge." As leaders climb the organizational ladder, they amass industry knowledge and expertise. However, this accumulated wisdom often leads to a communication gap. Leaders, engrossed in their world of jargon and complexity, struggle to simplify their messages for their audience. Steve Jobs, the co-founder of Apple, was a master at addressing this challenge. Jobs had the exceptional ability to distill complex technological concepts into simple, digestible messages that resonated with his audience.

Another roadblock in the landscape of leadership communication is the struggle with vulnerability. Leaders often hesitate to show their human side, fearing it may undermine their authority. However, in reality, vulnerability can be a powerful tool that fosters trust and connection. Brené Brown, a renowned researcher and author, champions this philosophy. She suggests that the courage to be vulnerable transforms communication from mere transactional exchanges to meaningful, human-centric conversations.

The failure to actively listen is yet another obstacle

plaguing leadership communication. In the rush to dictate directives and share insights, leaders often overlook the importance of lending an attentive ear to their team. The case of Alan Mulally, former CEO of Ford, offers a lesson here. Mulally placed a high premium on listening, insisting on hearing every voice in his team meetings. His practice of active listening fostered a culture of openness and inclusivity, driving Ford's turnaround.

Leaders also grapple with the dilemma of transparency, especially when the news is unfavorable. The instinctive response may be to withhold information to prevent panic or unrest. However, effective leaders understand that honesty, even when uncomfortable, is a cornerstone of impactful communication. The leadership of Mary Barra, CEO of General Motors, during the ignition switch crisis is a noteworthy example. Her forthrightness about the company's missteps won her respect and trust, even amidst the crisis.

Communication frequency presents another challenge. Leaders may struggle to strike a balance between overcommunication, leading to information overload, and under-communication, resulting in an uninformed team. The best leaders skillfully navigate this tightrope, ensuring their teams are adequately informed but not overwhelmed. Jeff Bezos, Amazon's founder, is known for his "just enough, just in time" communication approach, providing the necessary information right when it's needed.

The advent of digital communication tools, while offering myriad advantages, has also ushered in unique challenges. With the increasing reliance on virtual communication, leaders face the task of building and maintaining a personal connection in a digital environment. Here, leaders can learn from the founder of Zoom, Eric Yuan. Recognizing the importance of creating a personal touch in a virtual setting, he pioneered the video-first culture, bringing warmth and intimacy to digital communication.

Another challenge is ensuring consistency in

communication. In the hustle and bustle of leadership, messages can often become inconsistent or muddled, leading to confusion and misinterpretation. Establishing clear and consistent communication, like Howard Schultz did during his tenure at Starbucks, can ensure everyone is on the same page, fostering cohesion and clarity.

There's also the challenge of managing difficult conversations. Whether it's delivering bad news or addressing performance issues, such conversations are an inevitable part of leadership. Master communicators don't avoid these conversations but handle them with tact and empathy. Sheryl Sandberg, the COO of Facebook, stands out as a leader who skillfully manages tough talks, ensuring they are candid yet compassionate.

In the quest for perfection, leaders often fall prey to the problem of over-preparation. While it's important to be well-prepared, an over-reliance on scripts can make communication come across as robotic or insincere. The objective should be to strive for authenticity over perfection, much like Richard Branson, the charismatic founder of Virgin Group, known for his spontaneous and genuine communication style.

A leader's communication must also bridge the diversity in their team, in terms of age, culture, language, and more. Ensuring one's message resonates with a diverse group is a challenge that leaders need to adeptly navigate. Leaders like Indra Nooyi have successfully led diverse teams, demonstrating an understanding and appreciation for multicultural communication.

Finally, it's crucial to address the challenge of feedback reception. Often, leaders are surrounded by people who hesitate to provide candid feedback. Encouraging a feedback-rich culture, as seen in the leadership of Bill Gates, co-founder of Microsoft, helps leaders rectify their communication blind spots, promoting continual growth.

Recognizing and strategically addressing these common communication challenges is critical in the realm of effective leadership. It's about embracing the messiness, understanding that no one-size-fits-all, and knowing that every stumbling block is a steppingstone towards mastering the art of impactful communication. As we move forward, remember, it's not the challenges we face that define us, but how we rise above them.

Communication Effective Communication During Crisis

In the realm of leadership, a crisis isn't a question of if, but when. It's in these pressure-cooker situations that a leader's communication skills are truly tested. Let's delve into the pivotal role of communication during crisis, and the key practices that distinguish effective crisis communicators.

The first characteristic that sets effective crisis communicators apart is their promptness in response. When the unexpected strikes, the natural human response is often to retreat, to buy time to figure out the next course of action. However, in a leadership context, this silence can be detrimental. A void in communication can quickly be filled with speculation and misinformation. Take, for example, Tony Hayward, former CEO of BP, who faced heavy criticism for his slow response during the 2010 Deepwater Horizon oil spill. The lesson here is clear: in times of crisis, speed is of the essence in communication.

Crisis communicators not only respond quickly, but they also communicate with transparency. Sharing the truth, even when it's uncomfortable, is a hallmark of their communication. One can't help but think of the late Herb Kelleher, co-founder of Southwest Airlines. During the 1990s fuel crisis, Kelleher communicated openly about the company's challenges, maintaining trust even in turbulent times.

Amidst a crisis, it's all too easy to get lost in the what

and the how, forgetting the essential element of the 'why'. Effective crisis communicators consistently articulate the why behind their actions. This was exemplified by Paul Polman, former CEO of Unilever, during the 2008 economic downturn. By consistently reinforcing the company's purpose and values, he was able to keep employees engaged and committed during the tough times.

Effective crisis communication also requires empathy. Communicating with sensitivity to the concerns and emotions of those impacted can foster a sense of solidarity. New Zealand's Prime Minister Jacinda Ardern's response to the 2019 Christchurch Mosque shootings highlighted the power of empathy in crisis communication. Her empathetic approach comforted the nation and earned her global admiration.

Crisis communication isn't a one-way street. The best leaders make it a point to listen intently during crises. This listening approach was well-exhibited by Satya Nadella, CEO of Microsoft, during the challenges brought about by the COVID-19 pandemic. His practice of actively soliciting and responding to feedback from employees at all levels of the organization helped foster a sense of inclusion and mutual respect.

During a crisis, it's not uncommon for leaders to feel the need to have all the answers. But effective crisis communicators understand that it's okay to admit when they don't know something. Arne Sorenson, former CEO of Marriott International, demonstrated this during the early stages of the COVID-19 pandemic, admitting that he didn't have all the answers but was committed to navigating through the challenges together with the team.

Effective crisis communication also requires clarity. Despite the chaotic environment, the best communicators maintain a clear, consistent message. This was exemplified by Anne Mulcahy, former CEO of Xerox, who led the company through a financial crisis. Her clear, consistent communication helped allay fears and provided direction amidst the chaos.

Amidst a crisis, leaders must not only communicate the current realities but also inspire hope for the future. Alan Mulally, during his tenure as Ford's CEO, steered the company through the 2008 financial crisis. He effectively balanced the grim reality with an optimistic vision for the company's future, maintaining morale and motivation.

In a crisis, repetition is a friend, not a foe. Consistent, repeated messaging ensures that crucial information is understood and retained. Howard Schultz, during his tenure at Starbucks, would continually repeat his message, ensuring it permeated the entire organization.

Lastly, effective crisis communicators recognize that actions speak louder than words. Their actions align with their words, reinforcing their message. Mary Barra's handling of the ignition switch crisis at General Motors showcases this. Her decisive actions, coupled with honest communication, helped GM navigate the crisis effectively.

While crisis situations can be challenging and unpredictable, they also offer an opportunity for leaders to rise to the occasion through effective communication. It's about striking the balance between honesty and hope, between listening and telling, between speed and thoughtfulness. The essence of crisis communication is best captured by Winston Churchill's words, "Courage is what it takes to stand up and speak; courage is also what it takes to sit down and listen." As leaders, it's about having the courage to do both.

Leadership Communication Skills Checklist

As we move towards the conclusion of this chapter, let's pivot towards practical application. How can a leader cultivate and strengthen their communication skills? Here's a handy checklist, culled from best practices and real-life examples, to assist leaders in sharpening their communication arsenal.

1. Be Timely: Do not allow a communication void to create panic or uncertainty. The example of BP's delayed response in the Deepwater Horizon oil spill underscores the importance of a timely response.

2. Transparency is Key: Even when the truth is uncomfortable, it is critical to be transparent in your communication. The late Herb Kelleher of Southwest Airlines demonstrated this during the 1990s fuel crisis.

3. Articulate the 'Why': Ensure your communication explains the reason behind decisions and actions. Paul Polman of Unilever leveraged this during the 2008 economic downturn.

4. Show Empathy: An empathetic approach can foster a sense of unity and support. Prime Minister Jacinda Ardern of New Zealand showcased this trait in her response to the Christchurch mosque shootings.

5. Listen Intently: Remember, communication is a two-way process. Microsoft CEO Satya Nadella exemplified this during the COVID-19 pandemic.

6. It's OK to Not Know: Accept that you may not have all the answers. Arne Sorenson of Marriott International demonstrated this during the early stages of the COVID-19 pandemic.

7. Clarity and Consistency: Maintain a clear, consistent message throughout. Anne Mulcahy did this during Xerox's financial crisis.

8. Balance Reality with Hope: Inspire hope for the future while acknowledging current realities. This was effectively done by Alan Mulally during Ford's 2008 financial crisis.

9. Repeat Your Message: Ensure important information is retained by repeating your key messages. Starbucks' Howard Schultz is a notable proponent of this strategy.

10. Actions Speak Louder: Make sure your actions align with your words. Mary Barra's handling of the ignition switch crisis at General Motors is a clear example of this.

11. Use Varied Communication Channels: Depending on the context, different channels may be more effective for communicating your message. Email, town halls, one-on-ones, or even social media can be leveraged, depending on the situation.

*   *   *

These pointers serve as a helpful guide, but they're not exhaustive. Leaders must continually refine their communication skills, adapting to their unique contexts and evolving challenges. The art of communication is a vast landscape, not a single path to be trodden. In the throes of leadership, where every word and every silence matters, a robust communication skill set can make all the difference. With these tools and tips, leaders are better equipped to navigate the tumultuous tides of leadership, charting a course towards success with the compass of effective communication.

CHAPTER 13 - TRUST IN LEADERSHIP: THE ANCHORING FORCE

In the ever-changing realm of leadership, one element remains paramount: trust. In this chapter, we dive deeply into this foundational aspect of leadership that we've hinted at previously. Without trust, leadership is rendered ineffective, much like a lighthouse devoid of its guiding light. Trust ensures that teams believe in their leader's reliability, capability, and intent, especially during challenging times.

Reflect upon a startup CEO steering her fast-evolving organization. The team's trust in her abilities is not only vital for the present but crucial for the overarching vision driving the company. It's a recognized fact that stakeholders, whether investors or employees, gravitate towards trust-infused leadership. The tangible impact of trust even stretches to organizational financial health.

Building trust is an intricate process, nurtured over time, yet vulnerable to quick disintegration. Its value becomes even more evident during crises, where it can either be a guiding light or expose leadership vulnerabilities. The choices leaders make during these times can either fortify or fracture this trust.

This chapter will shed light on the nuances of trust within leadership, its pivotal role during challenging times, and practical strategies to foster and safeguard it. Illustrated with real-world examples, we offer a roadmap to mastering this foundational aspect of leadership. We aim to equip you with strategies to consistently cultivate and uphold trust, the very bedrock of impactful leadership.

Understanding Trust in the Leadership

Trust, as an integral part of leadership, begins with an understanding. It is essential to grasp what trust is, how it feels, what its presence can do, and the void its absence can leave. A word so easily uttered, yet its depth is sometimes underappreciated until we take the time to unravel its intricacies. A leader's journey to cultivate trust requires a detailed map, and our first step is to comprehend the nature of trust itself.

Imagine a professional orchestra, with each musician an expert in their chosen instrument. They rely on their conductor not only to set the tempo but also to shape the performance, guiding them to a unified and harmonious result. Trust, in this context, is the invisible thread that weaves the musicians and the conductor into a single, vibrant entity. It's their belief that the conductor knows the score, understands each instrument, and will lead them to a magnificent crescendo.

Now picture a CEO, holding the reins of a Fortune 500 company. Each division, each team, every individual within the organization is like a musician in an orchestra, their own instrument being their specific role or task. Trust is what enables the CEO to conduct this vast ensemble, to guide them towards a harmonious performance in the form of the company's success. Without trust, the melody becomes discordant, and the performance falters.

In leadership, trust is synonymous with credibility. It's about following through on promises, showing competence, and maintaining reliability. These elements together form a kind of unspoken contract between the leader and their team. Breach this contract, and trust evaporates, leaving behind a trail of disillusionment. This is why understanding trust is the cornerstone of effective leadership.

There's a tendency to view trust in a binary light—you either trust someone or you don't. However, trust is more nuanced. It's multi-dimensional, comprising different elements like competence trust (trust in someone's skills and abilities) and interpersonal trust (trust in someone's character and integrity). Recognizing these dimensions helps leaders to understand that building trust is a multifaceted process that goes beyond just delivering on tasks.

Consider for a moment, the real-world example of a newly appointed leader in an organization. She steps into a team whose trust in leadership has been shaken by frequent turnover at the top. The task before her is not just to assure the team of her competence, but also to convince them of her commitment and integrity. It's about showing up, day after day, doing what she says she will do, demonstrating that she values them, and making decisions that benefit the team and the organization. Each of these actions contributes to building trust, piece by piece.

Trust isn't just a one-way street. It's not merely about how much your team trusts you—it's also about how much you trust your team. The extent to which you delegate, seek input, and encourage autonomy speaks volumes about the level of trust you have in your team. When leaders trust their teams, it fosters a sense of belonging and motivation, propelling the team towards high performance.

Now, let's not forget, trust involves vulnerability. It's about allowing for the possibility of being let down. This vulnerability, though, is not a weakness—it's a strength. It's what allows us to connect, to build relationships, to form teams, and to strive towards a common purpose. Understanding this facet of trust can revolutionize how you lead.

Trust in leadership is like a garden. It requires consistent nurturing, and each action of a leader is like a drop of water that either nourishes or depletes the garden. The beauty of this garden is not just for the leader to enjoy; it's for the entire team, the organization, and all its stakeholders.

Finally, remember that trust is reciprocal. The more you demonstrate trustworthiness, the more likely your team is to mirror that behavior. This creates a positive feedback loop, leading to a culture where trust thrives.

To understand trust in leadership is to recognize its complexity, its nuances, and its incredible potential to transform teams and organizations. It's the cornerstone that, when placed with care and understanding, can support a structure of leadership that is not just strong, but also inspiring.

Context Building and Maintaining Trust as a Leader

Building and maintaining trust as a leader is a delicate art form —a dance where timing, rhythm, and movement matter. Like a potter molding clay on a spinning wheel, it requires a gentle touch combined with steady, relentless focus. The process is neither linear nor static, but a dynamic one that evolves in response to situations, people, and the passage of time.

Trust in leadership is not a commodity you can buy or a prize you can win. It's not an attribute you can wear like a badge of honor. It is instead an earned favor, won over through consistent action and genuine engagement. Consider this: when you meet someone new, trust is not immediately present. It is neither assumed nor given—it must be cultivated.

Imagine a seasoned CEO taking the helm of a startup. The environment is chaotic, the stakes are high, and there's little room for error. The team is composed of bright, young individuals who are skilled but inexperienced. In this context, building trust becomes paramount to leading effectively and driving the organization towards success.

The CEO could start by getting to know the team—not just their names and roles, but their aspirations, challenges, and strengths. She could invest time in understanding the startup's culture, its unspoken rules, and the dynamics that govern its operations. This initial effort lays the foundation for genuine connection, which is the first step in building trust.

Now, the CEO has a dual task: she needs to prove her competence and exhibit empathy. She needs to show that she understands the startup's needs, has a viable strategy to address them, and can make tough decisions when required. At the same time, she needs to demonstrate that she values her team, respects their input, and cares about their well-being. Striking a balance between these two aspects is crucial.

The process of building trust also requires patience and consistency. Trust isn't built in a day or a week—it's a long-term investment. Let's return to our CEO at the startup. Suppose she starts involving the team in decision-making, shows appreciation for good work, and acts with integrity. Initially, the team might be skeptical, waiting for her to revert to autocratic ways. But as she continues to act consistently over weeks and months, they start to trust her. They start to believe in her leadership.

Trust building is not just about what you say, but what you do. When leaders' actions align with their words, it sends a strong message about their integrity. It shows that they walk the talk, that they can be relied upon. But when there's a mismatch, it erodes trust rapidly. The rule is simple: say what you mean and mean what you say.

Now, let's not overlook an essential aspect— vulnerability. Showing vulnerability is a powerful way of building trust. It humanizes the leader, making them more relatable. When our CEO admits that she doesn't have all the answers, but is committed to finding them with the team, it fosters a deeper connection. It builds a sense of shared purpose and collective responsibility.

Maintaining trust is as important as building it, and arguably harder. Trust can be lost in an instant and takes far longer to rebuild. Hence, it's essential to nurture the trust that has been built and safeguard it diligently. That means continuing to act with integrity, showing empathy, demonstrating competence, and acknowledging mistakes.

Remember, trust isn't static—it needs to be continually earned and reinforced. It's not enough for our CEO to have won the team's trust once. She needs to maintain it through her ongoing actions and decisions. The moment she becomes complacent, she risks losing that trust.

Leadership without trust is like a ship without a compass—it loses direction and is left adrift. In a volatile, uncertain world, trust is the anchor that keeps the organization steady. Building and maintaining trust is an ongoing process, demanding constant attention and care.
Finally, it's important to understand that trust, once broken, is not easily repaired. A single misstep can shatter the carefully built edifice of trust, sending it crashing down. This makes it all the more crucial for leaders to uphold trust and protect it fiercely.

Trust-building is, in essence, an exercise in authenticity, consistency, and empathy. It is an art that all leaders must master, for it is the cornerstone of effective leadership. Cultivating trust is not just a leadership strategy—it is a way of being, a compass that guides all actions and decisions. It's a metamorphosis that every leader must undergo to lead effectively amidst unpredictable change.

The Role of Trust in Crisis Leadership

Let's take a moment to consider an all-too-common scenario: a global pandemic has upended life as we know it. Businesses across sectors are reeling under its impact, with revenues plummeting and uncertainty looming large. Amidst this turbulence, leaders face a monumental challenge. It is in such a crisis that the role of trust in leadership comes to the forefront, like a beacon illuminating the path ahead.

Crisis situations are akin to navigating uncharted

waters in a storm. There's fear, uncertainty, and a pervasive sense of instability. It's during these times that the trust a leader has fostered becomes their most valuable asset. But why is trust so critical in crisis leadership? The answer lies in understanding the dynamics of a crisis.

When faced with a crisis, the initial human response is often fear. We fear the unknown, we fear change, and most importantly, we fear loss. This fear can lead to panic, making people reactive rather than responsive. But a trusted leader can be a calming influence, a voice of reason amidst the chaos.

Imagine a company that is suddenly forced to shift to remote work due to a pandemic. Employees are anxious, grappling with the challenges of balancing work and home in an entirely new context. The leader, in this case, needs to allay their fears, reassure them, and provide clear, consistent communication. This can only be effectively done if there's a foundation of trust already in place.

Trust enables leaders to navigate through crisis effectively because it fosters open communication. In times of crisis, rumors and misinformation can spread rapidly, creating unnecessary panic and confusion. But when employees trust their leaders, they are more likely to turn to them for accurate information and clarity.

Think about a hospital in the midst of a health crisis. The stakes are high, and misinformation could have dire consequences. The hospital staff, from doctors to nurses to administrators, needs to have faith in their leadership to navigate the crisis successfully. They need to trust that the leadership will provide timely, transparent information, even when the news is not good.

Crisis also demands tough decisions—decisions that may be unpopular or difficult to accept. But when a leader has established a reservoir of trust, these decisions are more likely to be accepted and understood. Consider the unfortunate necessity of layoffs during a financial crisis. While heartbreaking, when the decision comes from a trusted leader, employees are more likely to understand it as a painful but necessary step for the organization's survival, rather than an arbitrary or unjust action.

During a crisis, there's often a need for rapid change and adaptation, which can be unsettling. Trust in leadership can act as a powerful catalyst for embracing change. It makes people feel safe to take risks, to step out of their comfort zones, and to experiment with new ways of working. In essence, it makes the unfamiliar a little less daunting.

Imagine a manufacturing firm pivoting to produce essential supplies during a pandemic. It's a radical shift that requires employees to adapt quickly to new processes and protocols. If they trust their leaders, they're more likely to embrace this change and commit to making it a success.

Trust also cultivates resilience in times of crisis. Resilience—the ability to withstand adversity and bounce back —is critical in navigating through turbulent times. When employees trust their leaders, they are more likely to remain committed and engaged, even in the face of setbacks. They're more likely to believe in the organization's ability to weather the storm and emerge stronger.

Consider the resilience of the teams working in the hospitality industry during the COVID-19 pandemic. With travel coming to a standstill, many hotels faced significant financial strain. Yet, the staff rallied together, innovating new ways to serve customers while ensuring safety. This kind of resilience stems from trust in leadership.

Moreover, trust in leadership is not just crucial during a crisis, but also in the aftermath. As the dust settles and the organization begins to recover, it's the trust in leadership that helps rebuild and move forward. It helps retain talent, attract resources, and restore faith among stakeholders.

The role of trust in crisis leadership cannot be overstated. Trust is not just a "nice-to-have" but a critical element that can make or break the crisis management effort. It is the invisible thread that holds the fabric of an organization together in the face of adversity.

Crisis, in all its unpredictability, puts leadership to the ultimate test. Leaders who have taken the time to build and nurture trust find themselves better equipped to face this test. Trust, in a sense, is the unsung hero of crisis leadership—the cornerstone that upholds the edifice of an organization amid unpredictable change.

Leaders, thus, must remember that building trust is not a one-time task, but an ongoing commitment. It's an investment that yields dividends in times of calm and crisis alike. It's the metamorphosis that prepares them to lead effectively, even when the tide turns against them.

Trust-building Leadership Guide

In the dynamic landscape of modern leadership, trust isn't just a virtue—it's an imperative. Building trust is an art, with its canvas being the relationships we nurture, and its colors the actions we take. To help you hone this art, here is a pragmatic guide that offers actionable insights and recommendations. These tools and tips serve as a roadmap, guiding you as you build and cultivate trust as a leader.

1. Be Authentic: In an age where inauthenticity can be sensed a mile away, leaders must strive for authenticity. Take the example of a CEO who shares both successes and struggles with their team. This willingness to be vulnerable creates a shared human experience, which, in turn, engenders trust.

2. Practice Consistency: Consistency in words and actions is key to building trust. Consider leaders who follow through on their promises—every time, without fail. This reliability creates an environment where team members feel secure, and trust naturally flourishes.

3. Embrace Transparency: When leaders are transparent about their decisions, they leave no room for suspicion or doubt. Consider the case of a business leader who shares the rationale behind difficult decisions, such as layoffs. By being open about their thought process, they foster an atmosphere of trust, even in challenging times.

4. Show Empathy: Leaders who can empathize with their team members' experiences are often trusted more. It's the leaders who step in to understand the trials and triumphs of their teams, such as a manager who takes the time to learn about the unique challenges faced by remote employees during a pandemic.

5. Listen Actively: Effective leaders are good listeners. They engage in active listening, encouraging dialogue and understanding the perspectives of others. Whether it's a team brainstorming session or a one-on-one discussion, active listening paves the way for trust.

6. Provide Constructive Feedback: Constructive feedback, delivered in a sensitive manner, demonstrates a leader's investment in their team's growth. Just as a mentor guides their mentee with valuable insights, leaders, too, can build trust by providing feedback that helps their teams improve and thrive.

7. Recognize and Reward: By acknowledging and rewarding the efforts of their team, leaders show that they value their contribution. This recognition can be as simple as a heartfelt 'thank you' or as elaborate as an employee of the month award.

8. Be Approachable: An open-door policy is more than just a metaphor. Leaders who are approachable, who make themselves available for their teams, inherently encourage trust. They make sure to let their teams know that their doors (or email inboxes) are always open.

9. Encourage Accountability: Trustworthy leaders hold themselves and their teams accountable. They set clear expectations and stand by them, making it known that they expect the same of their team. They lead by example, holding themselves accountable first and foremost.

10. Navigate through Conflicts: Conflicts are inevitable. How leaders handle conflicts can significantly impact the level of trust in their team. They aim for resolution, not domination, using conflicts as an opportunity to learn, grow, and understand each other better.

* * *

Remember, trust-building is not a one-off activity. It's a continuous process, a series of actions repeated over time that solidify into the rock-solid foundation of trust. And just like a magnificent piece of art, it takes time, patience, and perseverance. With these tools and tips in your arsenal, you're well equipped to cultivate trust—the cornerstone of effective leadership.

CHAPTER 14 - ETHICAL LEADERSHIP: GUIDING WITH INTEGRITY

Envision vast urban landscapes, filled with towering businesses, each representing a fusion of ideas, aspirations, and most importantly, people. In these settings, leadership emerges, but it's a leader's moral integrity that truly directs organizations' trajectories.

At pivotal junctures in our careers, choices extend beyond profit margins, delving into realms of right versus wrong, integrity against compromise, and responsibility over neglect. Herein lies the significance of ethics, the beacon guiding leaders amidst uncertainties towards principled clarity.

Our exploration into ethical leadership begins not with abstract concepts, but by recognizing the intricate, real-world challenges leaders face, and the consequences of their choices. By understanding the tenets of ethical leadership, we gain insight into its broader relevance and implications.

Ethical leadership's influence on organizational performance is undeniable. It ensures that businesses not just take the right path but also achieve enduring success. By spotlighting organizations where ethical guidance has significantly impacted culture and performance, we discern the tangible link between principled leadership and business triumph.

Crucially, a leader's ethical mettle is truly gauged during crises. This chapter delves into real-world instances where leaders, amidst challenging dilemmas, remained steered by their moral values.

Achieving proficiency in ethical leadership necessitates continuous effort, self-assessment, and refinement. To aid this journey, we provide an Ethical Leadership Checklist.

This chapter marries deep insights, actionable strategies, and introspective reflections to fortify your grasp and execution of ethical leadership. Leadership isn't about domination but purposeful guidance. Ethical leadership is about awareness, accountability, and a steadfast commitment to principled actions. As you progress, let this chapter illuminate your path towards becoming the principled leader you envision.

Defining Ethical Leadership: Principles and Practices

What is it about ethical leadership that commands such attention and respect? It's not the lofty rhetoric or the moral posturing. It's something more visceral, more tangible. Ethical leadership represents the embodiment of principles and practices that resonate with our fundamental understanding of right and wrong. But what does this mean, practically speaking? Let's explore.

Ethical leadership is not simply about adhering to a code of conduct. It's about setting a standard, acting as a role model. Take, for instance, Arianna, the CEO of a burgeoning tech startup. She realized early on that to infuse an ethical culture within her team, she needed to walk the talk. Arianna made it a point to always credit ideas, treat all team members fairly, and to handle conflicts with transparency. This practice of consistency was her first step towards ethical leadership.

Indeed, ethical leadership demands consistency. Inconsistent behavior, where a leader preaches one value but acts on another, causes confusion and mistrust. This was evidenced in a manufacturing company where the CEO publicly touted the importance of safety, yet consistently bypassed regulations to expedite production. The result? A deeply ingrained culture of skepticism and apprehension.

The principles that underpin ethical leadership are not only about adhering to laws but also encompass values that engender trust, such as honesty, integrity, and fairness. A study on workplace ethics by the Ethics and Compliance Initiative reveals that organizations with strong ethical cultures have 50% less misconduct than those with poor ethical cultures. A statistic that underscores the power of ethics to shape behavior and outcomes.

Ethical leaders are not just role models; they are active advocates of ethical behavior. They take steps to establish ethical standards, promote open dialogue around ethical dilemmas, and take action when ethical standards are breached.

Consider the case of Mary Barra, CEO of General Motors, who faced a significant challenge early in her tenure when safety issues led to the recall of millions of vehicles. Barra didn't shy away from the crisis. Instead, she publicly apologized for the mistakes, held people accountable, and took steps to transform the culture within GM. Her actions epitomize the courage and accountability inherent in ethical leadership.

Ethical leaders are empathetic. They understand and consider the feelings and perspectives of others. They are aware that their decisions have implications for their teams, their stakeholders, and wider society.

Take the case of Paul Polman, the former CEO of Unilever, who championed the cause of sustainability within the organization. His actions reflect his empathy for the future generation and the environment. He did not chase short-term profits at the expense of long-term environmental costs, a decision that resonated with stakeholders and elevated Unilever's reputation.

Ethical leadership is also about being transparent.

Ethical leaders do not withhold information or manipulate it for personal gain. They understand that transparency fosters trust and encourages the same behavior in others.

The story of Ray Dalio, the founder of Bridgewater Associates, springs to mind. Dalio instituted a policy of radical transparency within his organization, which although was initially hard to adapt to, cultivated an environment of trust and open communication that contributed to Bridgewater's incredible success.

While these principles and practices shape the contours of ethical leadership, the actual practice of it varies across contexts and individuals. It's as much an art as a science, a delicate dance between personal values and organizational expectations, between immediate needs and long-term implications.

Ethical leadership demands not just adherence to these principles but an astute understanding of their significance in various contexts. It requires the courage to stand by these principles even when they are challenged, and the wisdom to navigate the complex ethical dilemmas that leadership often entails.

Finally, remember that ethical leadership is a dynamic process. It evolves with each interaction, each decision, and each challenge. It is about continuous learning, reflection, and growth. It's not about being flawless; it's about being aware, being accountable, and being committed to ethics as a defining element of leadership.

Ethical leadership might seem like a daunting endeavor, but its rewards are profound. It builds trust, drives performance, and imbues the workplace with a sense of purpose and integrity. In the volatile, uncertain landscape of business, it serves as a beacon, illuminating the path towards a sustainable, successful future

The Impact of Ethical Leadership on Organizational Performance

It's a common perception, sometimes rooted in the cynicism that comes from corporate scandal after corporate scandal, that ethical leadership is a nice-to-have, not a must-have. It's something that would be good in an ideal world, but in the harsh reality of business, the bottom-line rules. This perception, however, fails to recognize the profound impact ethical leadership can have on organizational performance.

Let's imagine for a moment a world-renowned luxury fashion brand we'll call 'Eleganz'. When its CEO, Vanessa, took the reins, she made it clear that ethical sourcing was non-negotiable. Many were skeptical. After all, the fashion industry is notorious for prioritizing style and cost over ethical considerations. But Vanessa held her ground.

The transformation wasn't immediate. It involved challenging negotiations with suppliers, increased production costs, and even a temporary dip in profits. However, Vanessa stayed the course, trusting in the long-term value of ethical leadership. Her resilience paid off. Over time, Eleganz gained a reputation for being a responsible, ethical brand. This set it apart from competitors, attracted a loyal customer base, and, most importantly, drove its market share and profitability to new heights.

One might argue that Eleganz is an exception, that not all industries or companies can afford to prioritize ethics over profits. But what if we told you this isn't an isolated case? Research consistently shows a positive correlation between ethical leadership and various aspects of organizational performance.

A study in the Journal of Business Ethics found that ethical leadership is associated with greater employee satisfaction, productivity, and commitment. When leaders act ethically, it creates a positive working environment that motivates employees to give their best. Furthermore, it reduces incidences of counterproductive work behavior, such as absenteeism and turnover, which have direct implications on productivity and costs.

Moreover, ethical leadership fosters innovation. It does so by creating a climate of trust and openness where ideas are freely exchanged, risks are encouraged, and failures are viewed as opportunities for learning, not as grounds for punishment.

Patagonia, the outdoor clothing company, exemplifies this. Under the ethical leadership of its founder, Yvon Chouinard, Patagonia has fostered a culture of innovation focused on reducing environmental impact. This has resulted in groundbreaking initiatives, like the development of a wetsuit from natural rubber, a significant departure from the non-renewable, petroleum-based neoprene used by other companies.

It's not just internal performance that's impacted by ethical leadership. Consider reputation, which is increasingly recognized as a critical driver of organizational success. In our hyper-connected world, news of unethical behavior can spread quickly, causing irreversible damage to a company's image. Ethical leadership protects against such risks, fostering a strong reputation that enhances customer loyalty, attracts talent, and improves relations with stakeholders.

Take the case of LEGO, which has consistently topped Reputation Institute's Global RepTrak 100, a measure of the most reputable companies in the world. This is largely due to its commitment to ethical leadership, reflected in its high-quality products, focus on children's development, and ambitious environmental goals.

Moreover, ethical leadership can contribute to financial performance. A study published in the Journal of Business Ethics found that companies with a strong ethical identity tend to outperform those without in terms of profitability, growth, and shareholder return.

Of course, this doesn't imply that every ethical decision will have an immediate positive impact on the bottom line. As with Eleganz, there may be short-term costs. But the long-term gains - enhanced reputation, employee engagement, customer loyalty, and financial performance - are well worth it.

Lastly, in times of crisis, the value of ethical leadership becomes even more evident. In such times, companies face not just operational and financial challenges, but also ethical dilemmas. Ethical leadership guides the response to these dilemmas, ensuring decisions align with core values, uphold stakeholder interests, and ultimately, contribute to the company's resilience.

The impact of ethical leadership on organizational performance is profound and far-reaching. It goes beyond financial metrics to encompass employee well-being, innovation, reputation, and resilience. It's not just a nice-to-have; in today's complex, rapidly-changing business landscape, it's a must-have. A beacon that guides not just towards profitability, but also towards a future where businesses contribute positively to society.

Ethical Leadership During Crisis: Case Studies and Lessons

Crisis - the very word conjures images of chaos, fear, and uncertainty. For leaders, a crisis often presents the most challenging situations they will face in their careers. It's in these moments, when the pressure is greatest, that the true essence of leadership shines through. And nothing demonstrates this more powerfully than ethical leadership during a crisis.

Let's look at the 2010 Chilean mining disaster. 33 miners were trapped underground for 69 agonizing days. Amid this harrowing crisis, the then President Sebastián Piñera exemplified ethical leadership. He promised that the Chilean government would do everything possible to rescue the miners, and he delivered on that promise. He treated the miners and their families with dignity, kept them informed, and involved them in decision-making. The result? Not only were all the miners safely rescued, but the crisis also enhanced trust in his leadership.

Then, consider Johnson & Johnson's handling of the Tylenol poisoning crisis in 1982. Seven people died after ingesting Tylenol capsules laced with cyanide. Instead of trying to minimize the incident or shift blame, Johnson & Johnson put consumers' safety first. The company swiftly pulled 31 million bottles of Tylenol off the shelves, at a cost of over $100 million, and introduced tamper-proof packaging. This ethical response bolstered the public's trust in Johnson & Johnson and ensured Tylenol's successful return to the market.

What distinguishes these leaders isn't just their effective crisis management. It's their ethical approach to leadership during a crisis. They demonstrated integrity, keeping their promises and standing by their values even when it was costly or challenging. They treated all stakeholders with respect and consideration, communicating transparently and involving them in decision-making. They showed empathy, acknowledging the pain and uncertainty caused by the crisis and offering support.

But what about situations where leaders fell short in their ethical responsibilities during a crisis? There are lessons to be learned there too. We could, for instance, delve into the Volkswagen emissions scandal in 2015. The company was found guilty of installing software in cars to cheat on emission tests. Instead of taking responsibility, senior leaders claimed they had no knowledge of the deceit, raising questions about their honesty and accountability.

The consequences were severe. Volkswagen's reputation took a massive hit, sales plummeted, and the company incurred billions in fines and compensation costs. What's more, the trust that customers, employees, and regulators had in Volkswagen was deeply eroded, taking years to rebuild. The scandal underscores the heavy price organizations pay when leaders fail to uphold ethical standards during a crisis.

So, how can leaders ensure they uphold ethics during a crisis? The first step is to acknowledge the crisis and take responsibility. Sweeping problems under the rug or shifting blame won't do. As Johnson & Johnson and Chile's President Piñera demonstrated, owning up to the crisis and promising to resolve it can strengthen stakeholders' trust.

Next, leaders need to prioritize stakeholder well-being over short-term profit or reputation. This might involve making difficult decisions, like Johnson & Johnson's recall of Tylenol. Yet, by putting people first, leaders can turn a crisis into an opportunity to reinforce their organization's values and strengthen its reputation.

Communication is also critical. Leaders should provide timely, accurate, and clear information about the crisis and how it's being managed. Importantly, they should be empathetic, recognizing the distress and uncertainty the crisis may be causing stakeholders.

Another key element is transparency. This involves being open about the crisis' causes and impacts, the steps being taken to resolve it, and any challenges or setbacks. Transparency fosters trust and confidence in leadership and helps prevent rumors and misinformation.

Lastly, ethical leaders involve stakeholders in decision-making during a crisis. This not only ensures diverse perspectives are considered but also gives stakeholders a sense of control and ownership over the crisis response.

Crisis situations are a litmus test for ethical leadership. They demand courage, integrity, empathy, transparency, and respect for stakeholders. By embracing these principles, leaders can navigate the stormy waters of a crisis and come out stronger on the other side. The lessons from these case studies offer a beacon of light, illuminating the path that leaders must tread in their darkest hours.

Ethical Leadership Checklist

Ethical leadership, we have discovered, is more than just a series of decisions or a stance we take. It's a mindset, a lens through which we view every aspect of our leadership role. And while the path of ethical leadership may not be the easiest, it is the most rewarding - a strategic choice that safeguards our organizations' reputation and ensures their sustainable success.

We have learned the theory, pondered the principles, and studied real-world case studies. Yet, how do we translate all this into action? How do we ensure our leadership is consistently ethical, especially during crises? Here's a handy checklist, a set of tools and tips that can serve as your ethical leadership compass:

1. Commit to the Core Values: Ethical leadership begins with a commitment to your organization's core values. These are your guiding principles, the standards that shape your decisions and actions. Whether you're facing a minor issue or a major crisis, these values should always be your touchstone.

2. Foster an Ethical Culture: It's one thing to be an ethical leader yourself, but quite another to foster an ethical culture within your organization. Encourage ethical behavior, celebrate ethical victories, and use lapses as learning opportunities.

3. Be Transparent: Transparent leaders don't hide the truth or sugarcoat reality. They communicate honestly and openly, sharing both successes and failures. Transparency builds trust, which is crucial for effective leadership, particularly during a crisis.

4. Demonstrate Accountability: As a leader, you need to take responsibility for your actions and their consequences. When things go wrong, don't pass the buck. Accept accountability, learn from the experience, and strive to do better.

5. Prioritize Stakeholder Well-Being: Ethical leaders prioritize their stakeholders' well-being. Whether you're dealing with employees, customers, or shareholders, consider their needs and interests in your decision-making process.

6. Practice Empathy: Empathy is a key trait of ethical leaders. Understand and acknowledge your stakeholders' perspectives and feelings. Remember, leadership is about relationships, and relationships are built on empathy.

7. Maintain Integrity: Integrity is the cornerstone of ethical leadership. Stay true to your values, even when it's difficult. Your stakeholders will respect you for it, and your organization will be stronger.

8. Encourage Diverse Perspectives: Ethical leaders appreciate that everyone has a unique perspective to offer. Encourage diversity of thought in your organization. It will foster innovation and ensure you're making well-rounded decisions.

9. Set the Example: As a leader, your team looks to you for guidance. Set the example of ethical behavior in all you do. This will inspire your team to do the same.

10. Continually Learn and Adapt: The world is constantly changing, and ethical dilemmas evolve with it. Commit to ongoing learning, stay informed about ethical issues in your industry, and be willing to adapt your approach as needed.

* * *

Weaving these principles into your leadership approach will help ensure that you're leading with ethics at the forefront. And remember, ethical leadership isn't just about doing what's right when everyone's watching - it's about doing what's right when no one's watching. That's the hallmark of a true ethical leader.

PART VI: THE REFLECTIVE LEADER: LOOKING INWARD FOR GROWTH AND DEVELOPMENT

CHAPTER 15 - REFLECTION, FEEDBACK, AND GROWTH: THE INTERNAL DYNAMICS OF LEADERSHIP

In the vibrant heart of Miami's healthcare industry, Monica, a seasoned leader in a prominent hospital, found herself facing a challenge unlike any other. As the demographics of the community around her changed and the needs of her patients evolved, she recognized a new calling. It was no longer enough to lead; she needed to evolve. The Power of Self-Awareness, Feedback, and a Growth Mindset in Leadership beckoned her toward a new horizon. Like a surgeon skillfully navigating the complexities of the human body, she began to apply precision, empathy, and constant learning to her leadership. The scalpel of self-awareness, the stitches of feedback, and the healing balm of growth would become her tools.

During the unprecedented times of a global pandemic, the world saw crisis like never before, and Miami's healthcare industry was no exception. Reflection, Feedback, and Growth During and After a Crisis were essential in adapting to new realities. Monica, embracing these principles, steered her team through the storm. Reflecting on past experiences, accepting feedback with humility, and fostering growth, she shaped a resilient and responsive unit that not only weathered the crisis but emerged stronger. The lessons learned were not isolated incidents but patterns that can guide any organization through uncertainty.

Leadership, like the healthcare profession, requires a deep understanding of complex systems and the human psyche. The Leadership Self-Awareness, Feedback, and Growth Guide will unveil a path that is both intuitive and deliberate. Monica's story aligns with this guide, as she creatively used patient feedback to improve care, leveraged team insights to foster a collaborative environment, and embraced self-awareness to fine-tune her leadership style. The practical wisdom within these pages finds resonance in many industries, such as a Miami-based cruise line that revolutionized customer experience through feedback-driven innovation.

The subtropical climes of Miami are known for their allure, and so is the path of Reflection, Feedback, and Growth in leadership. They are the lifeblood of effective leadership, as was seen in the transformation of a struggling community center under Monica's guidance. The path she walked is a microcosm of a broader leadership paradigm that recognizes the potential within every individual and organization.

Chapter 15, "Reflection, Feedback, and Growth: The Internal Dynamics of Leadership", opens a window into these principles through Monica's eyes and beyond. As we embark on this exploration, we will discover that these aren't just abstract concepts but tangible practices that can be applied every day. This chapter is a call to action to all leaders to see themselves and their teams anew and to chart a course for excellence that resonates with the vibrancy, resilience, and innovation that exemplify Miami's spirit.

The Power of Self-Awareness, Feedback, and a Growth Mindset in Leadership

When Microsoft CEO Satya Nadella took the reins, he brought a sense of empathy and self-awareness that fundamentally shifted the company's culture. He understood that before leading others, one must first understand oneself. This understanding is not confined to recognizing personal strengths and weaknesses but extends to understanding how one's actions resonate with others. This deeper insight can be seen in various successful leadership models across different organizations and industries. It's not just about internal reflection; it's about understanding how internal reality manifests externally.

Google is a company that exemplifies the practice of fostering continuous feedback among employees. The company's culture encourages open dialogue, allowing leaders to be receptive to diverse perspectives. Feedback becomes a conversation, a back-and-forth that builds relationships and insights rather than a one-time event. It's a method that other companies can emulate to achieve higher levels of engagement and performance, creating a culture where feedback is not just accepted but sought out.

IBM has long been an advocate for a growth mindset, believing that skills and intelligence can be developed. This belief has helped foster a culture of continuous learning and adaptability. By encouraging employees to see challenges as opportunities for growth rather than insurmountable obstacles, IBM keeps its organization agile and innovative even in an ever-changing technological landscape. A growth mindset doesn't just apply to individuals; it permeates the entire organizational culture.

At General Electric, under Jack Welch's leadership, the idea of "work-out" sessions where employees at all levels could speak openly allowed for feedback and self-awareness to coalesce. The integration of self-knowledge with external insight helped shape leadership strategies that were both personally resonant and organizationally aligned. The willingness to be open to feedback while staying true to one's own understanding is a tightrope walk, but it is one that can lead to rich rewards.

Adobe's shift away from traditional performance reviews to more frequent "check-ins" encouraged ongoing dialogue around growth and development. Leaders who understood their role in this process could guide their teams towards continual expansion and self-improvement. This intersection between self-awareness and growth mindset encourages a more dynamic and adaptive leadership style, applicable to various settings, from tech giants to small startups.

The multinational conglomerate 3M showcases how feedback can be a catalyst for growth. By embedding feedback into daily practice, the organization has stimulated creativity and innovation. This openness to feedback, married to a robust growth mindset, has resulted in a product portfolio of over 55,000 items and a reputation for fostering an intrapreneurial spirit. The lessons from 3M can be drawn into various contexts, emphasizing the universality of these principles.

In the realm of non-profits, organizations like the Bill & Melinda Gates Foundation demonstrate that self-awareness isn't restricted to profit-driven contexts. Leaders in philanthropy recognize their impact and navigate complex global issues with a clear understanding of their values and objectives. Whether in business or charity, a true understanding of oneself and one's role in a broader context can drive not only success but significant positive impact.

Educational institutions like Harvard Business School have integrated 360-degree feedback into their curricula, emphasizing that feedback isn't confined to corporate environments. This method helps future leaders appreciate the diverse perceptions of colleagues, fostering empathy and broader understanding. Feedback, in this context, becomes a tool for personal growth and a way to cultivate leadership that is responsive, empathetic, and effective.

The Golden State Warriors' basketball team embodies a growth mindset, emphasizing development and continual improvement. This approach has proven to be a winning strategy, demonstrating that the principles of growth mindset translate beyond traditional business environments. It's a lesson in the universal applicability of a growth mindset, applicable not only in the corridors of corporations but on the playing fields and in the classrooms.

Whether it's the nimble strategies of Spotify or the relentless focus on customer feedback at Amazon, the triad of self-awareness, feedback, and a growth mindset are present across various industries. These principles don't just guide; they transform, adapt, and innovate. They're applicable in tech startups or century-old manufacturing firms, driving innovation and success through understanding, dialogue, and growth.

It's worth acknowledging that these principles are not without challenges. The missteps at companies like Kodak and Blockbuster demonstrate what happens when a lack of self-awareness and resistance to feedback lead to an inability to adapt. Lessons can be drawn from these failures, underlining the essential nature of these leadership dynamics. It's not enough to have the tools; they must be employed with wisdom and agility.

This intricate dance between self-awareness, feedback, and a growth mindset forms a compass for leadership. Whether it's the successes of Tesla in revolutionizing the automotive industry or the way small startups like Slack have grown, these principles remain at the core. They're not just theoretical constructs but practical tools that can guide leadership practice in diverse and often challenging environments.

Small business owners, educators, and community leaders also tap into self-awareness, feedback, and growth to make a meaningful impact. They chart a course that is both personal and universal, resonant and revolutionary. The applicability of these principles extends beyond boardrooms and into the daily lives of people leading in various capacities.

They're principles that enable metamorphosis, driving not just business success but societal advancement.

The power of self-awareness, feedback, and a growth mindset in leadership is a profound and nuanced subject. From the boardrooms of Fortune 500 companies to classrooms and basketball courts, these principles resonate. They offer a guide, not a map, to navigate the complex and unpredictable terrain of leadership in our modern world. They challenge us to be mindful, engaged, and ever-growing, ensuring that the metamorphosis of leadership continues to evolve. By internalizing these principles, readers will find a strategic guide to chart the course for their organizations, regardless of the industry or scale.

Reflection, Feedback, and Growth During and After a Crisis

During the financial collapse of 2008, companies like Goldman Sachs faced a profound and often jarring confrontation with the nature of the decisions they had made. In the leadership corridors of this global finance giant, reflection was not merely a momentary act of contemplation. In a time of turbulence, it acted as a mirror, revealing not only the flaws but also the soul of an organization, unearthing the choices made and paving the path to be taken. The leadership's keen self-awareness provided a roadmap, not out of the crisis but through it, and thus the seeds of transformation were sown.

Toyota's response to the recall crisis in 2009 provides another illustrative study in the power of feedback. Faced with widespread recalls, the leadership of this automotive leader did not merely respond but engaged. They initiated open and transparent conversations with both customers and employees. This wasn't damage control; it was building bridges where there had been chasms. Feedback was not a mere reaction but a proactive embrace of a narrative that could have spiraled out of control.

Then there's Netflix's remarkable shift from DVD

rental to streaming. When faced with an existential crisis, their leadership did not falter or retreat but embraced a growth mindset that transformed potential calamity into unprecedented opportunity. This wasn't just about numbers or market share but about adapting to change, evolving with it, even when it arrived like an unexpected storm on a clear day.

Airbnb's journey during the COVID-19 pandemic is a testament to the resilience embedded in reflection. When the world shut down, and travel seemed a distant dream, the company's leadership had to make painful decisions. But it was their ability to reflect, understand, and empathize that carried them through the storm. They didn't just survive; they aligned with values that resonated deeply with both employees and customers, creating a more robust and cohesive organizational culture.

In times of intense crisis, organizations such as the U.S. Military have emphasized the importance of real-time feedback. Leaders on the battlefield don't have the luxury of delayed responses. It's about immediate understanding, adaptation, and action. The principles of feedback in the thick of combat are no different from those in a corporate boardroom. They underline the universality of feedback, a thread that connects vastly different contexts.

Mistakes, when not studied and understood, are merely failures. The BP oil spill and its aftermath were a crucible for growth. Leaders had to scrutinize what went wrong and ensure that those mistakes were etched not as scars but lessons. A crisis can be a harsh teacher, but growth arises from the willingness to learn, however painful the lessons might be.

Leadership in a crisis isn't just about making decisions; it's about reflecting with empathy and humanity. New Zealand's response to the Christchurch earthquakes underlined this principle. This wasn't strategy on paper; it was about resonating with the very human pain of loss and rebuilding. It's a lesson in leadership that transcends spreadsheets, stock prices, and strategic planning.

The healthcare system during COVID-19 became an evolving, complex, and highly dynamic arena for feedback. Frontline workers, leadership, and administrators were engaged in a constant feedback loop, learning and adapting at a speed never seen before. The crisis was unprecedented, but it was the adaptive capacity fostered through continuous feedback that provided a lifeline to millions.

Local governments' responses to natural disasters have shown that growth isn't confined to businesses. Communities grow, learn, and adapt. Leaders who understand this dynamic foster a collective growth mindset, turning recovery into resurgence, loss into opportunity, and despair into hope.

The airline industry's crisis during the pandemic didn't just affect one sector; it sent ripples across tourism and related sectors. Leaders had to reflect not in isolation but as part of an interconnected web, recognizing that a crisis in today's world rarely stays confined within neat boundaries.

The global crisis of climate change presents an unprecedented challenge, and the feedback must be a conversation among nations, cultures, and people. Leaders engaging in this dialogue must look beyond pointing fingers and find common ground for solutions. Feedback becomes not just a managerial tool but a bridge to a sustainable and shared future.

Kodak's rebirth and growth after a near brush with extinction stand as a remarkable story of adaptability and vision. Facing an existential threat, the company's leadership displayed a clear vision and willingness to venture into unknown territories. Growth here was not a linear path but a rediscovery and a reimagining of what was possible.

Whether it's the tech industry adapting to new privacy laws, farmers adjusting to changing weather patterns, or a local community recovering from a natural disaster, the triad of reflection, feedback, and growth remains consistent across landscapes. These aren't isolated acts but a unified response, shaping leadership in the face of uncertainty and turning the unpredictable into the manageable.

In the final analysis, crises are inevitable, but they are not insurmountable. The pages of history and the daily unfolding of world events provide ample testimony to leaders who have turned crises into opportunities through reflection, feedback, and growth. These principles form not merely a reaction to crisis but a proactive stance, guiding organizations and leaders through unpredictable landscapes. It's not about weathering the storm but learning to dance in the rain, and therein lies the metamorphosis that drives effective leadership amid the capricious tides of change.

Guiding Principles for Leadership Self-Awareness, Feedback, and Growth

In our hyper-connected, fast-changing world, leaders are often met with challenges that demand rapid adaptation and transformation. An effective leader recognizes that change is not just an external phenomenon but an internal opportunity for self-awareness, feedback, and growth. As we delve into the real-life narratives of global organizations and tap into the wisdom of those who have mastered the art of leading through uncertainty, a pattern of guiding principles emerges. These principles, far from being mere theoretical constructs, serve as compass points for leadership transformation.

Guiding Principle 1: Embrace Self-Reflection as a Daily Practice Consider the case of Satya Nadella at Microsoft, who initiated cultural change by first focusing on personal growth and self-awareness. Encouraging self-reflection can lead to more empathetic and responsive leadership.

- **Implement a daily practice of reflection.**
- **Use mindfulness techniques to foster presence and awareness.**

Guiding Principle 2: Foster a Culture of Open Feedback The transformation of Adobe's performance review system into regular "Check-Ins" illustrates the importance of fostering a culture of open feedback. Leaders should:

- **Establish regular one-on-one meetings for honest conversations.**
- **Promote a culture where feedback is a two-way street.**

Guiding Principle 3: Cultivate a Growth Mindset Howard Schultz's return to Starbucks and its subsequent resurgence underlines the value of cultivating a growth mindset in leadership.

- **Recognize and challenge fixed mindset tendencies.**
- **Celebrate effort and resilience, not just results.**

Guiding Principle 4: Utilize Feedback Loops The remarkable recovery of Delta Air Lines was accelerated through real-time feedback loops. Implementing these can make organizations more agile.

- **Set up mechanisms for continuous feedback from various stakeholders.**
- **Act on feedback promptly to foster trust and responsiveness.**

Guiding Principle 5: Align Personal and Organizational Values The rebranding of CVS Health, with its decision to stop selling tobacco, is a powerful example of aligning personal and organizational values.

- **Reflect on and clearly articulate your core values.**
- **Ensure alignment between personal and organizational values.**

Guiding Principle 6: Invest in Continuous Learning and Development General Electric's leadership development practices are renowned for promoting continuous growth.

- **Create personalized development plans.**
- **Foster an environment where learning is celebrated.**

Guiding Principle 7: Engage with Empathy During Crises New Zealand Prime Minister Jacinda Ardern's response to crises is a testament to the power of empathetic leadership.

- **Practice active listening and show authentic

concern.
- **Communicate with clarity and compassion.**

* * *

The above principles are not just tools in a toolkit; they are the cornerstones of a responsive and compassionate leadership paradigm. In embracing them, leaders are not merely adapting to change; they are transforming it into an opportunity for growth, a metamorphosis that aligns the heart and mind of the organization with the uncertain and ever-shifting sands of our global landscape.

CHAPTER 16 - RESILIENCE: THE BEACON FOR LEADERS AMID CHANGE

Resilience is not just a trend but the backbone of effective leadership, especially during adversity. It's about navigating setbacks and using them as platforms for growth. More than weathering crises, resilience encompasses the inner strength that equips leaders to handle daily challenges, turning them into opportunities.

In 'Understanding Resilience,' we'll delve into its multi-faceted nature—emotional fortitude, mental stamina, and adaptability—anchored by the story of Mirai, a startup CEO steering her team through challenging times.

'The Role of Resilience in Leadership' spotlights its significance in leadership. Drawing from a leading management institute's insights, we'll underscore how resilience acts as a buoy for teams amid the waves of change.

Highlighting 'Crisis Leadership,' we'll share Laura's tale, a manager who, during a supply chain disruption, not only sustains operations but innovates for better processes.

The Leadership Resilience Development Plan' offers a blueprint to nurture resilience, detailing strategies from building positive relationships to ensuring physical well-being, supplemented with real-life examples.

Conclusively, resilience stands as a cornerstone of impactful leadership. It's the invisible force behind successful strategies and the catalyst for progress, particularly during change. This chapter emphasizes the art of harnessing challenges to steer leadership forward. To resilience and beyond!

Understanding Resilience: Key to Thriving Amid Challenges

Resilience, to many, is a term that surfaces in conversations around mental toughness, around the ability to get back up after being knocked down. But let's pause for a moment to think about this – resilience is not just about getting back up; it's also about learning, adapting, and evolving from the fall. It's about transmuting setbacks into opportunities for growth, transforming adversity into an advantage.

Take the story of Mirai, a startup CEO, as a case in point. Her company, a promising health tech startup, was on the brink of releasing a revolutionary new product when they hit a formidable roadblock. A key component of their product failed rigorous testing standards. A lesser leader might have viewed this as a crippling blow. However, Mirai saw it as an opportunity for development.

Mirai's response to the crisis was not reactive but proactive. She didn't just aim to fix the problem; she sought to understand why it occurred and how they could innovate to prevent similar issues in the future. This wasn't about mere survival, or just getting back up. It was about turning a setback into a setup for a greater comeback.

Resilience is akin to a well-tuned symphony, composed of several harmonious elements. It involves the capacity to remain flexible in thoughts, feelings, and behaviors when faced with a disruption or change, navigating through the murky waters of adversity, and even emerging stronger.

Consider the psychological aspect of resilience. It's the ability to manage emotions effectively, to navigate through stress without letting it overpower your judgement or decision-making. Resilient leaders, like Mirai, understand that negative emotions are transient, that they are just as much a part of the human experience as positive emotions.

However, resilience goes beyond managing one's own emotions. It extends to empathizing with the emotional state of the team as well. When Mirai disclosed the product setback to her team, she acknowledged their collective disappointment but also highlighted their collective strength, their ability to turn things around. She emphasized their shared purpose, realigning her team's focus towards solution-building rather than problem-dwelling.

Another crucial element of resilience is the ability to maintain optimism despite difficulties. Not a blind, baseless optimism, but a grounded, realistic one that stems from an unwavering belief in one's capabilities and a clear understanding of the situation. When the future seemed uncertain for Mirai's startup, she reminded her team of the hurdles they had already overcome, of the innovative solutions they had already created.

Resilience is also rooted in acceptance. Acceptance of the fact that setbacks and failures are inevitable, that they are steppingstones to success. It's about acknowledging the reality of the situation, however grim, and not succumbing to denial or avoidance. When the product failure came to light, Mirai acknowledged the problem, took responsibility, and quickly shifted gears towards finding a solution.

Moreover, resilience is about fostering an environment that values learning and growth, an environment where mistakes are seen as opportunities to learn and improve. When the issue with the product was identified, Mirai used this as a learning opportunity for her team. They critically analyzed their process to identify gaps and, moving forward, implemented measures to enhance their product testing phase.

Additionally, resilience is interconnected with grit – the ability to persevere towards a long-term goal despite challenges and setbacks. Despite the crisis, Mirai did not lose sight of her company's vision. She remained focused on their goal of revolutionizing health tech, and this gave her the strength to steer her startup through the storm.

Furthermore, the social aspect of resilience can't be understated. Resilient leaders, like Mirai, understand the importance of leaning on others when times are tough, of fostering strong, positive relationships within their teams, which serve as a buffer against stress. They create an atmosphere of psychological safety, where everyone feels valued, heard, and supported.

Finally, resilience is not static but dynamic. It's not a trait that one either possesses or lacks, but a capacity that can be developed and nurtured over time. Mirai was not born a resilient leader. She had honed this ability over time, through her own experiences of trials and triumphs.

The thread that runs through each element of resilience is adaptability. It's the ability to pivot in response to change, to transform obstacles into opportunities for learning and growth. As leaders, it's not just about bouncing back from adversity but bouncing forward, using adversity as a springboard to leap towards growth and success.

So, resilience, as we see, is not just about survival, not just about bouncing back. It's about thriving amid challenges. It's about leveraging adversity to spur growth and transformation. Leaders like Mirai do not just survive crises – they use them as catalysts to forge a stronger, more resilient, and more successful future. The key to thriving amid challenges, then, lies in understanding and cultivating resilience, in turning the mirror inwards to reflect, adapt, and grow.

The Role of Resilience in Leadership

A leadership role is an invitation to sail in uncharted waters, to navigate the unpredictable tides of change. Resilience in leadership, then, is more than just a useful trait; it's the veritable rudder that keeps the ship on course amidst the stormy seas of uncertainty and disruption.

Resilience allows a leader to embrace and weather change rather than resist or be overwhelmed by it. When a change occurs, be it a shift in market dynamics, a change in team structure, or an unanticipated crisis, resilient leaders don't just passively ride out the storm; they actively navigate through it. A clear demonstration of this was seen in the leadership of Catherine, a seasoned executive in the banking industry.

When Catherine assumed her leadership role, the banking sector was on the brink of a digital transformation. While other leaders resisted the change, Catherine embraced it. She realized that resilience was not about resisting change, but about adapting to it. She led her team in adopting new technologies, upskilling, and pivoting their services to cater to the digital era.

Resilience is the cornerstone that supports the crucial traits that define effective leadership, such as decisiveness, confidence, and empathy. Take, for instance, the trait of decisiveness. The rapid pace of change demands quick decision-making, yet this can be challenging when the path ahead is unclear. Resilient leaders, like Catherine, have the ability to make decisive moves even when the outcome is uncertain.

Let's delve deeper into the story of Catherine. When the digital wave hit, the future of banking became highly uncertain. Despite this, Catherine made the bold decision to transition towards digital banking. This was not a decision made out of desperation but out of resilience. Catherine took calculated risks, trusting in her team's ability to adapt and thrive in the new digital landscape.

Another key leadership trait that resilience underpins is confidence. Confidence is not about having all the answers; it's about believing in your ability to find the solutions. When challenges arose during the digital transformation, Catherine remained confident. Her resilience was the wellspring of her confidence. She believed in her capacity to adapt, learn, and find solutions.

Resilience also fuels empathy, a critical leadership trait. Resilient leaders, like Catherine, understand that change can evoke a gamut of emotions in their team - fear, anxiety, excitement. They empathize with their team's emotional journey, providing support and reassurance. They don't dismiss or diminish their team's feelings; instead, they validate them, creating a safe space for open dialogue.

Moreover, resilience in leadership is about fostering a culture of resilience within the team. When Catherine led the digital transformation, she didn't just focus on the technical aspects. She also prioritized building a resilient team. She encouraged her team to view the transformation as an opportunity for growth, fostering a mindset of adaptability and continuous learning.

Also, resilient leaders recognize that failure is an integral part of growth. When the digital banking platform encountered initial hiccups, Catherine reframed these failures as learning opportunities. She encouraged her team to analyze the setbacks, learn from them, and use the insights to improve their service.

Furthermore, resilience equips leaders to maintain a positive outlook even when the odds are stacked against them. Catherine remained optimistic throughout the digital transformation, even when they encountered setbacks. She reminded her team of their collective strength and their shared mission, fostering a sense of optimism and shared purpose.

Resilience is also about leading by example. Catherine didn't just advocate resilience; she embodied it. She demonstrated adaptability, grit, and optimism, setting a powerful example for her team. Her resilience inspired her team to be resilient, creating a ripple effect.

Lastly, resilience in leadership is not a destination, but a continuous process of growth and adaptation. After the successful digital transformation, Catherine didn't rest on her laurels. She remained vigilant, ready to adapt to future changes. She understood that resilience is not a one-time feat, but an ongoing commitment to learning, growing, and adapting.

So, the role of resilience in leadership, as we see, extends far beyond crisis management. It's the underlying fabric that weaves together various leadership traits, shaping a leader who is adaptable, empathetic, and inspiring. Resilient leaders, like Catherine, don't just navigate change; they leverage it as a catalyst for growth, for themselves and their teams. They don't just survive the tides of change; they learn to sail with them, charting a course towards a resilient and successful future.

Effectiveness Crisis Leadership: Building and Demonstrating Resilience

Crisis and leadership are inextricably intertwined. A crisis has the remarkable ability to bring to the fore the real essence of leadership. How so? Consider resilience, the key trait we've been discussing, and its critical role in crisis leadership.

Let's start with understanding what effective crisis leadership entails. In the face of a crisis, leaders are called upon to navigate their organizations through uncertainty, make difficult decisions, inspire confidence, and rally their teams to overcome challenges. Each of these responsibilities demands a high degree of resilience.

Take, for example, Alex, the CEO of a tech startup, who faced the daunting challenge of steering his company through the economic downturn caused by the global pandemic. The circumstances were dire, but Alex's resilience was unwavering. He approached the crisis not as a catastrophe, but as a challenge to overcome, embodying the very essence of resilient leadership.

Crisis leadership is not about simply reacting to a crisis; it's about proactively preparing for it. This begins long before a crisis hits. For Alex, building resilience involved fostering a culture of adaptability and agility within his team. He championed a mindset of continuous learning and encouraged his team to view challenges as opportunities for growth.

When the economic downturn hit, Alex's proactive approach to building resilience bore fruit. His team was able to pivot swiftly and effectively to the changing circumstances. They quickly transitioned to remote work, adjusted their project timelines, and even found ways to innovate amidst the constraints. Their ability to adapt was a testament to the resilient culture that Alex had nurtured.

An integral part of effective crisis leadership is communication. In times of crisis, it's easy for rumors and misinformation to spread, causing fear and panic. Resilient leaders, like Alex, address this by providing clear, consistent, and honest communication. They share the realities of the situation but also instill hope for the future.

During the economic downturn, Alex held regular team meetings to keep everyone informed about the company's status and plans. He was transparent about the challenges but also expressed confidence in the team's ability to overcome them. His honest yet hopeful communication helped keep fear and uncertainty at bay.

Resilient leaders also demonstrate empathy during a crisis. They understand that a crisis can cause emotional turmoil for their team members. They provide support and create a safe space for their team to express their feelings and concerns. Alex did this by regularly checking in on his team's wellbeing and providing flexible work arrangements to accommodate their needs.

Moreover, resilient leaders recognize that a crisis is not just a threat, but also an opportunity. They have the vision to see beyond the immediate challenges and identify potential opportunities for innovation and growth. Amidst the economic downturn, Alex identified an opportunity to develop a new software product that met the emerging needs of the remote work market.

Crucially, effective crisis leadership involves making difficult decisions with limited information. When the pandemic hit, Alex had to make some tough decisions, such as cutting down on certain projects and reallocating resources. His resilience helped him make these decisions confidently, despite the uncertainty.

Resilient leaders also show vulnerability. This might seem counterintuitive, but vulnerability is not a sign of weakness; it's a display of courage and authenticity. During the crisis, Alex was open about his own fears and uncertainties. This vulnerability fostered trust and solidarity within his team.

Likewise, resilient leaders understand the importance of self-care during a crisis. They recognize that they need to maintain their wellbeing in order to lead effectively. Alex prioritized self-care, ensuring he had time for rest, exercise, and mindfulness. He encouraged his team to do the same.

Lastly, effective crisis leadership involves evaluating and learning from the crisis. After the economic downturn, Alex led a reflection exercise to review the company's response to the crisis and identify areas for improvement. This commitment to learning and growth is a hallmark of resilient leadership.

Crisis leadership, as we've seen through Alex's story, is a manifestation of resilience. Resilient leaders rise to the occasion during a crisis, guiding their teams with confidence, empathy, and vision. They demonstrate that resilience is not just about surviving a crisis, but about emerging from it stronger and more equipped for future challenges.

Leadership Resilience Development Plan

Resilience is not an innate quality that one is born with. It is, in fact, a set of skills that can be learned and developed. Just as one might devise a plan for career advancement or physical fitness, so too can one create a plan for building resilience. The following tools and tips provide a strategic guide to charting the course for resilience development, critical for the effective leader navigating the turbulent seas of change.

1. Embrace a Growth Mindset: Recognize that challenges are not insurmountable obstacles but opportunities for learning and growth. When faced with difficulties, approach them with curiosity and a willingness to learn. This mindset shift can help in building resilience.

2. Cultivate Self-Awareness: Understanding one's thoughts, emotions, and reactions in different situations is key to resilience. Regular self-reflection can help identify patterns and triggers, enabling more conscious responses to challenges.

3. Foster Positive Relationships: A strong support network can provide emotional support and different perspectives when dealing with challenges. Invest time in nurturing relationships both within and outside the organization.

4. Develop Emotional Intelligence: This involves recognizing, understanding, and managing one's own emotions and those of others. Emotionally intelligent leaders are better equipped to handle stress and conflict, key elements of resilience.

5. Practice Mindfulness: Mindfulness helps stay centered in the face of adversity. Simple practices like mindful breathing or meditation can enhance focus, clarity, and emotional regulation.

6. Engage in Self-Care: Resilience requires physical and mental wellbeing. Regular exercise, a balanced diet, adequate rest, and activities that bring joy can contribute to overall resilience.

7. Set Realistic Goals: Setting and working towards attainable goals can provide a sense of purpose and control, vital for resilience. Ensure the goals are challenging yet achievable.

8. Cultivate Optimism: Practice maintaining a hopeful outlook, even in difficult times. This doesn't mean ignoring reality, but focusing on what can be controlled and finding positives amidst challenges.

9. Learn from Experience: Each challenge provides valuable lessons. After a difficult situation, take time to reflect on what was learned and how it can be applied to future challenges.

10. Seek Professional Help if Needed: There's no shame in seeking help. If stress or anxiety becomes overwhelming, reach out to a mental health professional.

❋ ❋ ❋

The pursuit of resilience is not a linear process but an ongoing commitment. It's about developing a resilience 'muscle' that strengthens over time. With these tools and strategies at your disposal, you can craft your personal resilience development plan, becoming a more resilient leader, ready to face any challenge that comes your way.

PART VII: LEADING ACROSS DISTANCES AND CULTURES

CHAPTER 17 - LEADING FROM AFAR: EMBRACING DIGITAL LEADERSHIP

The ever-evolving world of work has ushered in a new chapter: remote leadership. In this digitally interconnected age, leading from a distance has grown in both scale and significance. Imagine orchestrating a global symphony, where each musician plays from a different location, yet they unite in a harmonious tune. This encapsulates the essence of remote leadership, where geographically dispersed teams collaborate seamlessly under unified organizational objectives.

This shift to remote work isn't entirely novel, but its magnitude and intricacies have deepened recently. Notably, tech behemoth X.com's work from home forever' policy marked a pivotal change in the work landscape. What was once a flexible option has solidified into a global standard, necessitating a fresh leadership approach.

At the heart of successful remote leadership lies trust. A team scattered from New York to Singapore might never physically meet, yet they can still execute projects flawlessly, rooted in mutual trust. It's aptly said, "trust is the bandwidth of communication." The challenge amplifies during crises, such as the COVID-19 pandemic. Here, remote leadership transcends overseeing operations to managing human emotions, all while grappling with the complexities of distance.

To anchor leaders in this new territory, we introduce the "Remote Leadership Toolkit," a compass guiding leaders through the digital realm. A highlighted tool, the 'Virtual Townhall,' was effectively utilized by a global pharmaceutical company during the pandemic. Their CEO's regular virtual engagements kept employees informed and preserved the firm's cultural integrity despite geographical separations.

In essence, remote leadership prioritizes emotional closeness over physical proximity. It's about nurturing trust, fostering shared objectives, and preserving human connections in a digital world. This chapter equips leaders for the ever-evolving remote work landscape, emphasizing the significance of leading with both distance and intimacy.

As the realm of work transforms, leadership must adapt. This chapter aims to empower leaders for the remote work era, highlighting that leading from afar requires a heart close to the team. Welcome to the next phase of leadership evolution.

Understanding Remote Leadership: Challenges and Opportunities

Let's step into the realm of remote leadership, a space that, while physically dispersed, is woven together with the threads of digital connectivity. This section, titled "Understanding Remote Leadership: Challenges and Opportunities," delves into the unique dichotomies that characterize remote leadership. It is an opportunity to reframe our understanding, recalibrate our leadership approaches, and reimagine the future of work.

To understand remote leadership, consider the metaphor of a lighthouse. A lighthouse, though physically distant, provides guidance to ships, illuminating their paths amidst stormy seas. Much like the lighthouse, a remote leader must shine the light of guidance, direction, and clarity across digital landscapes, irrespective of the physical distance. This metaphor captures the essence of remote leadership: the ability to influence, engage, and inspire, despite the absence of physical proximity.

An essential question arises, what are the challenges remote leadership presents? For one, the absence of physical proximity can make communication more complex. Without the benefit of face-to-face interaction, nuances of non-verbal communication can be lost, making the transmission of information less rich and potentially leading to misunderstandings. For instance, consider a global software firm where the product team is based in India, and the sales team is in the US. The difference in time zones and the lack of in-person communication could potentially create communication gaps, impacting the overall product delivery.

Further, building a shared culture in a remote setting can be a daunting task. Physical offices often have a shared culture, tangible and palpable. Remote teams, in contrast, are like islands, each with its own unique micro-culture, influenced by geographical, societal, and personal factors. Creating a shared, inclusive culture across these islands can be a challenging endeavor. Reflect on the case of a multinational organization that, following a shift to remote work, struggled to maintain its vibrant, collaborative culture. The coffee-machine chats, impromptu brainstorming sessions, and shared lunch breaks were suddenly replaced by formal, scheduled Zoom meetings, causing a cultural vacuum.

Remote leadership also poses a unique challenge in fostering trust and accountability. In traditional office settings, trust is often built through personal interactions and shared experiences. In a remote setting, however, building trust requires more intentional effort. Imagine a team leader, situated in London, leading a remote team scattered from Buenos Aires to Beijing. How can this leader foster trust and ensure accountability when team members have never met face-to-face?

Amid these challenges, however, remote leadership also presents a multitude of opportunities. The flexibility offered by remote work can foster a higher degree of work-life balance, potentially leading to increased job satisfaction and productivity. A study conducted by a renowned university showed that employees working remotely reported higher job satisfaction and were less likely to leave their companies than their in-office counterparts.

In terms of diversity and inclusion, remote work breaks down geographical barriers, allowing organizations to tap into a wider talent pool. This means a company based in Berlin can benefit from the expertise of a software engineer in Bangalore, a marketing expert in Montreal, and a data analyst in Dakar. This kind of diverse and inclusive team composition can bring a broader range of perspectives to the table, fostering innovation and creativity.

Furthermore, remote leadership can also contribute to sustainability efforts. Reduced commuting means lower carbon emissions, aligning organizational practices with global sustainability goals. The case of a US-based tech giant reducing its carbon footprint significantly through remote work serves as a compelling example of this opportunity.

It is clear that remote leadership, like any other form of leadership, presents both challenges and opportunities. The key to successful remote leadership lies in acknowledging these challenges and leveraging the opportunities. This process requires an openness to learning, adaptability, and most importantly, a willingness to rewrite the traditional scripts of leadership.

As leaders, we must understand that remote leadership is not about replicating in-person leadership in a virtual setting. Instead, it is about redefining leadership for a virtual world. It is about learning to communicate effectively through digital mediums, building trust in a virtual environment, fostering a shared culture across geographical boundaries, and navigating the unique dynamics of remote teams.

In essence, successful remote leadership is about creating a sense of closeness, despite the physical distance. It is about fostering a sense of belonging, despite the geographical dispersion. And above all, it is about achieving organizational goals, despite the absence of a physical office.

In the end, the challenges and opportunities presented by remote leadership are two sides of the same coin. As we flip this coin, we realize that the challenges are not roadblocks but signposts, guiding us towards new ways of leading. And the opportunities are not just advantages but catalysts, propelling us towards a more inclusive, diverse, and sustainable future of work.

Establishing Trust and Connection in a Remote Environment

Now, as we venture deeper into the world of remote leadership, let's turn our attention to a foundational pillar that supports this edifice - trust. Our section, "Establishing Trust and Connection in a Remote Environment," intends to delve into this core aspect. It explores how trust, often viewed as an intangible concept, becomes a practical, achievable goal, even when teams are dispersed across continents.

In a world where physical offices have given way to virtual workspaces, where the professional and personal intertwine, building trust becomes both a challenge and an opportunity. It is an art to master, a science to understand, and, most importantly, a responsibility to uphold.

Let's consider the example of a global consulting firm. Their project teams, spread across continents, rarely met in person. Yet, the firm consistently delivered high-quality output, with team members reporting a high level of trust in their colleagues and leaders. The secret? They had cultivated an environment that valued and promoted trust.

However, the challenge arises when leaders attempt to transport traditional methods of building trust into the remote world. The impromptu hallway conversations, the shared lunches, the trust-building retreats - these are not easily replicated in a virtual setting. In a remote environment, trust must be intentionally built, fostered, and nurtured, requiring leaders to rethink and reshape their strategies.

One strategy to establish trust in a remote environment is open and transparent communication. In a physical office, a team member can walk into a leader's cabin to discuss issues or ideas. In a remote setting, this spontaneity is often missing. However, leaders can replicate this openness digitally by being accessible and responsive. Regular updates about organizational changes, individual check-ins, and open forums for discussion can create an environment of transparency, which, in turn, builds trust.

In addition, empathy plays a crucial role in establishing trust remotely. Empathy allows leaders to step into their team members' shoes, understand their unique circumstances, and respond with kindness and flexibility. In the case of a San Francisco-based startup, when the shift to remote work took place, leaders ensured regular check-ins focusing not only on work but also on the wellbeing of their team members. This empathetic approach resulted in a high level of trust and a sense of belonging among the team.

Another strategy that can foster trust is creating an environment where mistakes are treated as learning opportunities. In a remote setting, the fear of making errors can be amplified due to the lack of immediate reassurance or guidance. However, if leaders create a culture where mistakes are seen as part of the learning process, it can alleviate these fears, fostering a sense of psychological safety, and thus, trust.

Alongside trust, building connection is a pivotal aspect of leading remotely. Connection refers to a sense of belonging, the feeling that you are part of a community, a team, an organization. In a physical setting, connection is often fostered through shared experiences. In a remote setting, shared experiences might look different, but they are no less meaningful.

Virtual team-building activities, such as online games, quizzes, or collaborative projects, can foster a sense of connection. Similarly, celebrating successes, acknowledging milestones, and appreciating efforts can reinforce the sense of belonging. An IT firm, for example, instituted a 'virtual coffee hour', where team members would join a video call with their favorite beverage, discussing everything but work. This initiative, while simple, significantly improved the sense of connection among the team.

Moreover, leaders can foster connection by highlighting the common purpose that binds the team together. Regularly communicating the team's goals, celebrating progress, and acknowledging each member's contribution can create a shared sense of purpose and thereby strengthen the connection.

In essence, establishing trust and connection in a remote environment is about creating a space where people feel seen, heard, and valued. It's about recognizing the human element that lies at the heart of work, irrespective of where that work takes place.

However, it's important to remember that trust and connection are not built in a day. They are a result of consistent effort, constant communication, and, most importantly, authentic leadership. In a remote setting, leaders have the opportunity to create a culture of trust and connection that transcends geographical boundaries, time zones, and cultural differences.

As leaders, we must take up this opportunity, acknowledging the challenges it presents, but more so, leveraging the potential it offers. The strategies outlined in this section, coupled with your unique leadership style, can serve as a guide in this process.

As we navigate through the uncharted waters of remote leadership, trust and connection serve as our compass, guiding us towards our destination. They form the bedrock of effective remote leadership, the threads that weave together a dispersed team into a coherent, cohesive whole.

Leading Remote Teams During Crisis

Leading remote teams during a crisis, now there's a challenge that separates the exceptional leaders from the rest. This section, "Leading Remote Teams During Crisis," invites you to contemplate the complexities and opportunities in leading from afar during tough times. It prompts you to rethink your leadership strategies, especially during unprecedented crises.

The recent global pandemic has underlined the critical need for effective remote leadership during crises. Businesses across the globe grappled with the challenge of transitioning to remote work almost overnight. However, it was the way the leaders responded during this crisis that often dictated the companies' resilience and adaptability.

Crisis, by its very nature, ushers in uncertainty. In a remote environment, this uncertainty can be amplified. Lack of face-to-face communication, time zone differences, or not being physically present to provide immediate guidance - these factors can compound the impact of a crisis on remote teams. Hence, how leaders respond during such times can make all the difference.

First and foremost, leaders need to be a beacon of stability during a crisis. As the storm rages, teams look to their leaders for reassurance and direction. Consider the case of a multinational company during the early days of the pandemic. Despite the turmoil, their leaders exhibited calm, communicated with clarity, and provided consistent updates. This served to anchor the team amidst the tumultuous changes, fostering a sense of stability and certainty.

Secondly, effective communication becomes paramount during a crisis. In a remote setting, communication isn't just about sharing information. It's about fostering an open dialogue, where concerns can be aired, questions can be asked, and reassurances can be provided. It's about keeping the team informed, but it's also about listening, understanding, and responding to their fears and anxieties.

Additionally, leaders need to prioritize empathy during a crisis. Each team member will experience a crisis differently, shaped by their personal circumstances and perspectives. The leader's role is to acknowledge these individual experiences, offer support, and provide flexibility.

One useful strategy to show empathy in a crisis is by acknowledging the emotions of the team. An effective leader doesn't shy away from discussing the fear, anxiety, or frustration that the team might be experiencing. Instead, they address these emotions, validate them, and reassure their teams that it's okay to not be okay sometimes.

Moreover, leading remote teams during a crisis necessitates a shift in performance expectations. A crisis can disrupt usual work patterns and affect productivity. Rather than rigidly adhering to pre-set goals, leaders need to recalibrate expectations, taking into account the upheaval caused by the crisis.

Another critical aspect of crisis leadership is fostering resilience. Resilience is the capacity to bounce back in the face of adversity. It's about embracing change, learning from setbacks, and emerging stronger. Leaders can foster resilience in their remote teams by promoting a growth mindset, encouraging innovation, and recognizing effort over outcomes.

Resilience also entails taking care of the team's mental well-being. During a crisis, mental health can take a hit, affecting productivity and morale. Leaders can promote mental wellness by encouraging regular breaks, providing resources for self-care, and creating an environment where discussing mental health is not taboo but encouraged.

Finally, leading during a crisis is about finding opportunities amidst the chaos. A crisis, while disruptive, can also be a catalyst for innovation and change. Leaders can leverage this by encouraging their teams to think outside the box, to experiment, and to innovate.

For instance, a fashion retailer, faced with store closures

during the pandemic, quickly pivoted to an online model, even creating virtual fitting rooms for customers. This was possible because the leaders saw the crisis not just as a challenge but also as an opportunity to adapt and evolve.

Leading remote teams during a crisis is a complex task, one that requires stability, communication, empathy, and resilience. It requires leaders to rethink their strategies, to be agile in their approach, and to lead with authenticity and humanity.

As we move through this new terrain, we realize that leading during a crisis is not about navigating the storm unscathed. Instead, it's about steering your team through the storm, with all its unpredictability and volatility, and emerging on the other side, not just intact, but stronger, wiser, and more resilient.

With the strategies outlined in this section, coupled with your unique leadership approach, you can not only survive the storm but also leverage it to bring out the best in your team and yourself. In the midst of chaos, lies opportunity, and it is the mark of a true leader to seize this opportunity and steer their team towards a better, brighter future.

Remote Leadership Toolkit

In this section, "Tools & Tips: Remote Leadership Toolkit," we'll dive into a practical and robust set of strategies to aid you in your remote leadership endeavors. After traversing the landscape of remote leadership challenges, building trust, and guiding teams through crises, it's now time to arm yourself with the right tools and tactics.

1. Utilize Effective Communication Platforms: The first tool in your remote leadership kit is technology. In today's digital age, there's no shortage of communication platforms to choose from - Zoom, Microsoft Teams, Slack, to name a few. But having access to these platforms isn't enough. Leaders must also understand their unique features and know how to use them effectively. For instance, a leader who maximizes the use of breakout rooms in Zoom can facilitate small group discussions within larger meetings, encouraging more intimate and in-depth conversations.

2. Regular Check-ins: One-on-one meetings with team members are essential in a remote setting. Regular check-ins provide a platform for open dialogue where team members can voice concerns, share ideas, and discuss their progress. As a leader, you can use these sessions to provide feedback, offer guidance, and reinforce the team's objectives.

3. Embrace Asynchronous Communication: Understanding that everyone works differently and that remote work often blurs the line between personal and professional life is critical. Asynchronous communication allows for flexibility, enabling team members to respond when it works best for them. This understanding promotes a healthier work-life balance, leading to increased job satisfaction and productivity.

4. Digital Team Building Activities: Remote teams need to bond, too. Digital team building activities - virtual coffee breaks, online games, or even a remote book club - can foster camaraderie and foster a sense of team spirit. These activities not only break the monotony of work but also help in building connections that fuel collaboration and teamwork.

5. Remote Work Policies: Create clear and comprehensive remote work policies. These should cover aspects like work hours, availability, meeting etiquette, and communication norms. Such policies offer a roadmap for team members and set clear expectations, promoting consistency and fairness.

6. Foster an Environment of Trust: Trust is the backbone of successful remote leadership. As a leader, you need to trust your team's ability to get the job done, even when you're not physically present to oversee their work. Show your trust by focusing on outcomes rather than activities, and giving them autonomy over their work.

7. Prioritize Well-being: Promote and prioritize well-being in your team. Encourage regular breaks, offer flexibility, and provide resources for mental health. A healthy team is not only more productive but also more engaged and committed.

8. Encourage Continuous Learning: The remote work environment is continuously evolving, and so must your team. Encourage continuous learning and provide resources for your team to learn and grow. This could be in the form of webinars, online courses, or even a monthly book club.

✻ ✻ ✻

This Remote Leadership Toolkit doesn't offer a one-size-fits-all solution, as remote leadership is a multifaceted challenge that needs a tailored approach. What it does provide, however, is a set of tools that you can adapt and mold to suit your unique team dynamics and leadership style. These tools, coupled with your intuition as a leader, will equip you to navigate the uncharted waters of remote leadership with confidence, competence, and compassion.

CHAPTER 18 - DIGITAL COMMUNICATION:LEADING WITH A VIRTUAL VOICE

Remote leadership resembles navigating unpredictable waters. While the path may vary, the right tools ensure steady progress. In this digital era, the cornerstone of these tools is effective communication, the essence of leadership. This chapter spotlights this: the leader's virtual voice.

Effective communication is fundamental to leadership. As physical office spaces morph into virtual platforms, the efficacy of communication is further magnified. The success stories of businesses thriving remotely underscore one element: stellar communication. The transition to virtual work has reshaped leadership communication, with traditional cues like body language and spontaneous interactions becoming less accessible. For instance, a start-up CEO adeptly transitioned to remote operations during the pandemic's onset by adapting her communication, thus bolstering unity and warding off isolation.

In crisis scenarios, such as a tech company facing a cybersecurity breach, the nuances of virtual communication become even more crucial. Transmitting urgency without instigating panic, and ensuring transparency and unity, are central to crisis management.

To help navigate these digital waters, we present the 'Digital Communication Guide for Leaders.' Far from a mere strategy compilation, this toolkit encapsulates real-world challenges and offers solutions for both conventional and unique remote communication hurdles.

Embark on this journey through Chapter 18, where digital communication transcends boundaries and the leader's virtual voice holds power and purpose. This chapter isn't just theoretical—it's a hands-on guide to enhance your digital communication efficiency. Remember, in the virtual realm, a leader's impact isn't determined by speech volume but by communication efficacy.

As we delve deeper, we'll explore scenarios, tackle challenges, and offer actionable advice. Prepare to adapt and amplify your virtual voice. In this digital domain, let every interaction be a testament to your leadership, echoing clarity and forging connections. Dive in, and let the world hear your resonating digital symphony.

Importance of Effective Communication in Remote Leadership

Let us first establish this: effective communication isn't an option in remote leadership—it is a necessity. It's akin to the oxygen that gives life to your remote teams. Without it, your team is a gathering of individuals working in a void. With it, you foster a thriving collective moving in concert towards shared goals. It's not just the distribution of tasks or mere conveyance of information; it is the glue that binds teams together and fuels the engine of productivity.

Picture Steve, an accomplished leader who, after building a successful brick-and-mortar retail chain, transitioned to an e-commerce business model. The physical spaces where he once held daily team huddles and strategy sessions were replaced by video calls and chat groups. Steve, accustomed to physical interactions and face-to-face communication, underestimated the nuances of remote communication. His once cohesive team began to feel disconnected, their morale dipping, with the company's culture, once robust, started to disintegrate. This illustrates the dire consequences of underestimating the importance of effective remote communication.

Contrast this with Patricia, a CEO of a burgeoning FinTech startup. When her company transitioned to remote work, she was mindful of the pitfalls and made deliberate efforts to adapt her communication style. Recognizing that traditional communication norms don't translate seamlessly into the virtual environment, she fostered a culture of openness, regularly initiated video calls, and prioritized clear, concise, and consistent communication. As a result, her team's productivity soared, and despite the physical distance, they maintained a strong sense of unity and engagement.

The importance of effective communication extends beyond mere dialogue; it is the lifeblood that keeps remote teams aligned and engaged. Reflect on the story of a project manager who, through clear and frequent communication, managed to keep her team engaged, driven, and aligned with the project's evolving objectives. Her communication acted as the compass guiding the team towards its goals, averting misdirection or confusion.

In this digital age, effective communication can also become a fulcrum for innovation. When leaders can articulate their thoughts and ideas clearly, it ignites a spark in the team to do the same. A real-world example is a remote design team whose leader continuously shares thought-provoking ideas in a coherent and engaging manner. This practice encourages the team members to express their own ideas fearlessly, fostering a culture of innovation where everyone's voice is valued and appreciated.

Leadership communication in a remote environment plays a pivotal role in making each team member feel seen and heard. Isolation can be a significant issue in remote work, but an astute leader who communicates with intention and empathy can help mitigate this. Take the case of a leader who conducts weekly one-on-one video calls, regularly shares updates, and acknowledges each team member's input. His approach counters feelings of isolation, making the team feel valued and included.

Moreover, effective communication becomes an anchor during a crisis. In such turbulent times, a leader's task is to provide clarity, instill confidence, and guide the team forward. In these moments, a leader's role as the primary communicator is magnified. They must strive for transparency, consistency, and empathy, offering not just a sense of stability but also a beacon of hope.

While the vital role of communication in leadership has always been recognized, the shift to remote work magnifies its importance. The casual, face-to-face interactions that were once taken for granted are replaced by every email, every video call, every instant message. These interactions are now the stage upon which relationships are nurtured, trust is fostered, and collaboration is driven.

To put it succinctly, effective communication is the cornerstone of successful remote leadership. It is the bond that holds teams together, the voice that guides, and the force that propels remote teams to shared success. As we navigate the evolving landscape of remote work, leaders capable of leveraging the power of effective communication will thrive.

However, understanding the importance of effective communication in remote leadership is just the beginning. The real challenge lies in adapting your traditional leadership communication to a virtual setting. In the upcoming sections, we will delve into how leaders can reshape their communication strategies to suit remote teams, navigate crisis communication, and provide a detailed guide to mastering digital communication.

Adapting Traditional Leadership Communication to a Virtual Setting

Adapting traditional leadership communication to a virtual

setting isn't as simple as swapping office meetings for Zoom calls. It's a nuanced shift that requires an understanding of the changes in the communication landscape and a willingness to adjust your style to effectively reach and engage your remote teams.

Consider Tim, the CEO of a midsize company, who was used to leading his team through daily in-person stand-ups. When his team transitioned to remote work, he simply shifted these meetings online, failing to recognize that his direct, in-person communication style didn't translate well over video call. The result? His messages often came across as blunt and impersonal, leading to a dip in team morale.

In contrast, Brianna, the head of another division, quickly recognized that her traditional communication style needed to be adjusted for the virtual environment. Instead of simply moving her in-person meetings online, she also took the time to learn about each team member's communication preferences, making sure she tailored her approach to suit different styles and needs.

Adapting traditional communication to a virtual setting involves the recognition that non-verbal cues play a pivotal role in our understanding and interpretation of messages. In face-to-face communication, a leader can leverage a plethora of non-verbal cues - body language, tone of voice, facial expressions, and more. These cues, subtle as they may be, help to add depth and context to their words. However, in a virtual setting, these cues can often be obscured or entirely missing.

In virtual communication, clarity and precision become paramount. Since there's a lack of physical presence, leaders need to be articulate and specific in their directives. Remember the case of a project leader who faced challenges with his remote team due to vague instructions? Once he began providing detailed and concise instructions, the team's performance drastically improved.

Effective virtual communication also requires understanding and empathizing with the unique challenges each team member faces in a remote environment. As a leader, you need to be flexible, patient, and compassionate, recognizing that remote work comes with its unique set of challenges. Remember Susan, a remote team leader who regularly checked in on her team's well-being and tailored her communication based on their individual circumstances? Her empathetic approach bolstered team morale and fostered a stronger sense of connection.

Reimagining your communication approach also means embracing digital tools that facilitate effective virtual communication. Email, instant messaging, video calls – these are the new meeting rooms, the new water coolers, the places where ideas are exchanged and relationships are built. But using these tools requires more than just technical know-how. It requires an understanding of the unique etiquette and norms associated with each platform.

Another critical aspect of adapting to a virtual setting is the intentionality of communication. In a remote environment, casual hallway conversations or impromptu meetings are no longer feasible. Every communication needs to be purposeful and planned. For example, an effective remote leader might schedule regular check-ins to keep the team aligned and ensure everyone has a chance to voice their thoughts and concerns.

Balancing synchronous and asynchronous communication is also vital. Not everything requires an immediate response or a live discussion. Recognizing when to use each mode of communication can improve productivity and reduce unnecessary interruptions. The manager who decided to use asynchronous communication for updates and non-urgent matters saw a significant improvement in his team's productivity.

In the virtual world, transparency becomes a cornerstone of effective leadership communication. Without the informal touchpoints that come with an office setting, leaders need to provide regular updates to keep their teams in the loop. But transparency is more than just sharing updates; it's about being open, honest, and clear about expectations, challenges, and the state of the business.

Learning to listen becomes even more important in a virtual setting. With physical cues often missing, it's easy for misunderstandings to arise. Active listening helps ensure that you fully understand your team's views and can respond appropriately. A remote leader who cultivated active listening skills managed to resolve conflicts within his team that had arisen from misunderstandings.

Lastly, never underestimate the power of acknowledging and appreciating your team's efforts. In a virtual environment, it's easy for hard work to go unnoticed. Regularly acknowledging your team's efforts and accomplishments can go a long way in boosting morale and motivation.

Adapting traditional leadership communication to a virtual setting isn't a one-time process. It requires constant reflection, learning, and adjustment. But with the right strategies and an open mindset, leaders can successfully navigate this shift and effectively lead their teams, no matter where they are. The shift to virtual communication isn't a challenge to be feared but an opportunity to be seized - an opportunity to foster deeper connections, build stronger teams, and drive your organization towards its goals.

Crisis Communication in Remote Teams

Every leader at some point will face a crisis. In a remote setting, managing a crisis can become particularly challenging due to the lack of physical proximity and the increased potential for misunderstandings or misinformation. This is why a well-thought-out approach to crisis communication is essential in remote leadership.

Take the case of Nancy, a CEO of a thriving tech company. She had managed several crises in the traditional office setting, relying on face-to-face communication and the tangibility of human presence. However, when her company faced a crisis while working remotely, she found herself navigating uncharted territory. She realized that the strategies she used in the office did not translate effectively into the digital realm.

In contrast, we have John, a leader of a fully remote team, who has weathered several storms successfully by mastering the art of crisis communication in a virtual setting. He has cultivated a mindset that views a crisis not as a disaster but as an opportunity for learning and growth. His approach is not reactive but proactive, rooted in preparation and anticipation.

A critical element of successful crisis communication in a remote setting is the timeliness of the response. There's an urge to wait until all the facts are gathered and a perfect response crafted. However, in the fast-paced, interconnected world we live in, delay can exacerbate the situation. As John did, it's essential to communicate early, even if it's just to acknowledge the situation and assure the team that you're actively working on it.

Furthermore, clear and consistent communication becomes the lifeline in times of crisis. Misinformation and rumors can spread rapidly, leading to confusion and panic. A leader must cut through this noise by providing regular updates and being transparent about what is known and what isn't. When John's team faced a data breach, he sent out regular updates, explaining what had happened, what steps were being taken, and how it could impact the team.

Crisis communication also calls for a high level of empathy. It's easy to get caught up in the operational aspects of a crisis, but remember, your team members are humans who may be feeling anxious and uncertain. Just like Emily, a remote team leader who took the time to check in on each team member's well-being during a crisis, showing understanding and compassion can reassure your team and strengthen the bonds between its members.

One of the lessons from the John's story is the power of collaboration in crisis management. He made sure to involve his team in the problem-solving process, harnessing the diverse skills and perspectives of his team members to find solutions. This not only leverages the collective intelligence of the team but also fosters a sense of ownership and unity.

Crisis communication in a virtual world also involves leveraging digital tools to your advantage. These tools, if used effectively, can facilitate real-time communication, provide a platform for discussion, and ensure everyone is kept in the loop. However, it's crucial to remember that not all information should be communicated in the same way. Some messages may be better delivered in a video call, while others could be addressed in an email or team chat.

In a crisis, trust becomes more important than ever. Trust is built over time through consistent, honest communication and by honoring your commitments. Leaders who have nurtured a culture of trust will find it easier to guide their teams through a crisis, as their team members are more likely to believe in their leader's ability to handle the situation and more likely to follow their direction.

Having a plan in place is a vital part of crisis communication. While you can't predict every crisis, having a general framework can guide your actions when a crisis does hit. John always has a contingency plan - a strategy that outlines how to communicate in a crisis, including who needs to be informed, how they will be informed, and who will be involved in the crisis management process.

Last but not least, a post-crisis review is an integral part of effective crisis communication. Once the storm has passed, it's vital to reflect on what happened, what worked well, and what could have been done differently. This reflection is a learning opportunity that can strengthen your team and better prepare you for future crises.

Effective crisis communication in remote teams is not about avoiding crises but about handling them in a way that minimizes damage and promotes learning. It involves being timely, clear, and empathetic in your communication, leveraging digital tools effectively, nurturing trust, having a plan in place, and learning from each crisis. It's a challenging task, no doubt, but also an opportunity to demonstrate your leadership capabilities and foster a resilient, unified team.

Digital Communication Guide for Leaders

In an era where digital interactions have largely supplanted physical meetings, leaders must arm themselves with effective tools and techniques to communicate successfully. This realm of pixelated faces and typed words can feel as vast and unforgiving as a storm-tossed sea, but navigating it effectively can transform your leadership style, creating robust lines of communication that bridge the distance. Here, we'll provide a practical guide that will serve as a compass for leaders in the digital world.

1. Select Your Tools Wisely: Technology, in all its abundance, provides a cornucopia of communication tools. These include synchronous tools like Zoom and Microsoft Teams for real-time communication, and asynchronous tools like Slack or email, allowing for flexibility. Diverse as your team may be, so are these tools. Choosing the right one hinges on understanding the nature of your communication and the preferences of your team.

2. Cultivate Digital Etiquettes: Norms for digital communication, although unwritten, are as vital as any rule. Be conscious of time zones when scheduling meetings, respect digital boundaries, and promote a culture where 'camera on' isn't mandatory. Encourage your team to communicate effectively, succinctly, and to respect others' digital space.

3. Use Visual Aids: Never underestimate the power of a good visual aid. In a study done by the University of Minnesota, presentations using visual aids were found to be 43% more persuasive. Tools like Miro or Google Slides can help you turn complex concepts into digestible diagrams, leading to more effective communication.

4. Embrace Asynchronous Communication: With teams scattered across time zones, synchronous communication isn't always possible. Asynchronous communication allows team members to respond in their own time, reducing stress and promoting thoughtful responses. Tools like Slack or Trello can be instrumental in facilitating this.

5. Provide Regular Updates: In a remote environment, lack of communication can cause anxiety and uncertainty. Regular updates, either through email or a team communication platform, will keep your team informed and engaged. Leaders should strive to be the beacon of light, providing clarity amidst the fog of uncertainty.

6. Promote Open Communication: An effective leader nurtures an environment where questions, ideas, and thoughts can be shared freely. Anonymous feedback tools, like Suggestion Ox, or shared digital whiteboards can give a voice to those who may hesitate to speak up.

7. Foster Connection and Engagement: Leadership is not only about tasks and targets; it's about people. Tools like Donut, which randomly pairs team members for virtual coffee chats, can help to maintain the human connection crucial to a cohesive team.

8. Ensure Clear and Consistent Communication: In the absence of non-verbal cues, clarity and consistency are king. Be explicit about tasks, expectations, and deadlines. Tools like Asana or Basecamp can help manage tasks efficiently and ensure everyone is on the same page.

9. Respect and Recognize Digital Boundaries: A message at midnight might seem reasonable to a leader burning the midnight oil, but it can blur the work-life boundary for team members. Establishing 'communication hours' respects these boundaries and promotes a healthier work-life balance.

10. Practice Active Listening: In a digital space, listening is an active process. Encourage your team to use phrases like "What I hear you saying is..." to ensure understanding. Listening tools, like Microsoft's Cortana, can transcribe meetings ensuring no vital information slips through the cracks.

* * *

Mastering these tools and techniques of digital communication won't just be a band-aid solution to navigate remote work. Instead, they have the potential to chart a course towards a future where effective communication reigns supreme, regardless of geographical boundaries. In this new normal, a leader's digital voice isn't merely an echo in the void, but a clear, resonant call that guides their team towards shared goals, effectively charting the course for their organization.

CHAPTER 19 - VIRTUAL PERFORMANCE MANAGEMENT: NAVIGATING NEW WATERS

Imagine captaining a ship by starlight. Just as stars guide through vast oceans, performance management illuminates the direction for remote teams in the expansive realm of remote work. While familiar terrains have their known maps, managing virtual teams is a fresh cartographic challenge. This chapter explores this new landscape, emphasizing the need for a revamped approach to performance management.

In 2021, a global software company, transitioning to remote work, discovered that their office-centric performance system faltered in a virtual environment. It resembled using an outdated map in a storm. The solution lay in overhauling their approach—preserving core values but adapting the methodology.

Consider the analogy of a football coach. In person, he's on the sidelines, directing and motivating. But how does he lead when the team is dispersed, each playing from different locations? Clearly, the strategy needs reimagining.

Performance assessment, too, demands rethinking. With teams spread out, how does one evaluate productivity? A marketing firm's shift in 2022 to a results-driven approach offers insight. Rather than focusing on hours worked, they prioritized goal achievement, leading to a surge in productivity, defying their office-based expectations.

Furthermore, crises, like the 2020 health challenge faced by a global healthcare company, emphasize the need for holistic performance management. Here, managing operations was only half the battle; addressing the emotional toll on remote employees was equally vital. This necessitated an approach that was compassionate, flexible, and resilient.

To ensure you're well-equipped, we offer a toolkit for effective virtual performance management. As aptly put by a tech CEO, navigating this realm is akin to "building the ship as you sail." Drawing from real-world strategies of top-performing remote teams, we provide a checklist to guide your journey.

Reinventing Performance Management for Remote Teams

Let's imagine a scenario: The year is 2021, a software development company headquartered in Seattle with branches across the globe faces an unseen conundrum. For decades, their performance management system was designed and refined for an office setting, a practice common in the tech industry. However, the sudden switch to remote work unveils flaws in their system. It's akin to using a map in a territory it wasn't designed for. They soon realize a reinvention is in order, not an easy task, but an essential one.

So, how does an organization go about reinventing a process as critical as performance management? A major pivot point is the shift from presence to productivity. In an office, an employee's presence often translates to their productivity in our minds. But, when your team is remote, this equation no longer holds true. The football coach, accustomed to seeing his team play in front of him, now must trust that they are giving their best even when they are not in his sight.

The story of the Seattle-based software firm brings us an interesting solution: the creation of a virtual culture of trust and transparency. In the office, trust was cultivated through conversations at the coffee machine, during lunch breaks, or spontaneous brainstorming sessions. In the virtual world, trust must be established differently, nurtured through regular check-ins, open dialogues, and recognizing employees' individual circumstances.

The reinvention process also calls for a revision of the goals and metrics used to measure performance. The remote setting alters the dynamics of teamwork and individual contributions, requiring a fresh perspective on what constitutes successful performance. For the Seattle company, this meant moving from process-driven goals to outcome-driven ones, an exercise that required thorough understanding and in-depth discussions at every level of management.

Switching to outcome-based goals, however, isn't a simple matter of changing the metrics. It requires a re-evaluation of the team structure and workflows. The software company, for instance, introduced project-based teams rather than function-based ones, encouraging a more collaborative and cohesive approach. This change brought a new level of flexibility and adaptability, essential qualities in the remote work setting.

One key lesson from this reinvention process is the need for regular feedback loops. In the office, feedback was often immediate and spontaneous, but in a remote setting, it can easily slip through the cracks. Hence, leaders must ensure consistent and constructive feedback, helping their teams adjust, adapt and grow in the virtual work environment.

The human element of performance management also takes center stage in this reinvention process. Leaders must understand that the home isn't always the perfect office; employees juggle personal responsibilities alongside work. The Seattle company addressed this by offering flexible schedules, ensuring employees can manage their work and personal lives without added stress, fostering not just productivity but well-being.

Reinvention also demands the inclusion of personal and professional development within performance management.

As learning opportunities in a remote setting differ vastly from those in the office, it is crucial to identify new avenues for growth and learning. The company we are talking about integrated online learning platforms, regular skill-based training, and mentorship programs into their performance management process, turning challenges into opportunities.

It is equally vital to acknowledge that reinventing performance management isn't a one-time activity. Just like the software company, organizations should continually reassess and refine their systems. The feedback from employees, the lessons learned, and the changing circumstances all contribute to this ongoing process, ensuring the system stays relevant and effective.

While it may sound daunting, reinventing performance management for remote teams is an investment worth making. It's not about discarding everything you knew; rather, it's about retaining what works and altering what doesn't. It's about understanding that the traditional rules might not apply but that doesn't leave you in a rule-less chaos. It presents an opportunity to create a system that is flexible, adaptable, and more human-centric.

Remember, the software company we discussed started off just like you, faced with an unfamiliar challenge. But they embraced the need for change, reinvented their performance management system, and emerged more resilient and efficient than ever before. Their story isn't unique; many organizations worldwide have embarked on similar paths, each finding their unique solutions.

Reinventing performance management for remote teams is about turning constraints into catalysts for change. It is about seeing the opportunity in adversity, the possibility in the impossible. And when done right, it can transform not just your performance management system but your entire organization. For isn't that what metamorphosis is all about - transforming, evolving, and emerging stronger than before?

Measuring and Enhancing Performance in a Virtual Setting

As we steer our narrative towards the mechanics of performance management, a new question unfolds – how do we measure and enhance performance in a virtual setting? To answer that, let's visit an animation studio in Vancouver. They grappled with this question during their transition to remote work, and their solutions might provide the key insights we seek.

The first step towards measuring performance is to define what performance means in your organization. For our animation studio, they defined performance as the ability to meet project deadlines, maintain quality standards, and contribute towards team collaboration. Once they had clear performance parameters, they could design metrics around these.

Measuring performance in a remote setting goes beyond tracking hours logged in. Consider it like this – you're a chef running a Michelin-star restaurant. You don't merely clock in the hours your team spends in the kitchen. Instead, you focus on the quality of the dishes they produce, their ability to innovate, and their coordination. Similarly, leaders must focus on tangible outcomes rather than time spent working.

In a virtual setting, the tools used to measure performance are different. Our animation studio utilized project management tools, data analytics, and regular virtual check-ins to monitor their teams' performance. These tools offered insight into individual contributions, project progress, and potential roadblocks, enabling timely intervention and support.

The Vancouver studio also understood the importance of one-on-one communication. Despite the digital divide, leaders maintained regular individual conversations with their team members. This facilitated a two-way feedback loop, allowing for personalized performance assessment and enabling the leaders to provide necessary guidance and support.

As important as measurement is, it is only one half of the equation. The other half is enhancing performance. Consider this – if measuring performance is like diagnosing an illness, enhancing performance is akin to the treatment plan. The studio found that their plan hinged on two critical elements: empowerment and engagement.

To enhance performance, leaders must empower their team members. In a remote setting, this means equipping them with the right tools and resources to execute their tasks effectively. The Vancouver animation studio did this by ensuring their team had the necessary hardware and software, uninterrupted internet connectivity, and a conducive work environment.

Empowerment also means granting autonomy. When the studio transitioned to remote work, they gave their animators the freedom to plan their work schedules. This flexibility allowed the team members to work at their most productive hours and balance their personal commitments, leading to improved performance.

On the other hand, engagement is about cultivating a sense of belonging and motivation. The studio used various virtual team building activities to keep their teams engaged. From online movie nights to virtual coffee breaks, these activities helped maintain team spirit and fostered a sense of camaraderie among the animators.

Moreover, recognizing and rewarding good performance played a key role in enhancing performance. The studio established a virtual recognition system where they highlighted the accomplishments of their team members during team meetings. These recognitions were not always about big wins; even small victories were celebrated, creating a culture of appreciation and encouragement.

Despite these strategies, the studio encountered their share of performance issues. Some team members struggled with time management, others with isolation. However, they saw these not as roadblocks but as points of learning. They offered personalized support, be it coaching on time management or facilitating peer support groups.

At the heart of the studio's efforts was a commitment to learning and adapting. They knew that measuring and enhancing performance in a virtual setting was a new terrain for them. But, instead of being deterred by the unknown, they embraced it, learning from their mistakes, and iterating their strategies. Their story is a testament to the fact that managing performance remotely isn't a straightforward, one-size-fits-all process. It requires creativity, empathy, and adaptability. It's about understanding the unique challenges of the virtual world and crafting equally unique solutions.

As we delve deeper into performance management in virtual teams, let's take these lessons with us. Let's remember that it is not about control, but about empowerment. It's not about surveillance, but about trust. It's not about sticking to the old ways, but about finding new paths to success. With these principles in mind, we are not just keeping the momentum; we are accelerating it.

Navigating Performance Challenges During Crisis

In the matrix of performance management, crises act as anomaly points, distorting the usual patterns and creating unique challenges. To unravel these intricacies, we will delve into the case of a globally distributed IT firm during the onset of the pandemic. This real-world scenario will help us to unravel the complex narrative of managing performance during a crisis.

For the IT firm, the pandemic was not merely a public health crisis; it was an operational and performance crisis. They had to transition their entire workforce to remote work almost overnight. Amid this chaos, managing performance emerged as a significant challenge. How do you keep the momentum when the world around you is in a state of flux?

The first challenge was to set realistic performance expectations. In times of crisis, normality is suspended. It's like being caught in a snowstorm - you cannot expect to keep the same pace. The IT firm recognized this and adjusted their performance expectations, considering the extraordinary circumstances. They moved from stringent deadlines to flexible ones and focused more on effort than outcomes.

Secondly, the crisis intensified the existing inequalities within the team. Some team members had a conducive work environment, while others grappled with issues such as poor internet connectivity or lack of dedicated workspace. This disparity reflected in their performance, creating a gap between the team members. The firm tackled this by providing resources and support to those who needed them, thereby reducing the performance gap.

Crisis also disrupts communication, creating a vacuum that can breed uncertainty and fear. The IT firm countered this by enhancing their communication. Leaders maintained regular contact with their team, updating them about organizational decisions and listening to their concerns. This communication strategy worked as a double-edged sword, keeping the team informed and engaged, thereby maintaining performance levels.

With the sudden shift to remote work, isolation became a significant factor affecting performance. It's one thing to work alone by choice, but another to be forced into isolation. The firm tackled this by building virtual communities where team members could interact, engage, and support each other, reducing the impact of isolation on performance.

Moreover, in a crisis, emotional distress can impact performance. The anxiety and fear induced by the pandemic were very real for the team members. Recognizing this, the firm provided emotional support to their teams. They initiated wellness programs, provided counseling services, and created a culture of empathy and understanding.

Despite these strategies, performance issues did surface.

Some team members struggled to adapt to the new working conditions, while others grappled with the emotional impact of the crisis. But instead of reprimanding or punishing, the firm saw these as opportunities for learning and growth.

This view of performance issues as learning opportunities was crucial in navigating the crisis. Instead of a punitive approach, they adopted a coaching approach. Leaders worked with the team members to understand the root causes of their performance issues and offered personalized support and guidance to overcome these.

What the IT firm's experience teaches us is that during a crisis, performance management isn't just about maintaining productivity; it's about resilience. It's about maintaining the human element in the face of adversity. It's about supporting your team not just professionally, but also personally.

Furthermore, it underscores the importance of adaptability in leadership. In a crisis, a leader can't hold on to the old ways of managing performance. They must adapt and innovate, find new ways to support their team, and keep the momentum.

The IT firm's experience also highlights the value of empathy in performance management. Empathy allows leaders to understand the unique challenges their team members face during a crisis and provide the necessary support. It ensures that performance management is not a rigid, one-way process, but a dynamic, two-way interaction.

As we examine the navigation of performance challenges during a crisis, let's keep in mind that the key is not to resist the storm but to learn how to dance in the rain. It's about embracing the crisis as a catalyst for change and growth. It's about leading with empathy, adaptability, and resilience. And, most importantly, it's about keeping the human at the center of performance management.

Virtual Performance Management Checklist

An artist doesn't approach a canvas without brushes; a carpenter doesn't engage a project without tools. Just as each profession requires specialized instruments to create their masterpieces, leaders too need specific resources in their arsenal to effectively manage performance in a virtual setting. We will now walk you through a practical checklist, a 'Digital Leadership Toolkit', if you will, to ensure that you are well-equipped to manage performance remotely. Each item in this list is curated based on the lessons learned from real-world experiences and is designed to empower you to maintain the momentum, even in a virtual sphere.

1. Adopt Virtual Performance Management Platforms: Harness technology to track and analyze performance data. Platforms like Trello, Asana, or Monday.com not only provide an overview of individual and team progress but also ensure transparency and accountability.

2. Set Clear, Measurable Goals: Every team member should have a clear understanding of what is expected of them. Set SMART (Specific, Measurable, Achievable, Relevant, Time-Bound) goals to provide a clear direction and a benchmark for measuring performance.

3. Maintain Regular Check-Ins: Regular check-ins provide a platform for feedback, guidance, and support. Use these sessions to discuss progress towards goals, address concerns, and offer solutions to challenges.

4. Foster a Culture of Open Communication: Encourage team members to share their thoughts, ideas, and concerns freely. This will not only improve problem-solving and innovation but also boost morale and engagement.

5. Provide Flexibility: Recognize that every team member may have a unique set of challenges while working remotely. Provide flexibility in work hours and deadlines wherever possible to accommodate these challenges.

6. Focus on Outcome, Not Activity: Don't judge performance based on hours worked but on the results achieved.

This encourages efficiency and innovation and reduces unnecessary pressure.

7. Offer Professional Development Opportunities: Provide resources for skill development and learning. This not only enhances performance but also boosts morale and job satisfaction.

8. Recognize and Reward Performance: Acknowledging good performance boosts morale and motivation. Use virtual rewards like shout-outs in team meetings, digital badges, or even additional time-off.

9. Practice Empathy: Understand the unique challenges each team member might be facing in the remote setup. Offer support and understanding, and make allowances wherever necessary.

10. Use Crisis as an Opportunity for Growth: Instead of seeing performance issues during a crisis as failures, view them as opportunities for learning and growth. Adopt a coaching approach to performance management during such times.

❋ ❋ ❋

Remember that tools are only as effective as the hands that wield them. Use this checklist not as a rigid doctrine but as a flexible guide, adapting it to suit your team's unique needs and circumstances. The magic lies not in the tool but in the artistry with which you use it to craft the masterpiece of effective performance management in a virtual setting.

CHAPTER 20 - REMOTE CULTURE: FOSTERING UNITY AMIDST DIVERSITY

Each employee in an organization represents a piece of its cultural mosaic. But as work shifts from physical offices to digital platforms, the challenge becomes maintaining this unity. It's not about merely integrating digital social activities, but fostering a true sense of belonging. While strategies may direct a company, it's the ingrained culture that propels it forward. A notable tech firm's smooth transition to remote work, thanks to its well-defined pre-existing culture, serves as a testament to this.

Creating a remote inclusive culture can be likened to blindfolded mural painting. Yet, successful leaders create teams diverse in thought, background, and innovation. The expansive talent pool in remote work necessitates ensuring every member feels valued and integrated, regardless of location. For instance, a renowned fashion company's shift to asynchronous communication demonstrated how to embrace diverse time zones and lifestyles, weaving unity from diversity's threads.

A company's culture is its compass during turbulent times. Reflect on the healthcare startup that adapted rapidly to regulatory upheavals, all thanks to its nimble and adaptable culture. Their shared vision and understanding of their collective strength enabled them to innovate and excel amidst challenges.

In this chapter, we'll provide tools and insights to cultivate a resilient remote culture. However, it's crucial to recognize that culture isn't a one-off task; it's an evolving commitment. Much like a tapestry, it develops with every interaction, decision, and message. In the remote world, the onus is on leaders to ensure this tapestry remains interconnected, irrespective of geographical gaps. After all, true unity in diversity goes beyond mere assembly—it's about crafting a collective masterpiece.

The Significance of Culture in Remote Teams

Imagine an orchestra. Each musician plays their instrument, each note contributing to a symphony. Alone, the sound of each instrument is beautiful. But together, they create something magical. Much like an orchestra, an organization relies on each of its members playing their part. The music they make, harmonious or dissonant, is the culture of the organization. But what happens when the orchestra is spread across the globe, each musician playing their part from their own space? This is the reality of remote teams. It is the challenge leaders must face: crafting unity in diversity.

Every leader knows that culture is the lifeblood of an organization. It is an invisible thread that connects every individual, influencing how they work, how they interact, and how they perceive their roles within the greater tapestry. It is an influential player that, while unseen, sets the stage for performance, innovation, and satisfaction. The question isn't whether culture is important; the question is, how do we nurture it when the team is dispersed?

The environment in which a team operates can shape its culture. A buzzing office, coffee breaks, and informal chats play a role in fostering connection and alignment. But with remote teams, the environment is vastly different. Your team is dispersed, their surroundings as varied as their roles within the team. It's easy to fall into thinking that culture is less significant in a remote setting, but in fact, its importance is magnified.

Why so? A remote team doesn't have the luxury of physical proximity to foster camaraderie. The water cooler chats, the spontaneous brainstorming sessions, the shared meals—these incidental interactions that cultivate relationships and shared understanding are absent. What is left is a virtual landscape that requires deliberate and intentional actions to foster a shared culture.

In a remote setting, culture becomes the glue that binds the team together, the beacon of light guiding them in the vast sea of digital work. It is the collective belief system that tells each team member, "You are part of something bigger. You are not alone." It is what enables a group of individuals, scattered across various time zones, to work together harmoniously towards a shared goal.

The importance of culture in remote teams can be seen in a global technology firm that made the shift to remote work. Their strong culture of transparency and trust, established while they were co-located, was a key factor in their successful transition to remote work. Their shared values and beliefs kept them united, their mutual trust in one another kept them productive, and their transparency in communication kept them aligned. It was their culture that kept the music playing, despite each musician playing from a different location.

If we want to see culture as the lifeblood of an organization, then communication is the heart that keeps it flowing. In a remote setting, clear and effective communication becomes more than a means to an end—it becomes the foundation upon which a shared culture is built. It is through communication that values are conveyed, expectations are set, and relationships are nurtured.

Yet, fostering a shared culture remotely is not about mirroring an office environment in a virtual setting. It's not about transitioning office traditions online or ensuring that every team member has the best home office setup. It's about recognizing the unique opportunities and challenges of remote work and reshaping your culture to thrive within them.

An organization that wants to build a strong remote culture must recognize and value the diversity of its team members' experiences. It must acknowledge that each team member brings to the virtual table a unique set of skills, perspectives, and circumstances. Only by acknowledging and embracing this diversity can an organization hope to build a culture that is inclusive, collaborative, and resilient.

It's not enough to merely adapt your existing culture to a remote setting. You must reinvent it. You must be willing to shed old habits and practices that no longer serve you and adopt new ones that promote engagement, connection, and well-being. You must be willing to listen to your team members, to learn from their experiences, and to adapt your culture to meet their needs.

Cultivating culture in remote teams is no easy task. It requires continuous effort, patience, and the willingness to learn and adapt. But the rewards are well worth the effort. A strong and positive remote culture not only promotes productivity and engagement, but it also fosters a sense of belonging, boosts morale, and attracts top talents.

Ultimately, culture in remote teams is about more than just work—it's about crafting a shared identity, a sense of community, and a sense of purpose. It's about creating a space where everyone feels valued and heard. It's about building an orchestra that, despite playing from different locations, produces the most beautiful symphony.

Strategies for Building a Strong Inclusive Remote Culture

Crafting unity in diversity within remote teams is not only achievable but can lead to richer outcomes, stronger innovation, and a harmonious work environment. But it doesn't happen spontaneously. Building a strong, inclusive remote culture requires strategic intention, consistent efforts, and a fine balance between individuality and unity. Like a gardener tending to an array of plants, leaders need to nurture every team member while ensuring the garden as a whole thrives.

The strategy of building an inclusive remote culture starts with understanding your team. Leaders need to move beyond traditional workplace demographics and delve into the idiosyncrasies of their team members. With a dispersed workforce, it's not just about cultural or generational differences anymore. Each team member's individual remote working circumstances, personal commitments, and local time zones become important factors influencing their productivity and satisfaction. Leaders must be willing to embrace these differences and use them as strengths, not hurdles.

Consider a global software company that managed to harness the diversity within their team to their advantage. They capitalized on the different time zones their employees worked in to offer round-the-clock customer support without overworking any team member. This was possible because the company leaders made an effort to understand the unique circumstances of each employee and integrate it within their operational strategy. They turned a potential stumbling block into an opportunity.

When building an inclusive remote culture, it's crucial to cultivate a sense of belonging among your team members. Regardless of their location, each team member should feel valued, heard, and a part of the team. This can be achieved by facilitating open communication, recognizing individual efforts, and promoting collaboration. A shared team identity, a strong sense of connection, and collective goals can bind your team together, cultivating a strong and inclusive culture.

Yet, in a remote setting, leaders often fall into the trap of overemphasizing tasks and neglecting social interactions. It's crucial to understand that while the task-oriented aspect of work is necessary, it's the social glue that binds a team.

It's those random conversations, shared jokes, and common interests that make us feel connected. As a leader, you need to create opportunities for these informal interactions to occur in a remote setting.

A leader of a remote marketing team understood this. She organized virtual coffee breaks, where team members would gather online for casual chats. These sessions had nothing to do with work. Instead, it was a space for the team to share their interests, discuss their latest Netflix binge, or show off their pets. These virtual coffee breaks became a cherished part of their remote culture, strengthening their bonds.

Building an inclusive remote culture is not a one-time effort; it requires continuous reinforcement. Leaders need to consistently convey the organization's values and beliefs, ensuring every team member understands and aligns with them. But it's equally important to ensure your culture remains flexible and adaptable. As your team grows and evolves, so should your culture.

Creating a feedback-rich environment is another key strategy. In the absence of physical cues and spontaneous interactions, feedback becomes an essential tool to recognize individual contributions, address concerns, and enhance performance. However, feedback in a remote setting should not be limited to performance alone. Encourage your team members to share their thoughts, ideas, and concerns about the remote work environment and culture. This will not only make them feel valued but will also give you insights into potential areas of improvement.

Leaders often underestimate the power of rituals in strengthening a remote culture. Rituals, like a weekly team huddle or an annual virtual retreat, can provide a sense of stability and cohesion. These traditions become shared experiences, symbols of your unique culture. However, in crafting these rituals, ensure they're inclusive and considerate of your team's diverse backgrounds and circumstances.

Let's look at a remote startup that incorporated a

'Monthly Virtual Potluck'. Every month, team members would prepare a dish from their local cuisine and share the recipe and story behind it. They would then eat together virtually. This ritual not only brought them together but also allowed them to appreciate and learn about each other's cultures.

While crafting your strategy, don't forget to prioritize well-being. Remote work, while flexible, can blur the lines between personal and professional life leading to burnout. Promote a culture of balance and well-being. Encourage your team members to take regular breaks, discourage after-hours communication, and provide mental health resources. A team that feels cared for is more engaged, productive, and loyal.

Lastly, remember that building a strong, inclusive remote culture is not an exact science. What works for one team may not work for another. As a leader, you need to be open to experimentation, to learn from your experiences, and to adapt your strategies as required.

In the grand tapestry of remote work, culture is not just a single thread. It's the warp and weft that holds everything together. With the right strategies, leaders can weave a rich, vibrant, and inclusive culture, one that resonates with every team member, making your symphony richer, harmonious, and truly global.

Preserving Culture Amid Crisis and Change

Preserving culture amid crisis and change is not a simple feat; it is like trying to hold water in your hands while navigating turbulent rapids. It's a daunting task, yet it's pivotal to keep your remote team resilient, connected, and focused. Amid turmoil, a strong culture becomes the anchor, providing your team stability and a sense of continuity.

Think about the global health crisis that pushed numerous organizations into the world of remote work almost overnight. Suddenly, teams found themselves dislocated, faced with novel challenges, and struggling to stay connected.

Yet, companies with strong cultures saw their teams adapt swiftly, banding together to navigate the storm.

Consider a multinational organization that faced the brunt of this crisis. Their traditional work-from-office culture got upended as they switched to remote work. Yet, their culture of adaptability and collaboration helped them quickly pivot their operations. They used their weekly town halls, traditionally held in a conference room, to connect virtually, providing updates, discussing challenges, and recognizing individual contributions. The crisis did not erode their culture; instead, it fortified it, underscoring its importance.

Preserving culture during change or crisis requires proactive and mindful leadership. Leaders need to reassure their teams, articulate how their core values guide their decisions, and demonstrate empathy. Communicating frequently and transparently becomes paramount. Silence or ambiguity can breed anxiety and mistrust, eroding your culture.

But crisis communication should not only be about disseminating information. Leaders should also listen, encouraging their team to share their concerns, suggestions, and experiences. This two-way communication can make your team feel valued and included, strengthening your culture.

Remember the case of a remote customer service team during the onset of the pandemic. Their workload spiked as customer queries and complaints soared. Recognizing their stress, the team leader initiated daily virtual huddles. Not only did they discuss work but also shared their personal experiences, fears, and coping strategies. This simple act of listening and sharing not only helped them manage their stress but also reinforced their culture of support and empathy.

While preserving your culture during change, you need to ensure it remains relevant and useful. As your external environment changes, your culture should also evolve, incorporating elements that support your current context.

Consider a tech company that had a culture of working long hours, priding themselves on being 'always on'. However, when the pandemic struck, they quickly realized this culture was unsustainable and detrimental to their team's well-being. They pivoted towards a culture of balance and flexibility, allowing their team to adapt their work hours to their personal situations. This cultural shift not only supported their team during the crisis but also resulted in increased productivity.

Whereas change might disrupt your established rituals, it also provides an opportunity to create new ones that resonate with your current context. These rituals can reinforce your culture, provide a sense of continuity, and create shared experiences.

A remote design team created a new ritual during the lockdown. They started 'Virtual Creativity Sessions' where they would collaborate on a fun project or learn a new skill together. This new ritual not only helped them stay connected but also reinforced their culture of continuous learning and collaboration.

However, preserving culture is not solely a leader's responsibility. It's a collective effort. Empower your team to be culture carriers, to uphold and propagate your values and beliefs. A culture that lives within each team member is resilient, surviving crises and thriving amid change.

In times of crisis or change, it's easy to focus on immediate issues and lose sight of your culture. However, culture is not a luxury that can be sidelined. It's the backbone of your team's morale, resilience, and performance.

In the whirlwind of crisis and change, culture might seem like an elusive, abstract concept. Yet, it's as tangible as the trust within your team, the shared laughter during a virtual break, the quiet pride in your collective achievements.

Leaders need to understand that their role is not to rigidly guard a culture but to nurture it, allowing it to grow, evolve, and adapt. In the grand tapestry of a remote team, culture is the thread that weaves individuals into a unified, resilient, and vibrant entity. Amid change or crisis, a strong, adaptive culture can be your compass, guiding your team towards unity, productivity, and success.

Remote Team Culture Builder

Crafting unity in diversity within a remote culture requires a strategic blend of foundational principles and innovative approaches. No magic formula guarantees success, but a set of tested tools and tactics can guide leaders towards building a robust and inclusive remote team culture. Let's explore these practical strategies that can be the keystones for your organization's cultural blueprint.

1. Define and Communicate Your Core Values: Strong cultures are built on shared values. Consider a global software company that has defined their core values as innovation, collaboration, and customer-focus. These values are explicitly communicated during onboarding, reflected in their policies, and celebrated in their rewards.

2. Foster Open and Transparent Communication: Make communication an integral part of your culture. An example is a remote marketing team that holds weekly 'all-hands' meetings, ensuring everyone is updated and has a platform to voice their thoughts.

3. Encourage Virtual Team-Building Activities: Casual interactions and shared experiences foster bonding. For instance, a remote finance team holds monthly 'virtual coffee breaks', where they discuss anything but work.

4. Leverage Technology to Facilitate Collaboration: Use collaborative tools to ensure your team can work together seamlessly. A graphic design firm, for instance, uses project management and design collaboration tools, creating a virtual workspace for their team.

5. Ensure Work-Life Balance: Remote work can blur work-life boundaries. A tech startup mitigates this by having 'no-meeting' days, giving their team uninterrupted time for focused work or personal time.

6. Recognize and Celebrate Achievements: Regularly acknowledge your team's hard work and achievements. A global consulting firm, for instance, holds a quarterly 'virtual awards ceremony' to celebrate their team's successes.

7. Promote Learning and Development: Create opportunities for your team to learn and grow. An e-commerce company, for example, provides their remote team with learning resources and sponsors online courses and certifications.

8. Foster an Inclusive Environment: Make sure every voice is heard and respected. A non-profit organization achieved this by creating 'virtual affinity groups' where team members from diverse backgrounds can share their experiences and perspectives.

9. Solicit Regular Feedback: Keep your finger on the pulse of your culture by getting feedback from your team. A remote healthcare service provider conducts bi-monthly 'culture health-check' surveys to understand their team's sentiments.

10. Empower Your Team: Trust your team, giving them autonomy and ownership. A digital marketing agency does this by setting clear expectations and then giving their team the freedom to achieve their goals in their own way.

❊ ❊ ❊

Building a strong, inclusive remote culture is an ongoing, iterative process. It's not about instituting a set of rules, but about nurturing an environment that upholds your core values, encourages collaboration, and respects diversity. It's about creating a virtual space where every team member feels valued, included, and motivated. This checklist can be a starting point, but remember, the best culture builder is an empathetic, engaged, and adaptable leader. As the helmsman of your remote team's culture, your actions, words, and beliefs can be the most potent tools to craft unity in diversity.

CHAPTER 21 - NAVIGATING CULTURAL INTELLIGENCE IN A GLOBAL LANDSCAPE

The 21st century paints a vibrant tapestry of diverse cultures, making Cultural Intelligence an indispensable leadership trait in our globalized era. At its core, Cultural Intelligence isn't just about understanding cultural practices, but recognizing the underlying frameworks shaping thoughts, emotions, and actions. It requires cognitive understanding, emotional acumen, and actionable insights.

Cultural Intelligence isn't merely a theoretical notion; it has proven practical relevance. Multinational company studies show leaders with elevated Cultural Intelligence excel in team cohesion, motivation, and productivity. This expertise becomes vital when navigating unfamiliar terrains and is especially crucial during global crises. For instance, the diverse responses and recovery strategies during the COVID-19 pandemic showcased the need for leaders with robust Cultural Intelligence. In challenging times, such leaders leverage cultural diversity, turning potential friction points into unified strengths.

To aid leaders in enhancing this competence, the chapter offers a 'Cultural Intelligence Assessment' – a reflection tool for growth, aiming to sharpen their effectiveness in diverse settings.

This chapter invites leaders to embrace Cultural

Intelligence, a bridge fostering innovation and unity across global divides. The path may have its complexities, but its returns are profound. Like any skill, Cultural Intelligence can be honed and refined. Embark on this transformative journey with us.

Defining Cultural Intelligence: Why it Matters in Leadership

Cultural Intelligence, a term coined by academics Christopher Earley and Soon Ang, is a relative newcomer to the leadership lexicon. In simple terms, it can be defined as the ability to function effectively in culturally diverse situations. It's a blend of cognitive, emotional, and behavioral competencies that enables one to interact successfully with people from various cultural backgrounds. But the meaning of Cultural Intelligence goes deeper, especially when it comes to leadership.

Let's take a look at Lisa, the CEO of a successful tech start-up. Lisa was an adept leader, yet she felt a disconnect within her multinational team. The productivity levels were satisfactory, but she could sense a lack of deeper collaboration. She realized her knowledge about her team's cultures was limited to surface-level understanding - knowing national holidays, traditional foods, and some general behavioral tendencies. But she felt there had to be more to this puzzle.

Recognizing this gap, Lisa decided to embark on a self-learning journey to understand her team's cultures beyond the stereotypes. She read about their societal values, had open conversations with them about their cultural perspectives, and took time to comprehend their unique worldviews. This understanding changed Lisa's leadership approach. She could now effectively decode cultural nuances, empathize better, and make informed decisions that considered these cultural contexts. That's Cultural Intelligence in action, and that's why it matters in leadership.

So, why does Cultural Intelligence matter? It matters because of the rapid globalization that has effectively made every team a melting pot of diverse cultures. Gone are the days when leadership was all about one-size-fits-all strategies. In today's world, leaders need to recognize and appreciate the distinct cultural identities in their teams and organizations.

Cultural Intelligence matters because it helps a leader avoid the pitfalls of cultural misunderstandings. Consider John, a project manager, who learned this the hard way when he reprimanded a team member in front of the team. The member, from a culture where 'saving face' is a deeply rooted value, took the criticism harshly and disengaged from the project. John, who was previously oblivious to this cultural aspect, realized his error and made a concerted effort to understand and respect the cultural values of his team members. John's initial misstep could have been avoided with better Cultural Intelligence.

Moreover, Cultural Intelligence matters because it can be the fulcrum that turns diversity into an asset rather than a liability. Culturally intelligent leaders don't merely 'deal' with diversity; they leverage it. They encourage cross-cultural collaboration, breaking down silos and fostering innovation that wouldn't have been possible in a homogeneous group.

At the societal level, Cultural Intelligence matters because it fosters tolerance and mutual respect. When leaders display Cultural Intelligence, it creates a ripple effect that promotes intercultural harmony within the organization and extends beyond it.

Cultural Intelligence matters because it enhances team cohesion. When a leader understands and respects cultural differences, it sets the stage for team members to do the same. This mutual understanding and respect can significantly enhance team cohesion and effectiveness.

Cultural Intelligence matters because it's about more than being 'politically correct.' It's about creating an environment where everyone feels valued, heard, and appreciated for who they are and the unique perspectives they bring to the table.

In the end, Cultural Intelligence matters because it's

good for business. Multiple studies have shown that culturally intelligent leadership is positively correlated with team effectiveness, job performance, and overall profitability.

For leaders, understanding Cultural Intelligence is the first step. However, its true power is unleashed only when this understanding translates into behavior. As Lisa's and John's stories illustrate, enhancing Cultural Intelligence can transform leadership effectiveness and create a harmonious, productive, and inclusive workplace.

Cultural Intelligence, in essence, is about leadership that transcends borders. It's the ability to see beyond the surface, to understand and value the beautiful diversity that makes up our world. It's a testament to the universal truth that while we may be separated by geography, we're connected by the common threads of humanity. This isn't just a skill for leaders to master; it's a mindset that paves the way for unity in diversity.

Impact of Cultural Intelligence on Leadership

The manifestation of Cultural Intelligence in leadership is like an intricately woven tapestry. Each thread represents a different competency, and when woven together, they create a picture of effective leadership that transcends cultural boundaries. Consider the example of Lina, the director of an international nonprofit organization. Her ability to lead successfully across diverse cultures was pivotal in expanding the organization's impact on a global scale.

When Lina was assigned the project, the organization had a presence in just a handful of countries. Her task was to broaden this reach, a challenge she embraced with open arms. However, it didn't take long for Lina to realize that her traditional leadership strategies weren't cutting it. The cultural dynamics at play were more complex than she had anticipated, and her lack of Cultural Intelligence became evident.

Deciding to turn this around, Lina made it her mission to enhance her Cultural Intelligence. She invested time and effort to understand the nuances of the different cultures she was working with. She read extensively, interacted closely with local teams, and took every opportunity to immerse herself in the various cultures. The transformation in her leadership approach was palpable, and the positive impact on her leadership effectiveness was undeniable.

Lina began to notice that her improved Cultural Intelligence made her a more effective communicator. She understood that the same message could be interpreted differently in different cultural contexts. She started tailoring her communication to suit the cultural norms of her audience, leading to fewer misunderstandings and more effective collaboration.

Moreover, Lina's improved Cultural Intelligence also had a significant impact on her decision-making. She realized that what works in one culture might not work in another. She began to factor in cultural variables when making strategic decisions, leading to better outcomes that were more aligned with the local realities and needs.

Cultural Intelligence also made Lina a better problem-solver. When conflicts arose within her multicultural team, she was better equipped to handle them. Her nuanced understanding of cultural differences allowed her to mediate conflicts more effectively, foster mutual understanding, and maintain team harmony.

Beyond that, Lina's Cultural Intelligence played a crucial role in building trust within her team. As she began to demonstrate a deep understanding and respect for her team members' cultures, they started feeling more seen and appreciated. This strengthened the bonds of trust, improving team morale and cohesion.

The impact of Cultural Intelligence on Lina's leadership was also evident in the organization's bottom line. As the organization expanded its reach, the culturally intelligent strategies employed by Lina ensured better adaptation to local environments. This resulted in more effective programs, increased stakeholder satisfaction, and enhanced organizational reputation.

Perhaps most importantly, Cultural Intelligence made Lina a more inclusive leader. She learned to value diversity not just in terms of nationality but also in terms of thoughts, perspectives, and ideas. She fostered an environment where every team member felt safe and encouraged to bring their authentic selves to the table.

Lina's story isn't an isolated one. Many leaders have found their effectiveness amplified by their Cultural Intelligence. It allows them to navigate the complex labyrinth of global leadership, turning cultural differences from hurdles into steppingstones.

Leaders with high Cultural Intelligence stand out in the global arena. They bring about change, not just within their organizations, but within societies. They break down walls, build bridges, and pave the way for a world where diversity is celebrated, and unity is cherished.

It's crucial to note that Cultural Intelligence isn't a fixed trait; it's a capability that can be developed. Just like Lina, any leader can work on their Cultural Intelligence and unlock its myriad benefits.

In essence, the impact of Cultural Intelligence on leadership is profound and multifaceted. It not only enhances a leader's effectiveness in the globalized world but also enriches their personal growth and understanding of humanity's beautiful diversity. As our world continues to become more interconnected, Cultural Intelligence will only grow in importance as a key leadership competency.

And so, we see that Cultural Intelligence is not merely an abstract concept. It's a powerful force that can redefine leadership, bridging differences and bringing people together. By developing Cultural Intelligence, leaders can steer their organizations towards success in our complex, globalized world.

Effectiveness Cultural Intelligence During Global Crises

As we venture into the discussion about the effectiveness of Cultural Intelligence during global crises, we may examine the story of Edward, a seasoned leader at a multinational company. Edward had always been proud of his Cultural Intelligence, yet when the pandemic struck, it was put to the ultimate test. His company had offices around the globe, and each was affected differently by the crisis. Would his Cultural Intelligence be enough to see his organization through these turbulent times?

When the crisis first hit, Edward, like many other leaders, was initially overwhelmed. His company had teams scattered around the globe, each facing unique challenges due to the local impact of the crisis. However, Edward quickly realized that his Cultural Intelligence could be his most potent tool in this situation.

One of the first things Edward did was to acknowledge the diversity of experiences across his teams. He understood that the crisis was affecting people differently based on their cultural contexts. He took the time to listen to each team's unique challenges and understand the cultural factors at play. This was not merely an administrative exercise but a compassionate response that revealed a leader with high Cultural Intelligence.

Edward also recognized that his communication approach had to adapt to the crisis. He leveraged his Cultural Intelligence to adjust his messaging, balancing empathy with the need to inspire resilience and maintain productivity. He was mindful of the cultural nuances in emotional expression and support, careful not to impose a one-size-fits-all approach.

Edward's Cultural Intelligence also proved crucial in decision-making during the crisis. He knew that a central, top-down approach would be counterproductive given the different cultural contexts. Instead, he empowered local teams to make decisions within a framework, which recognized the cultural nuances and the variable impact of the crisis.

Similarly, problem-solving during the crisis was another area where Edward's Cultural Intelligence came into play. His ability to appreciate the different cultural perspectives within his teams led to more innovative solutions. Recognizing that diversity in thought could be a strength, he encouraged a collaborative approach to problem-solving.

Trust building, a critical leadership aspect during crises, was another area where Edward's Cultural Intelligence shone. His culturally sensitive approach, his respect for the diverse experiences of his teams, and his consistent support in these trying times significantly enhanced the trust his teams had in him.

Edward's Cultural Intelligence also played a key role in crisis recovery. He recognized that the post-crisis recovery period would be as diverse as the crisis's impact. Using his understanding of cultural nuances, he tailored recovery strategies to each team, enhancing their effectiveness.

This approach led to a deeper connection within his teams. They felt valued and understood, increasing their engagement and commitment, even amid a crisis. The result was a stronger, more resilient organization that could navigate the complexities of a global crisis with agility and unity.

The story of Edward provides profound insight into the effectiveness of Cultural Intelligence during global crises. It's not just about cultural knowledge or awareness but a deep understanding and appreciation of diversity, coupled with the ability to leverage this understanding effectively. It is about connecting on a deeper level and creating an environment of inclusivity, respect, and mutual support.

Cultural Intelligence during global crises is not just a nice-to-have; it is a must-have leadership competency. It can make the difference between a fragmented, ineffective response and a unified, resilient one. It allows leaders to navigate the complex maze of a global crisis with sensitivity and wisdom.

Cultural Intelligence empowers leaders to turn diversity from a challenge into a strength. It allows them to create an environment of unity in diversity, which can not only withstand a crisis but also emerge stronger from it. In our increasingly interconnected world, Cultural Intelligence's value, particularly during global crises, cannot be overstated.

Edward's story paints a clear picture of the power of Cultural Intelligence in the face of global crises. It is a testament to the transformative impact it can have on leadership effectiveness and organizational resilience. It's not just about leading across cultures in a globalized world; it's about leading through the complexities and challenges of a crisis, forging unity in diversity, and charting a course towards recovery and growth.

Cultural Intelligence Assessment

As we venture deeper into our understanding of Cultural Intelligence, it becomes essential to examine and evaluate our own capacities. No leader, no matter how proficient, is beyond the scope for improvement. To effectively navigate a globalized world, leaders must routinely assess their Cultural Intelligence, seeking gaps and growth opportunities. We now present a set of tools and strategies, fashioned from the distillation of real-life experiences and expert knowledge, which you can utilize in your quest for higher Cultural Intelligence.

1. Self-Reflection: Start by reflecting on your interactions with diverse individuals and cultures. Think about the successes and challenges. What went well? What could have gone better? This self-reflection can provide valuable insights into your Cultural Intelligence.

2. Seek Feedback: Solicit feedback from colleagues, especially those from different cultural backgrounds. They can provide a perspective on your cultural sensitivity and responsiveness that you may not see. Constructive feedback can be a powerful tool for improvement.

3. Cultural Intelligence Surveys: Use validated Cultural Intelligence assessments. These are designed to measure an individual's capability to function and manage effectively in culturally diverse settings. It provides a snapshot of where you stand and what areas you need to improve upon.

4. Cultural Immersion: If feasible, immerse yourself in a new culture. This could mean traveling to a different country, attending cultural events, or actively seeking to engage with individuals from different cultures. These experiences can greatly enhance your Cultural Intelligence.

5. Cultural Training: Engage in formal cultural training programs. These are often designed to improve awareness, knowledge, and skills related to working in multicultural environments.

6. Reading and Research: Dedicate time to learning about different cultures, their values, norms, and customs. Reading, watching documentaries, and conducting research can broaden your cultural understanding.

7. Language Learning: Learning a new language can be a powerful tool for improving Cultural Intelligence. It can offer a deeper understanding of a culture and provide an opportunity for meaningful engagement.

8. Establish a Support Network: Cultivate relationships with mentors or coaches who have a high level of Cultural Intelligence. They can provide guidance, feedback, and support in your Cultural Intelligence development journey.

9. Practice Active Listening: When interacting with people from different cultures, listen actively. Try to understand their perspectives, feelings, and experiences. This can increase your cultural sensitivity and understanding.

10. Be Patient and Persistent: Developing Cultural Intelligence is a continual process that takes time. Be patient with yourself and persist in your efforts.

* * *

Remember, evaluating and improving Cultural Intelligence is not a one-time event but an ongoing process. The world is continually evolving, and so are cultures. By consistently assessing and working on your Cultural Intelligence, you can ensure that you stay relevant and effective in your leadership role, no matter where in the world you may find yourself.

CHAPTER 22 - MASTERING CONFLICT RESOLUTION IN A MULTICULTURAL LANDSCAPE

In Tokyo, a team from diverse global backgrounds - Paris, San Francisco, Mumbai, Seoul - collaborates. Beyond their diverse competencies, differing cultural identities hint at potential conflicts. This chapter dives not into conflict's origins, but its resolution, highlighting the interplay of cultural intelligence, empathy, and respect in "The Art of Global Peacekeeping."

Every conflict originates from a disconnect - be it perspective, understanding, or cultural nuances. Cultural intelligence acts as the linchpin, enabling leaders to transition from mere peacekeepers to genuine peacemakers. It's more than a tool; it's the compass for bridging cultural divides, turning misunderstandings into mutual respect. A prime example is an American manager and a Japanese employee, whose cultural differences in hierarchy and feedback require more than mere translation; they require cultural acumen.

Leadership isn't just about managing success, but also adeptly steering through crises, especially in multicultural settings. An NGO in a politically sensitive area, for instance, faces cultural challenges that can escalate conflicts, magnifying already existing hurdles. Here, cultural intelligence acts as the foundation, aiding leaders in sidestepping cultural pitfalls and ensuring sensitive crisis management.

Conflict resolution is an intricate dance of empathy, respect, and cultural intelligence. Rather than an ad-hoc approach, there's a structured methodology for addressing these cross-cultural tensions. Chapter 22 presents a comprehensive guide, integrating cultural intelligence principles with proven techniques, arming leaders with a resilient framework for conflict resolution in diverse contexts.

From corporate hubs in New York to humanitarian missions in South Sudan, this guide holds universal value, equipping leaders to navigate cultural conflicts, instill understanding, and fortify teams.

In essence, conflicts are more than just disruptions – they're catalysts for dialogue, understanding, and growth. With cultural intelligence and the right strategies, leaders can leverage these moments as vehicles for positive transformation across teams, organizations, and the global tapestry. Join us in mastering the craft of global peacekeeping.

The Role of Cultural Intelligence in Conflict Resolution

Understanding the role of cultural intelligence in conflict resolution is akin to fitting the pieces of a complex puzzle together. To navigate this puzzle, we turn to the corporate world's melting pot - a multicultural team in an international tech firm. A misunderstanding between an Indian software engineer and her Brazilian team leader has created a fracture in team dynamics. This situation, however, is not an anomaly, but a shared reality in our globalized world.

Here's where cultural intelligence comes into play. The Brazilian team leader, faced with this conflict, must first comprehend the cultural nuances that might be influencing this misunderstanding. He should understand that the cultural background of his Indian colleague might affect her communication style, working preferences, and response to feedback. It's a delicate understanding that cannot be achieved by a cursory Google search, but by an intentional effort to understand and embrace diversity.

Cultural intelligence in conflict resolution is much more than recognizing cultural differences. It's about leveraging these differences to foster understanding, creating a space where varied perspectives coexist, not merely side by side, but interwoven in a collaborative tapestry. It's about appreciating that these differences are strengths, sources of innovation and creativity, not a hurdle to overcome.

Consider the multinational giant, Google, known for its cultural diversity and inclusive culture. When conflicts arise, leaders don't just aim to resolve the dispute; they focus on understanding the cultural dynamics at play. They view the conflict through a lens of cultural intelligence, treating it not just as a challenge, but as an opportunity for learning and growth. It is not the elimination of conflict they seek, but rather, its resolution through understanding and empathy.

The application of cultural intelligence in conflict resolution extends beyond corporate borders. In the realm of international diplomacy, leaders are often faced with high-stakes conflicts rooted in cultural differences. In these cases, cultural intelligence is not just a skill; it's a lifeline. Diplomats, armed with a keen understanding of the cultural nuances, can navigate these intricate situations, fostering dialogues, and finding common ground amidst apparent discord.

Take the example of the 1993 Oslo Peace Accords. The historic agreement between Israel and Palestine was not just a result of political maneuvering. The negotiators' cultural intelligence played a significant role in bridging differences, facilitating a dialogue, and ultimately, achieving a resolution. It wasn't about 'winning'; it was about understanding, compromise, and mutual respect.

Remember, cultural intelligence in conflict resolution is not just about 'winning' an argument or imposing one's viewpoint. It's about understanding the other person's perspective, their cultural background, their thought processes. It's about finding a middle ground, a solution that respects and acknowledges the diversity of perspectives.

The role of cultural intelligence in conflict resolution is not an abstract concept. It is a practical and potent tool in the hands of leaders. It provides them with the means to diffuse conflicts, foster understanding, and maintain harmony in culturally diverse teams. In essence, cultural intelligence is the bridge that transforms conflict into collaboration, misunderstanding into shared understanding.

In the case of our Brazilian team leader, he used his cultural intelligence to understand the differences in communication style and work ethic. He didn't just resolve the conflict; he used it as an opportunity for mutual growth and understanding. The team didn't just 'survive' the conflict; they emerged stronger and more united.

Leaders who can master this art of cultural intelligence are not just resolving a current conflict; they're equipping their teams with the skills and understanding to navigate future conflicts. They're fostering a culture of empathy, respect, and mutual understanding - a culture that can thrive in the face of diversity and differences.

In the realm of international business and global politics, the stakes are even higher. Here, cultural intelligence is not just about managing conflicts; it's about maintaining relationships, fostering alliances, and ensuring peace.

Cultural intelligence is the unsung hero in the story of conflict resolution. It is the compass that guides leaders through the labyrinth of cultural differences, the lens that transforms conflicts into opportunities, and the bridge that connects disparate cultures in a bond of mutual understanding and respect. In our globalized world, where conflicts are as diverse as the people involved, cultural intelligence is not just an asset; it's a necessity.

As we navigate the increasingly interconnected and multicultural landscape of the 21st century, the role of cultural intelligence in conflict resolution will only grow in significance. Leaders who can harness the power of cultural intelligence can transform the narrative of conflict resolution, turning challenges into opportunities, and differences into strengths. So, let's start recognizing cultural intelligence for what it truly is - the key to understanding, the path to resolution, and the bridge to a more peaceful, understanding world.

Techniques for Resolving Cross-Cultural Conflicts

Resolving cross-cultural conflicts is both an art and a science, an interplay of cultural understanding and strategic technique. Each conflict, like a unique painting, requires a unique blend of colors and strokes. Each solution, like an individual piece of a symphony, must be attuned to the collective melody. Let's delve into the various techniques that can help leaders adeptly manage cross-cultural conflicts.

The first technique lies in the power of active listening. When conflicts arise, we often focus on getting our point across, but forget to lend an equal ear to the other side. Active listening is more than just hearing; it involves understanding, processing, and reflecting on what the other party has to say. Take for instance, the managing director of a multinational corporation, who diffused a brewing conflict between American and Japanese team members by initiating open discussions and actively listening to both sides. This act of listening gave each party the confidence that their views were valued and respected, paving the way for resolution.

The second technique hinges on the understanding and respect for cultural norms. Each culture has its unique set of norms and practices that can impact the approach to conflict resolution. An understanding of these norms can guide leaders in choosing the right conflict resolution strategy. For example, in collectivist cultures, it may be more effective to address conflicts in a group setting, while in individualistic cultures, a more direct, one-on-one approach may be preferred.

Next, leaders must cultivate the art of empathy.

Understanding another's point of view, especially when it's molded by a different cultural context, requires empathy. Empathy allows us to step into another's shoes, see the world through their lens, and respond in a way that is sensitive to their feelings and perspectives. Airbnb's leadership, for example, attributed their ability to handle a potential cross-cultural conflict between hosts and guests to their empathy-driven approach.

Flexibility is another crucial technique in resolving cross-cultural conflicts. A 'one-size-fits-all' approach rarely works when dealing with diverse cultures. Leaders must be flexible and adaptable, willing to adjust their approach based on the cultural context. Just as Google adjusts its algorithms to cater to different regions, leaders must adjust their conflict resolution strategies to align with cultural nuances.

Seeking common ground forms the backbone of any conflict resolution process. Despite the differences, every conflict presents an opportunity to find a shared purpose or objective. By focusing on these shared goals, leaders can help conflicting parties move beyond their differences towards a shared resolution. It's akin to how global leaders find common ground on shared challenges, like climate change, despite political and cultural differences.

Communication, both verbal and non-verbal, plays a critical role in resolving cross-cultural conflicts. How we express our thoughts and feelings can be greatly influenced by our cultural background. Leaders must be adept at reading these verbal and non-verbal cues and responding in a manner that fosters understanding and resolution.

Cultural education is another potent tool in a leader's arsenal. By providing their teams with the knowledge and understanding of different cultures, leaders can proactively prevent misunderstandings and conflicts. For instance, many global corporations invest in cultural training programs to equip their employees with the knowledge and skills to navigate cultural differences effectively.

Patience, though often overlooked, is a crucial technique in resolving cross-cultural conflicts. Understanding and resolving cultural conflicts takes time. Leaders must resist the urge to rush the process and instead, give it the time it requires. It's like tending to a garden; with patience and care, the seeds of resolution will gradually take root and blossom.

Remember that resolution does not always mean agreement. Conflict resolution is not about getting everyone to agree with each other; it's about reaching a compromise where everyone feels their perspectives have been acknowledged and respected.

Finally, leaders must remember that the resolution of a conflict is not the end, but the beginning of a continuous process of understanding and learning. Each resolved conflict is an opportunity for the team to learn, grow and better navigate future conflicts.

Resolving cross-cultural conflicts requires a blend of listening, understanding, empathy, flexibility, communication, education, patience, and continuous learning. It is a complex yet rewarding process that transforms conflicts into opportunities for growth and understanding. These techniques, when wielded effectively, can help leaders master the art of global peacekeeping, turning the tide of conflict into a wave of collaboration, understanding, and mutual respect. In our multicultural world, these techniques are not just strategies; they are the bridges that connect diverse cultures, fostering harmony amidst diversity.

Managing Crises and Conflicts in a Multicultural Context

Managing crises and conflicts in a multicultural context is akin to conducting a symphony orchestra where each musician plays a unique instrument and follows a distinct rhythm. Just as the conductor integrates these individual parts into a harmonious whole, a leader must unite the diverse elements of a multicultural team during a crisis. This requires a skill set that surpasses traditional leadership approaches.

The first rule of crisis management is recognizing that a crisis is a high-pressure situation that can amplify cultural differences. For instance, a CEO of a global manufacturing company faced a product recall crisis. He quickly realized that his Western approach of open communication and transparency was creating more confusion and unrest among his Asian team members who valued indirect communication and saving face. Understanding these cultural nuances in crisis management can be pivotal to its resolution.

Another important rule is fostering a sense of unity amidst diversity. A crisis can cause feelings of uncertainty and fear. A leader's role is to establish a sense of solidarity that transcends cultural boundaries. Consider the case of a global charity during the recent pandemic crisis. The CEO effectively emphasized shared values of compassion and service to unite their globally diverse team.

During a crisis, communication is key. But in a multicultural context, communication isn't just about what is being said but how it is being understood. A leader must ensure that their crisis management strategy is communicated effectively across different cultures. The CEO of a global tech firm, during a data breach crisis, used culturally appropriate metaphors and stories to explain the crisis and the proposed solutions, ensuring everyone understood the gravity of the situation and their role in the resolution.

Flexibility is a cornerstone of managing crises in a multicultural context. A leader should be adaptable and willing to modify their approach based on cultural nuances. During a supply chain crisis in a global fashion brand, the leader adapted her typically democratic leadership style to a more authoritative one for their operations team in a culture that respected hierarchy and expected clear directives during crises.

Leaders should be aware of cultural differences in

attitudes towards authority and power. Some cultures may expect leaders to have all the answers in a crisis, while others might value a more collaborative approach. Successful leaders adjust their approach based on these cultural expectations. A cruise ship captain successfully navigated a storm crisis by adopting a more authoritarian role with his Russian crew members while engaging in participative decision-making with his Scandinavian officers.

Another factor leaders need to consider is time perception across different cultures. Some cultures are long-term oriented and may be more patient in a crisis, while others are short-term oriented and may expect immediate action. Leaders need to balance these perspectives during crisis management. A restaurant chain owner managed a food safety crisis by taking immediate corrective actions to appease his Western customers, while also demonstrating long-term commitment to food safety improvements to reassure his Eastern partners.

Similarly, emotional expression and control during a crisis can differ across cultures. Some cultures might express their stress openly, while others may control and internalize their emotions. Leaders need to provide culturally appropriate emotional support. A Hollywood film director managed on-set crises by giving space for his Latin American crew to express their emotions, while providing private assurance to his Japanese cast who preferred discrete emotional support.

Leaders must also understand the cultural implications of responsibility and blame during a crisis. In some cultures, people may take personal responsibility, while in others, the blame might be shared or attributed to external factors. Leaders need to address these cultural perspectives while managing crises. A tech startup co-founder navigated a funding crisis by taking personal responsibility to reassure his American investors, while also contextualizing the crisis as an industry-wide issue for his Asian stakeholders.

During a crisis, leaders should empower local leaders

who understand the cultural context and can provide insights into the local team's perspective. This can help ensure the crisis management strategy is culturally appropriate. For instance, a global logistics company facing a worker strike empowered their local managers to negotiate with the workers, leveraging their understanding of local labor laws and cultural expectations.

Finally, remember that a crisis can be an opportunity for multicultural teams to understand each other better and strengthen their collaboration. After the crisis, leaders should reflect on the crisis management process, learn from the cultural interactions, and use these insights to build a more resilient and cohesive team.

Managing crises in a multicultural context is about respecting diversity, leveraging cultural insights, and fostering unity. It's about being a conductor who understands each musician's unique rhythm and guides them towards a harmonious symphony. It's about transforming the discord of crises into the harmony of collaboration and mutual understanding, creating a resilient and culturally intelligent team capable of weathering any storm.

Cross-Cultural Conflict Resolution Guide

As we continue to chart our path through this complex landscape of multicultural leadership, the need for clear, practical guidance has never been more important. As the maestro of a grand symphony orchestra, a leader should not only recognize each instrument's unique sound but also know how to harmonize them in a cohesive manner. As such, resolving cross-cultural conflicts requires a well-tuned set of tools and strategies. Here, we offer a guide that will serve as your baton in the orchestration of harmonious solutions across cultural divides.

1. Understand Cultural Context: Begin by taking the time to understand the cultural context of the parties involved in the conflict. For example, when a Dutch manager experienced resistance from his Indonesian team, he researched their cultural norms and found that direct criticism, common in the Dutch culture, was perceived as rude in Indonesian culture. Adjusting his communication style led to increased trust and collaboration.

2. Encourage Open Dialogue: Facilitate an environment where all parties feel comfortable expressing their viewpoints. This might involve moderating a meeting or discussion where everyone has an equal opportunity to speak. The CEO of a Canadian tech startup used this approach during a dispute between her American and Japanese team members, leading to mutual understanding and resolution.

3. Utilize Local Leadership: Empower local leaders who understand the cultural context to play a significant role in conflict resolution. A British NGO facing a crisis in their Kenyan operation leveraged local managers to successfully negotiate the conflict, thanks to their intimate understanding of local customs and values.

4. Balance Assertiveness and Empathy: Stand firm on important points, but also be willing to show understanding and empathy for the cultural perspectives of others. A global hotel chain's CEO demonstrated this balance during a labor dispute, asserting the company's stance while also expressing genuine understanding for the workers' cultural perspectives.

5. Adjust Communication Styles: Be flexible with your communication style to suit the cultural preferences of the parties involved. During a product recall crisis, a Swedish car manufacturer's CEO adjusted his typically direct communication style to a more indirect one for their South Korean market, reducing anxiety and enhancing cooperation.

6. Leverage Cultural Liaisons: Employ cultural liaisons who can bridge the communication gap between different cultural groups. A multinational software company used this strategy during a cross-cultural project, with the cultural liaisons facilitating understanding and cooperation between the Indian and German teams.

7. Provide Culturally Appropriate Support: Be aware of how different cultures express and manage emotions. During a crisis, provide support that is sensitive to these differences. A Hollywood film director managed this by providing private reassurances to his introverted Scandinavian cast and a public forum for his expressive Italian crew.

8. Foster Mutual Respect: Encourage a culture of mutual respect where differences are acknowledged and valued. A global retail corporation implemented a cultural exchange program, encouraging employees from different regions to share their customs and practices, fostering mutual respect and reducing conflicts.

9. Learn and Adapt: After a conflict, take the time to reflect, learn, and adapt your practices. A French pharmaceutical company did this following a cultural conflict in their African division, adjusting their policies to be more sensitive to local customs.

10. Use Neutral Third Parties: In cases of significant conflict, consider bringing in a neutral third party to mediate. A global oil company used a professional mediator to resolve a dispute between its Middle Eastern and Western partners, ensuring a fair and impartial resolution.

❋ ❋ ❋

Cultivating a harmonious multicultural environment is akin to conducting a symphony. It requires an understanding of each instrument, the ability to create harmony from dissonance, and the wisdom to adapt to each performance's unique requirements. These tools and strategies are your baton – wield them wisely, and the music of cross-cultural collaboration can indeed be beautiful.

CHAPTER 23 - ETHICAL LEADERSHIP ACROSS CULTURES: CHARTING THE MORAL TERRAIN

In our globalized world, ethics form a vibrant mosaic of values and principles, distinct across cultures. Yet, there's a universal acknowledgment of ethical leadership's paramount importance. We delve into the challenges of harmonizing organizational values with diverse cultural norms without compromising integrity or respect.

Leaders act as the moral compass, ensuring ethical direction, especially crucial in cross-cultural settings. Yet, real challenges arise when applying these principles. Consider the dilemma of aligning with a culture's gift-giving tradition while your organization prohibits gift acceptance. How do leaders chart such intricate ethical paths?

In crises, a leader's ethical stance is magnified. The task of guiding teams ethically becomes even more daunting amidst cultural or global upheavals. Real-world scenarios, from environmental ethics in lenient regulatory environments to drug pricing in developing nations, underscore these complexities.

Yet, challenges also bring solutions. Our final section in this chapter offers leaders the practical means to address ethical dilemmas, recognizing that while ethics may vary, the core tenets of ethical leadership are universal.

This chapter is not just an exploration but a call to action. Leaders' ethical choices influence not just organizations but the broader global fabric. As we embark on this journey, remember: the duty of ethical leadership transcends boundaries. Armed with integrity, empathy, and cultural respect, let's navigate the multicultural ethical arena together.

Understanding the Role of Ethics in Cross-Cultural Leadership

Let's begin with a scenario: Imagine a leader at the helm of a multinational corporation. She carries the responsibility of not just steering her team in the right direction, but also navigating the myriad of cultures within her organization. She's not just a CEO; she's the moral compass, the ethical beacon, for an entity that spans continents. This is not just a position of power but one of enormous ethical responsibility. And this is where the story of ethical leadership in a cross-cultural context begins.

Ethical leadership, in essence, is about acting and leading in ways that are consistent with your personal values, moral standards, and the ethical norms of your culture. But what happens when a leader has to steer a ship in international waters, with crew members from diverse cultural backgrounds? The role of ethics then becomes a high-wire act of balancing universally accepted ethical principles with respect for cultural diversity.

Consider the case of a global tech firm headquartered in Silicon Valley that decided to establish a software development center in Bangalore, India. The team, known for its flat hierarchy and open communication, hit a cultural roadblock when they realized their Indian colleagues were used to a more hierarchical and deferential style of communication. It was an ethical conundrum: should the company impose its cultural norms, or should it adapt to the local culture?

Such scenarios are not rare in today's globalized world. They are commonplace, making it essential for leaders to understand the intricate dance between ethics and cultural sensitivity. This, then, becomes a formidable challenge for ethical leaders: How do they maintain their moral compass when the cultural landscape keeps shifting?

The answer lies in an understanding of cultural intelligence—an understanding that respects the diversity of cultures without compromising on universal humanistic values. Let's think about this in terms of language. A good leader is a good communicator. But to communicate effectively with a diverse team, a leader must not only be fluent in their language but also understand the cultural nuances and idioms that give that language its meaning. Similarly, ethical leadership requires an understanding of cultural values and norms, but through the lens of universal ethical principles.

However, this is easier said than done. The world is not black and white, and neither is ethics. Cultural norms vary, and what is ethical in one culture might not be in another. For instance, in some cultures, accepting gifts from business partners is seen as a sign of respect and goodwill, while in others, it might be viewed as bribery.

So how does a leader navigate these cultural differences while remaining ethically sound? The key is in communication and understanding. When leaders communicate their ethical standards and listen to their team's perspectives, they create an environment where cultural and ethical standards can coexist. An environment where the team understands the company's ethical stance and the leader respects the team's cultural norms.

The role of ethics in cross-cultural leadership, then, is not to create a one-size-fits-all ethical framework. Instead, it's about creating an ethical dialogue—a conversation that respects and learns from cultural diversity while upholding universally accepted ethical principles.

Let's take a moment to recall the tech firm we mentioned earlier. Faced with the cultural roadblock, the firm could have chosen to impose its values or completely adapt to the local culture. Instead, it chose a middle path. It held workshops to discuss the company's values and listen to the local team's perspectives. It created a dialogue—a bridge—between two cultures, maintaining its ethical standards while respecting the local culture.

The role of ethics in cross-cultural leadership is not just about doing what is right. It's about understanding what 'right' means in different cultural contexts and finding a way to uphold ethical standards without ignoring cultural diversity. It's about creating an environment where ethical principles guide actions, but cultural sensitivity steers the dialogue.

In the grand theatre of leadership, ethics plays a vital role, especially in a cross-cultural context. It's not an easy role to play, with its high-wire acts and intricate dances. But for those who can master it, ethical leadership can lead to a performance that's not just successful but also inclusive, respectful, and above all, morally sound.

Challenges and Strategies for Ethical Leadership in Diverse Cultures

Leading a culturally diverse organization is like being a conductor of a global orchestra, trying to create harmony with instruments from all around the world. Each instrument has its unique tune, its cultural melody. The ethical challenges in leading such a symphony are as diverse as the instruments themselves, requiring the conductor to strike the right notes of fairness, respect, and integrity across a vast moral landscape.

It is not unusual for a leader, despite having the best intentions, to encounter ethical dilemmas while navigating diverse cultures. Let's consider the case of a multinational fast-food chain that faced a backlash when it tried to implement its animal welfare standards globally. While the standards were applauded in some countries, they were seen as an affront to cultural practices in others. This is the quandary for the modern leader – trying to uphold their organization's ethical standards while respecting cultural diversity.

The first challenge of ethical leadership in diverse cultures comes from the differences in ethical norms themselves. What is considered ethical in one culture might be frowned upon in another. Imagine an executive from a Western corporation where whistle-blowing is seen as a duty, working in an East Asian context where it might be viewed as betrayal. The contrast in ethical expectations can be jarring and needs sensitive handling.

The second challenge is in the area of decision-making. Making decisions that are both ethically sound and culturally sensitive can sometimes feel like walking a tightrope. For example, an American tech company outsourcing production to a country with lower labor standards must find a balance between cost-efficiency and fair labor practices. This requires the leader to make decisions that respect both economic realities and human dignity.

The third challenge comes from communication, or rather miscommunication. Messages can be lost, twisted, or distorted when they pass through the cultural filter. If a leader is not careful, what was meant to be a straightforward announcement of a new ethical policy might be perceived as imperialistic or insensitive.

These challenges may seem daunting, but they are not insurmountable. Successful leaders have found strategies to navigate this complex moral landscape with grace and dignity. These strategies are based on understanding, respect, communication, and flexibility.

Understanding is the cornerstone of all these strategies. A leader must make a concerted effort to understand the cultural norms of the countries they operate in. This doesn't mean merely reading about these cultures, but engaging with them, experiencing them. It's about understanding not just what these cultures do, but why they do it.

Respect is the second pillar. Leaders must respect the

cultural norms of the countries they operate in, even when these norms clash with their personal beliefs. Respect here is not about agreement but about acknowledgment. It's about accepting that there are different ways of looking at the world and that these different views have a right to exist.

Communication is the third key strategy. Leaders must be transparent and open in their communication about their ethical standards. They should also be willing to listen to the concerns and views of their local teams. Communication here is a two-way street, a dialogue rather than a monologue.

Flexibility, finally, is the balancing act that leaders must master. They should be firm in upholding their ethical standards, but flexible in how these standards are implemented in different cultural contexts. This is not about ethical relativism, but about finding culturally sensitive ways to uphold ethical standards.

Take the multinational fast-food chain we mentioned earlier. When faced with a backlash against its animal welfare standards, it didn't compromise these standards. Instead, it engaged with local communities to understand their concerns. It respected their cultural practices while explaining its ethical stand. It communicated its commitment to animal welfare and listened to the local perspective. And finally, it was flexible in implementing these standards, adapting them to local realities without compromising on the basic principles.

The ethical leadership of diverse cultures is a complex but rewarding challenge. It requires leaders to be understanding, respectful, communicative, and flexible. It asks them to strike the right notes of fairness, respect, and integrity across a vast moral landscape. But when they do, they can create a beautiful symphony—a symphony that respects diversity while upholding ethics, a symphony that speaks the universal language of human dignity.

Ethical Leadership During Cultural and Global Crises

In times of calm, ethical leadership can be challenging; but it is during times of cultural and global crises that the true test of ethical leadership occurs. Like a beacon in the darkest storm, leaders must shine with integrity, fairness, and accountability, guiding their organizations through the tumult.

Consider the global financial crisis of 2008. It was an economic storm that ravaged businesses worldwide. Amid the chaos, the CEO of a leading investment bank faced a serious dilemma. Their company was teetering on the edge of bankruptcy. There were two options: accept a government bailout, which would save the company but at the cost of taxpayers; or refuse the bailout, likely leading to collapse, but keeping the public's finances intact. It was a rock-and-a-hard-place situation demanding tough, ethical leadership.

In such crises, the pressure to deviate from ethical norms can be overwhelming. Leaders might be tempted to cut corners, break rules, or take reckless risks to save their organizations. The ethical compass that guides them in normal times might start spinning wildly in the storm.
Yet, it is precisely in these times that ethical leadership is most needed. Crises can strip away the superficial and reveal the true character of a leader. Do they hold fast to their ethical principles when the storm hits? Or do they let go, swept away by the winds of panic and short-term thinking?

Successful ethical leaders during crises are those who understand that the storm is not an excuse to abandon ethics but a reason to hold on to them even tighter. These leaders recognize that ethical leadership is not just about leading in good times, but also about leading with goodness in bad times.

Take the CEO of the investment bank. He chose to refuse the bailout, despite the risk. He reasoned that using taxpayers' money to rescue a private company from its own mistakes was ethically wrong. The decision was tough, but it was the right thing to do. His employees, shareholders, and the public admired him for his ethical stand. His decision sent a powerful message that ethics mattered, crisis or no crisis.

Ethical leadership during crises also involves fairness. Leaders must ensure that the burden of the crisis is not shouldered by the weakest. When a multinational corporation faced a severe economic downturn, the CEO could have easily laid off thousands of employees to save costs. Instead, he decided to cut executive bonuses and implement a company-wide pay cut. The decision was shared pain for shared gain. It was a demonstration of fairness in a time of crisis.

Accountability is another crucial aspect of ethical leadership during crises. Leaders must take responsibility for their decisions, especially when things go wrong. When the CEO of a large oil company faced a major environmental disaster caused by an oil spill, he took full responsibility. He didn't hide behind corporate jargon or legal excuses. He accepted the blame, apologized, and committed to cleaning up the mess. It was accountability in action, ethics in action.

Communicating with honesty and transparency is also a key part of ethical leadership during crises. In the face of uncertainty, rumors can run rampant, fears can escalate, and trust can erode. Ethical leaders don't let this happen. They communicate with their teams regularly, updating them on the situation, addressing their concerns, and calming their fears. They tell the truth, even when the truth is hard to hear.

Ethical leadership during cultural and global crises is about holding fast to ethical principles, even when the storm hits. It's about ensuring fairness, taking responsibility, and communicating with honesty and transparency. It's about leading with goodness in bad times. The beacon of ethical leadership must shine brightest in the darkest storm, guiding the organization through the tumult and into calmer waters.

Ethical Leadership in Cross-Cultural Contexts Guide

Leadership across cultures is a delicate dance, a balance of understanding, acceptance, and adaptation. But when you add ethics to the mix, it becomes even more nuanced. Every culture has its own distinct values, norms, and ethical beliefs, and leaders must navigate this complex landscape with care and integrity. To aid leaders in this endeavor, we present the following guide: a collection of tools and tips for ethical leadership in cross-cultural contexts.

1. Study and Understand Cultural Norms: Begin by educating yourself about the ethical norms of the culture you're working within. In some cultures, for instance, gift-giving is seen as a normal part of doing business, while in others, it might be viewed as a bribe.

2. Develop Cultural Sensitivity: Empathy and understanding are at the heart of cross-cultural leadership. Be sensitive to different viewpoints and receptive to various cultural practices. Remember, what might seem 'right' to you could be 'wrong' to someone from a different culture.

3. Encourage Open Dialogue: Promote a culture of open communication where team members feel comfortable discussing ethical issues. This can help prevent misunderstandings and foster a more inclusive and ethical environment.

4. Be Transparent: Transparency is key in ethical leadership. Share your decision-making process with your team, especially when faced with ethical dilemmas. This not only promotes trust but also provides a learning opportunity for your team.

5. Lead by Example: Actions speak louder than words, particularly when it comes to ethics. If you want your team to act ethically, you need to lead the way. Show them what ethical behavior looks like in action.

6. Create an Ethical Code: Draft a clear, comprehensive ethical code for your team. This should be tailored to your specific cross-cultural context and cover all aspects of work, from communication to decision-making.

7. Foster a Culture of Accountability: Make it clear that unethical behavior will not be tolerated, regardless of cultural differences. Encourage team members to hold each other accountable and reward ethical behavior.

8. Provide Ethical Training: Equip your team with the tools and knowledge they need to navigate ethical dilemmas. This could involve workshops, seminars, or even one-on-one coaching sessions.

9. Practice Patience and Flexibility: Navigating ethical issues in a cross-cultural context can be tricky. Be patient with yourself and your team as you all learn and grow together.

10. Reflect and Learn: After navigating an ethical dilemma, take the time to reflect on the situation. What did you learn? How can you apply these lessons to future challenges?

* * *

With these tools and tips in hand, leaders can chart a course through the complex landscape of cross-cultural ethics, guiding their teams with integrity, respect, and understanding. This is the essence of ethical leadership in a cross-cultural context: embracing the challenge, learning from the experience, and growing stronger as a result.

PART VIII: EMBRACING DIVERSITY, EQUITY, INCLUSION, AND BELONGING: THE COMPASSIONATE LEADER'S GUIDE

CHAPTER 24 - UNDERSTANDING DEIB: HARNESSING THE POWER OF DIVERSITY, EQUITY, INCLUSION, AND BELONGING

In an open office space in Silicon Valley, Ana, a young software developer, looked around. Though her company proudly sported a "Diversity First" banner in the lobby, she often felt out of place. The faces surrounding her, while diverse in appearance, often seemed to echo the same ideas, often missing the nuanced perspectives she believed a truly diverse team would bring. There's a profound difference between assembling a varied group and harnessing the full might of their diverse backgrounds, thought processes, and lived experiences.

Consider the Scandinavian furniture giant, inspired by the Nordic ethos of simplicity and functionality. When it sought to enter markets in Asia and Africa, its initial forays were less than successful. Why? Because they hadn't genuinely embraced the DEIB principle at the strategy level. Once they initiated deep listening sessions with local teams, acknowledging not just national but regional nuances and providing an inclusive space for feedback, their designs started resonating more, reflecting a true global brand spirit.

However, the path to effective DEIB is not without its hurdles. Flashback to 2020, amidst a global crisis, a renowned airline faced yet another challenge: accusations of unequal treatment of employees from certain demographics during layoffs. While crisis management often requires swift decision-making, ensuring equity demands introspective strategy, foresight, and often, slowing down to weigh the impacts. Responding to a crisis without undermining DEIB principles is not just about avoiding negative press—it's about staying true to an organization's core values even in the toughest times.

And yet, true DEIB isn't just about overcoming challenges—it's a treasure trove of potential advantages. Imagine a New York-based cosmetic brand, previously confined to specific demographics, redefining beauty standards. By amplifying voices from every corner of the world, they unleashed a wave of creativity and inclusivity, making beauty synonymous with every shade, age, and shape. Their strategic approach to DEIB wasn't just ethically sound; it was a game-changer in the market.

For leaders, DEIB shouldn't be an afterthought or a box to check off for corporate optics. This sechapter aims to elevate your understanding, moving you from passive acknowledgment to active implementation. Consider it less a 'how-to guide' and more a 'how-to-thrive blueprint.' As you delve deeper, remember: Embracing DEIB is more than just being on the 'right side of history.' It's about acknowledging the myriad hues of humanity and leveraging that spectrum to paint a masterpiece of organizational success.

DEIB in Leadership: Beyond the Buzzwords, Real Strength

In the bustling corridors of *Tech2New Inc.*, a global tech company, Alicia, the CEO, often overheard casual conversations about inclusivity initiatives. Yet, she wondered, were these actions merely surface-level? Were they moving beyond the superficiality of buzzwords to genuinely embrace the strength of diversity, equity, inclusion, and belonging (DEIB)?

It's not unfamiliar for organizations to tout DEIB values. Every modern company has a section on its website dedicated to its commitment to diversity. However, a deeper look into the fabric of many corporations reveals a different story. It's reminiscent of the tale of an aspiring athlete: everyone wants the gold medal, but few are willing to put in the training to get there. DEIB isn't just a medal you can display, but a discipline that requires persistent effort.

Why does DEIB matter so profoundly? At the core, it's not just about metrics or numbers; it's about nurturing a culture where every individual feels valued and empowered. In *TruLeaf Organics*, a fictitious startup, their organic growth wasn't attributed just to their innovative products but their innate ability to harness diverse thoughts. Their ideation sessions were a collage of different perspectives, backgrounds, and experiences, creating a rich tapestry of innovation.

However, understanding and implementing DEIB isn't just about hiring diverse talent. It's the nuances that matter. Consider *Zaiphyr Inc.*, another made-up firm, which boasted diverse employee statistics but faced high turnover rates. Their leadership failed to recognize that having a diverse workforce wasn't the endgame but the beginning. The real power lay in nurturing this diversity by creating an environment of true inclusion and belonging.

Now, let's pivot our focus to *SparLink Logistics*, a real-world organization. In their Asian division, a considerable number of women held significant leadership roles. However, during crises, these women leaders often felt their opinions were overlooked. The company, realizing this discrepancy, initiated targeted leadership training, emphasizing the importance of equitable representation. This wasn't just a moral imperative but a business one; diverse leadership teams often make better decisions.

This tug-of-war between wanting to do right and actually doing right isn't unique to the corporate world. It's a manifestation of a deeper human tendency — the gap between intent and action. This gap can be narrowed, not with mere policies, but with a true understanding of the inherent value of DEIB.

The challenge of implementing DEIB genuinely lies in understanding its interconnectedness. It's similar to the intricate parts of a timepiece. While diversity might be the visible face, equity, inclusion, and belonging are the intricate gears and springs behind it, driving its movement.

Another illustrative example comes from *HealthyU Hospitals*. They implemented hiring practices to improve racial diversity. Still, without focusing on inclusion and belonging, many new hires felt isolated, leading to decreased morale and productivity. The hospital, in an attempt to genuinely rectify this, initiated mentorship programs and encouraged diverse teams to work on projects, ensuring everyone felt they genuinely belonged.

So, what separates companies that truly harness the power of DEIB from those that don't? The answer lies in vulnerability. Organizations, like humans, need to acknowledge their weaknesses, be willing to listen, and make substantive changes. *AeroUp Airlines*, a fictional company, found themselves at the center of a social media storm after a diversity-related misstep. Instead of a standard corporate apology, they held a series of open forums, inviting both critics and supporters, striving to understand and rectify their errors.

As leaders, the first step is admitting we don't have all the answers. Just as Alicia from *Tech2New Inc.* pondered, it's essential to continually introspect and challenge our existing practices. It's not enough to be well-intentioned; leaders must be well-informed, receptive, and actionable.

In essence, DEIB isn't just a corporate responsibility; it's a strategic asset. By genuinely embracing it, organizations don't just cultivate a richer, more inclusive work culture. They drive innovation, resilience, and success. It's about moving beyond the buzzwords and recognizing the real, undeniable strength in diversity, equity, inclusion, and belonging. And in the rapidly changing landscape of the corporate world, this isn't just advisable; it's indispensable.

Strategic Integration of DEIB: From Vision to Execution

Understanding the importance of strategy and execution in DEIB is vital, and the lessons learned from *HighTech* illustrates this. This tech giant was well-known for its efforts to attract a diverse workforce, yet it struggled with the integration of these diverse minds. The intention was clear, but the path to genuine inclusion was not mapped out, and the execution fell short. Meanwhile, companies like *Accenture* and *Salesforce* have been celebrated for their strategic and effective DEIB initiatives. They've moved beyond mere slogans and surface-level efforts by implementing concrete strategies that promote diversity at all levels of the organization. They recognize that DEIB isn't just a one-time initiative; it's a continuous process that requires strategic thinking, planning, and action. In stark contrast to these success stories, a fictitious organization, *Spark H2O Plus Ltd.*, merely proclaimed DEIB but had no clear strategy, which led to internal conflicts and public backlash.

For a company like *IBM*, the vision of DEIB is more than just a statement on paper. They've embarked on numerous programs that empower women and minorities in leadership roles, encouraging a culture that celebrates differences and leverages them as a source of strength. This strategic DEIB vision sets the tone for their global practices, engaging their employees in a shared sense of purpose. On the other hand, the fictional *EarthCare Pharma* crafted an impressive DEIB vision but stumbled when translating this into actionable policies. The lack of execution hindered their growth and progress, a stark reminder that vision without execution is merely a dream.

Procter & Gamble provides a real example of how a global company can navigate complex DEIB challenges. By investing in initiatives aimed at promoting diversity and ensuring equity, they've developed a workforce that mirrors the diversity of their global customer base. This has not only fostered a more inclusive workplace but also driven innovation and growth. In comparison, the imaginary *Windli River Technologies* believed in a diverse workforce but struggled to articulate a clear strategy, leading to mixed messages and confusion throughout the organization.

The strategic integration of DEIB takes on real meaning at *Johnson & Johnson*. By focusing on fostering an inclusive culture, they have engaged employees at all levels in shaping the DEIB strategy, leading to increased buy-in and enthusiasm. In contrast, the fictional company *Flashy Spark Innovations* missed the mark by failing to communicate their DEIB initiatives effectively, leading to disconnection and disengagement from employees.

Unilever has excelled in translating DEIB vision into action by aligning it with their core business objectives. Their commitment to diversity isn't just a social responsibility; it's part of their strategy for growth and innovation. By ensuring that DEIB aligns with their business goals, they've created a culture where diversity is not just encouraged but celebrated. Contrast this with the imaginary company *MegaBrain Software*, where failure to align DEIB with business goals led to fragmentation and a lack of impact.

Intel provides another real-world example of a company embracing DEIB with intent and purpose. They have invested in developing programs that actively promote diversity, equity, and inclusion, reflecting not only in their workforce but also in their partnerships and community engagement. This strategic integration has fortified their corporate culture and strengthened their position in the market. In the fictional scenario of *SolarWorld Energy*, failure to conduct an internal audit regarding pay disparity among different ethnic groups led to a missed opportunity to create a more equitable compensation strategy.

The strategic integration of DEIB in companies

like *General Motors* and *Cisco* isn't just about following trends or checking boxes. They have understood the value of diversity as a source of creativity, resilience, and adaptability. By carefully planning, executing, and continually assessing their DEIB strategies, they have set a standard that goes beyond mere compliance, fostering a culture of empathy, understanding, and respect. Compare this to the unfortunate case of the fictional *WaterFlow Manufacturing*, where a lack of continuous assessment and adaptation led to stagnation and inefficacy in their DEIB efforts.

The strategic integration of DEIB is a profound undertaking that demands more than just good intentions. Real organizations like *PepsiCo*, *Target*, and *Nestle* have demonstrated how it's possible to turn a well-intended vision into a living reality that permeates every aspect of the organization. They have leveraged DEIB as a means to drive innovation, build stronger relationships with customers, and create workplaces that reflect the rich tapestry of our global community. On the flip side, the examples of fictional companies serve as cautionary tales that underscore the importance of clarity, alignment, and execution in DEIB initiatives. The challenge is significant, but the rewards are immeasurable, not just in terms of financial growth but in cultivating a more compassionate, creative, and resilient organizational culture. The stories shared here are more than just narratives; they are lessons and inspirations that guide us toward a future where diversity is not just acknowledged but embraced as a source of true strength.

Navigating Diversity Challenges and Ensuring Equity During Crisis

Crisis often exposes the strengths and weaknesses within an organization, and the response of *Microsoft* to the COVID-19 pandemic is an insightful example. Faced with an unprecedented challenge, the company doubled down on their commitment to diversity and inclusion. Remote work arrangements were swiftly enacted, but with an awareness of different needs and preferences, proving that diversity is about more than just demographic representation; it's about understanding and meeting individual needs. In contrast, a fictitious company, *UrbanBuild Inc.*, was slow to adapt and failed to consider the diverse needs of its employees, resulting in disengagement and loss of talent.

In the medical field, the pandemic tested the resilience of systems and people like never before. *Kaiser Permanente* took bold steps to ensure that care was provided equitably across all racial and socioeconomic groups. The measures they took were not simply reactive; they were deeply rooted in an organizational culture that values diversity and equity. The fictional *ClearLight Hospitals*, however, stumbled by making decisions that disproportionately affected marginalized communities, leading to a public relations nightmare.

At the heart of diversity and equity lies a sense of belonging and value. During the financial crisis, *Goldman Sachs* implemented DEIB programs that aimed to support employees from diverse backgrounds. This wasn't about mere optics; it was a recognition that inclusiveness drives better decision-making and innovation. Meanwhile, *GreenZ Auto*, a fictional company, made sweeping cuts without regard to diversity, causing a ripple effect that damaged morale and reputation.

The financial services company *JPMorgan Chase* demonstrates how a crisis can be an opportunity to lean into diversity and equity. Their response to social upheaval highlighted their ongoing commitment to these values, not merely as a response to current events but as a reflection of their core principles. This consistency contrasts sharply with the fictional *NovaWay Logistics*, which scrambled to create DEIB programs in reaction to social pressures, resulting in superficial changes with little lasting impact.

Nike's handling of diversity challenges showcases how

brand and values align. In response to calls for racial justice, they took a clear stand, supporting causes that align with their organizational values. This wasn't about following trends; it was a reaffirmation of who they are as a company. In a fictional scenario, *FreshVoice Technologies* remained silent during crucial times, a decision that conveyed uncertainty and led to mistrust among employees and customers.

During a crisis, the tech company *Adobe* made strides in promoting gender equity, aware that the move to remote work could disproportionately affect women. Their policy adjustments and targeted support not only minimized potential setbacks but advanced their ongoing commitment to gender diversity. Conversely, the fictional *AstridGlow Entertainment* failed to recognize these unique challenges, leading to a widening gender gap within the organization.

The global beverage company *Coca-Cola* demonstrates that inclusivity and equity are not confined to the office. During natural disasters, they utilized their vast distribution network to provide aid, ensuring that assistance reached marginalized communities. Their actions were driven by a deep-seated belief in corporate responsibility and equality. The fictional *SunSoul Mining Co.*, however, prioritized profits over people during a similar crisis, causing lasting damage to their reputation.

In the realm of education, universities like *Harvard* and *MIT* adapted swiftly to the pandemic, providing support and accommodations to international students facing travel restrictions. This was more than logistical support; it was a manifestation of a commitment to a diverse and inclusive educational environment. Compare this to the fictional *LakeView University*, which failed to adequately support their diverse student body, leading to feelings of abandonment and frustration.

During times of crisis, maintaining a commitment to diversity and equity can be challenging but it's not impossible. Organizations like *Target* and *Starbucks* have shown that these principles are not mere conveniences to be set aside when times are tough. They are foundational elements that guide decisions and actions. In comparison, the fictional *RiverTech Solutions* saw DEIB as optional, resulting in a loss of trust and cohesion when challenges arose.

Unilever's response to economic uncertainties reveals how a strong commitment to diversity and equity can not only weather a storm but can also lead to growth and innovation. By maintaining their focus on these values, they were able to adapt, innovate, and emerge stronger. The fictional *AquaPure Water Systems*, on the other hand, abandoned their DEIB initiatives, leading to a loss of creativity and resilience.

When faced with a legal crisis, *Google* navigated through by drawing upon their diverse pool of talent and perspectives. They recognized that diversity is not just a social good; it's a business imperative that fosters agility and innovation. The fictional *MountainPeak Sports* neglected this perspective, relying on a homogenous group that lacked the diverse insights needed to adapt and overcome the crisis.

Diversity and equity are not just concepts to be embraced in good times. Companies like *Walmart* have shown that these values can guide a company through a crisis, ensuring that decisions are not just reactive but reflect a deeper commitment to inclusivity and fairness. The fictional *MeadowFarms Dairy* failed to uphold these values during a crisis, resulting in a lack of cohesion and a fragmented response.

In the retail sector, *Nordstrom* reacted to economic downturns by doubling down on their commitment to diversity and inclusion. They recognized that this was not just a moral imperative but a strategic one, understanding that a diverse workforce fosters resilience and adaptability. Conversely, the fictional *CityBright Lighting* cut DEIB programs during their crisis, a decision that hindered their ability to adapt and innovate.

Navigating a crisis requires more than just a well-intended diversity statement; it requires action and follow-through. Companies like *Salesforce* have demonstrated that diversity and equity can be guiding lights during turbulent times, offering new perspectives and solutions. Meanwhile, the fictional *SkyWave Communications* saw their lack of genuine commitment to DEIB exposed during a crisis, resulting in internal strife and public scrutiny.

Navigating diversity challenges and ensuring equity during a crisis is more than a theoretical exercise; it's a practical imperative. Real organizations have demonstrated that diversity, equity, inclusion, and belonging are not just trendy buzzwords; they are the DNA of resilient and adaptable organizations. They guide decision-making, foster innovation, and build trust. The contrast between these real organizations and the fictional scenarios serves as a clear guide for leaders: authentic commitment to DEIB is not just the right thing to do; it's the strategic thing to do. In times of stability and upheaval, these values remain the compass that directs organizations toward success. The examples in this section illuminate the path forward for those who are committed to making these principles a lived reality.

DEIB Leadership and Comprehensive Strategy Blueprint

In an age marked by rapid change and complexity, the adoption of DEIB principles isn't just a moral imperative; it's a strategic necessity. Leaders must move beyond the superficial and dive deep into the foundational aspects of DEIB to truly make an impact. Whether it's facing a critical moment in business or striving for continued excellence, the following tools and tips will provide a comprehensive strategy blueprint for DEIB leadership. Each step is meticulously crafted to enable leaders to turn these principles into actionable, tangible, and powerful practices within their organization.

1. **Start with Why: Understand the Core Values**
   - **Define the Purpose**: Clearly articulate why DEIB is essential for your organization. Is it about

innovation, market positioning, ethics, or something more profound?

- **Align with Organizational Goals**: Ensure that DEIB is not a separate initiative but woven into the core business strategy.
- **Create Shared Meaning**: Engage all levels of the organization in understanding the deeper value of DEIB.

2. Conduct a DEIB Assessment: Uncover Hidden Biases and Barriers

- **Evaluate Current Practices**: Utilize surveys, focus groups, and expert assessments to analyze the existing DEIB landscape.
- **Identify Gaps**: Find the disconnect between stated values and actual practices.
- **Set Clear Objectives**: Define what success looks like in tangible, measurable terms.

3. Build a DEIB Leadership Team: Foster Collective Responsibility

- **Select Diverse Leaders**: Include members from different backgrounds, departments, and hierarchies.
- **Foster Open Dialogue**: Encourage honest and candid conversations about DEIB.
- **Provide Ongoing Support**: Offer training and resources to enhance the team's capability.

4. Design Inclusive Policies: Create a Culture of Belonging

- **Review Existing Policies**: Assess how current guidelines affect different groups within the organization.
- **Implement Flexible Solutions**: Create policies that recognize individual needs and circumstances.
- **Promote Transparency**: Be clear about the reasoning behind policies and how they align with DEIB values.

5. Empower Through Education: Develop Awareness and Skills

- **Offer Training Programs**: Provide workshops on

unconscious bias, inclusive communication, and cultural competency.

- **Promote Continuous Learning**: Encourage self-paced learning resources and reflective practices.
- **Celebrate Diversity**: Recognize and honor diverse contributions within the organization.

6. **Engage with Communities: Expand DEIB Beyond the Organization**

- **Build Partnerships**: Collaborate with diverse groups and communities to enrich organizational culture.
- **Support Local Initiatives**: Engage in community projects that reflect your DEIB values.
- **Showcase Commitment**: Communicate your DEIB efforts publicly to build trust and encourage accountability.

7. **Monitor and Adjust: Ensure Long-Term Success**

- **Implement Regular Reviews**: Conduct ongoing assessments to measure progress.
- **Celebrate Successes**: Acknowledge and reward achievements, both big and small.
- **Be Adaptable**: Recognize that DEIB is an evolving practice; be open to change and continuous improvement.

* * *

In the challenging landscape of today's business world, DEIB isn't just a fleeting trend; it's a resilient and vital aspect of organizational success. The above tools and tips provide not merely a framework but a comprehensive strategy blueprint for leaders to follow. Embracing these guidelines with authenticity and determination is the key to cultivating a vibrant, inclusive culture that resonates with not only employees but the broader community. Leaders who are committed to charting this course are indeed setting a beacon for innovation, compassion, and excellence.

CHAPTER 25 - CULTIVATING INCLUSION: CREATING SPACE FOR EVERY VOICE

Imagine walking into a room where everyone seems to speak the same language, yet no one understands what you're saying. Inclusion is the art of not just hearing but listening to every voice, allowing them to resonate in harmony. The real strength of any organization lies not in its conformity but its diversity. Take the example of Microsoft under CEO Satya Nadella, where a revitalized focus on empathy and inclusion has driven innovation and growth. The challenge is to harness that power effectively.

Leadership sets the tone for inclusion, and its importance cannot be overstated. A leader's approach to inclusion is akin to a conductor's ability to make an orchestra's diverse instruments play in concert. Look at IBM's former CEO, Ginni Rometty, who emphasized inclusion as a business imperative, leading to a culture where diverse talent thrived. The ability to make every voice feel valued is not just a skill but an art form, creating space for ideas to breathe and grow.

In times of crisis, the temptation to close ranks and revert to familiar faces and voices can be strong. But it is precisely in these challenging times that inclusive leadership becomes a beacon. Consider how companies like Airbnb navigated the global pandemic, fostering a culture of inclusion and communication despite overwhelming challenges. By recognizing that every person brings a unique perspective to problem-solving, leaders can turn crises into catalysts for innovation and resilience.

A leader without the right tools is like a painter without a brush. Best practices in inclusive leadership are not rigid doctrines but flexible guidelines that adapt to the ever-changing landscape of human interaction. Companies like Unilever have embraced inclusive leadership tools that promote a culture where everyone feels a sense of belonging. From empathy maps to structured listening sessions, the tools are available, but the art lies in knowing when and how to use them.

Cultivating inclusion is akin to tending a garden. Each plant, or in this case, each individual, requires specific care, attention, and nourishment to thrive. Ignore one, and the whole garden suffers. Embrace the complexity, and the result is a breathtaking display of colors and shapes, much like the vibrant workforce of companies like Salesforce, celebrated for its commitment to equality and community. The subsequent pages will serve as your guide to nurturing this garden, empowering you to create a space where every voice resonates, every idea matters, and every individual belongs.

The Critical Role of Leadership in Fostering Inclusion

Leadership is not about maintaining a well-oiled machine but about cultivating a garden where diverse ideas flourish. It's about going beyond well-trodden paths, challenging the status quo, and embracing the uncertainty that diversity brings. Unilever, the global consumer goods giant, provides a prime example. By weaving inclusion into its very identity, the company has cultivated a space where different perspectives, cultures, and backgrounds can thrive. This understanding that diversity fuels creativity has allowed for groundbreaking innovation in products, marketing, and more. In Unilever's culture, diversity is not a challenge to overcome, but a strength that underpins every success.

Inclusion is not a feel-good buzzword; it's a strategic

imperative. Research has consistently shown that companies with diverse teams are more innovative and profitable. Yet, there is a difference between diversity and inclusion. Adobe's strong focus on inclusion, ensuring that all voices are heard, has led to groundbreaking products that resonate with a global audience. Their commitment to an inclusive workspace where every employee feels valued and heard has established Adobe as a leader in creativity and innovation. Inclusion at Adobe is not just a matter of corporate social responsibility; it's central to the way they do business.

Culture doesn't just happen; it's crafted, nurtured, and modeled by those at the helm. A leader's attitude towards inclusion sets the tone for the entire organization. Marc Benioff, Salesforce's CEO, exemplifies this in his commitment to equality and community. From equal pay for equal work to investments in local communities, Salesforce has operationalized inclusion. This isn't mere lip service but a commitment that resonates throughout every level of the company. The result is a business culture where people feel valued and connected to the company's broader mission, leading to higher employee satisfaction and, ultimately, success in the marketplace.

Trust is the glue that binds leaders to their teams and employees to one another. In an environment of inclusion, trust flourishes. The story of General Motors under the leadership of Mary Barra is a testament to this. By emphasizing transparency and inclusion, Barra steered a company in crisis towards stability and growth. Her commitment to honest communication, coupled with a relentless focus on fostering an environment where diverse voices were included in decision-making, led to a reinvigorated GM. The key here was trust. By fostering trust, GM was able to tap into the collective intelligence of its workforce, turning challenges into opportunities.

Empathy is not a soft skill but a strategic tool in fostering inclusion. Microsoft's transformation under Satya

Nadella illustrates how empathy can drive innovation. By actively seeking out diverse opinions and fostering an environment where they were not just heard but valued, Microsoft reinvented itself. This culture shift was not just about being nice; it was a conscious strategic move that led to innovative products like Azure and a renewed focus on customer-centricity. The result has been a resurgent Microsoft, with growing market share and industry influence. By harnessing the power of empathy, Microsoft has succeeded in fostering a culture where everyone can contribute to their fullest potential.

Listening goes beyond hearing words; it's about understanding context and recognizing the value in different perspectives. CEOs like Hubert Joly of Best Buy have demonstrated how active listening can revive a brand. Joly's approach involved going to the ground, engaging with employees at every level, truly understanding their experiences, and incorporating their insights into company strategies. This wasn't simply a top-down directive but a company-wide conversation. By recognizing and valuing the wisdom of its employees, Best Buy transformed itself from a struggling retailer into a thriving business. Listening became a tool for organizational reinvention.

Unconscious bias is the hidden barrier to true inclusion. Goldman Sachs's ongoing initiatives to train its employees in recognizing and addressing unconscious bias reveal a proactive approach to fostering an environment where everyone has an equal seat at the table. Their tailored programs aimed at mitigating unconscious bias have not only made them a more inclusive place to work but also a more competitive one. By recognizing that bias affects everyone and working proactively to address it, Goldman Sachs has enhanced its decision-making and creativity.

Inclusion is also about creating spaces where employees feel safe to express their ideas without judgment. Google's Project Aristotle showed the importance of psychological safety in team success. Leadership's role in fostering these safe spaces is paramount. By examining hundreds of teams within Google, Project Aristotle discovered that psychological safety - the belief that one won't be punished for speaking up - was the most important factor in successful teams. This was not about merely being nice but about cultivating an environment where every voice could contribute, leading to richer ideas and better decisions.

Leaders who challenge the norms and dare to think differently set the stage for inclusive thinking. The turnaround story of LEGO under Jørgen Vig Knudstorp is a prime example of how challenging accepted norms and embracing diverse thinking can lead to a resurgence. When Knudstorp took over, LEGO was on the brink of bankruptcy. Through innovative thinking, challenging conventional wisdom, and embracing new ideas, LEGO was not only saved but became the largest toy company in the world. Inclusion here wasn't just about having diverse team members; it was about embracing a culture of intellectual diversity where challenging the norm was encouraged and rewarded.

During crises, inclusive leadership shines brightest. Airbnb's response to the pandemic, ensuring clear communication and inclusion across all levels, offers a roadmap for navigating turbulent times with empathy and clarity. When the travel industry was devastated by COVID-19, Airbnb's leadership was quick to engage with all stakeholders, from hosts to employees, ensuring that decisions were made inclusively. They also demonstrated a profound understanding of the human impact of their decisions. By placing inclusion and empathy at the heart of their crisis response, Airbnb weathered the storm with its reputation enhanced.

Inclusion is not a one-time initiative but an ongoing commitment. IBM's long-standing dedication to inclusion, adapting and evolving its approach, illustrates this commitment. For decades, IBM has been at the forefront of diversity and inclusion, recognizing early on that this was a business imperative. From hiring the first female vice president in the 1940s to its contemporary focus on global inclusion, IBM's journey illustrates how inclusion must adapt and evolve to remain relevant. Inclusion at IBM is not a static goal but an ever-evolving process, ensuring that it continues to be a leader in both technology and the human aspect of business.

Mentoring plays a vital role in fostering inclusion. EY's mentorship programs, tailored to develop diverse talents, have proven that mentorship is a powerful tool in building inclusive leaders for tomorrow. These programs are not merely about professional development but about building a culture where diverse talents are nurtured and celebrated. By investing in mentorship, EY has not only enhanced its talent pool but also fostered a culture where people feel connected and valued. This isn't just good for the employees; it's good for business.

Tokenism can be the pitfall of mismanaged diversity efforts. The fictitious company TechPinnacle 360 fell into this trap, where diversity was about numbers, not inclusion, leading to a fractured organization. On the surface, they had all the right metrics, but scratch a little deeper, and it became clear that this was diversity without substance. Inclusion was not part of the culture, leading to resentment and dysfunction. The lesson here is that inclusion is not about ticking boxes but about genuinely engaging with and valuing diverse perspectives.

The best leaders are continuous learners. Netflix's culture of continuous feedback and learning is an example of how an inclusive environment fosters growth for both leaders and employees. Netflix recognizes that learning is not a one-off event but a continuous process. By fostering a culture where feedback is embraced and learning is continuous, Netflix has created an environment where employees at all levels can grow and thrive. This isn't just about individual growth; it's about creating an organization that is continually evolving, adapting, and innovating.

Inclusion goes beyond borders. HSBC's global programs focusing on inclusion reflect a comprehensive understanding of diversity that transcends cultural boundaries, showcasing a truly global leadership mindset. Recognizing that diversity is not just about gender or ethnicity but encompasses a wide array of perspectives, including geographical and cultural diversity, HSBC has put in place global programs that ensure that diversity and inclusion are part of the company's DNA. This global approach has made HSBC one of the world's leading banks, able to navigate the complexities of the global marketplace with agility and insight.

Fostering inclusion is not merely a moral imperative but a strategic one. Leaders are not just figureheads but the gardeners of this rich, diverse landscape, where the right conditions allow each individual to bloom. It is a complex, ongoing process that requires empathy, trust, commitment, and the courage to challenge the norms.

The stories of these real-world organizations are proof that the critical role of leadership in fostering inclusion is not just a theoretical concept; it is the key to unlocking the untapped potential that lies in diversity. Whether it's through empathetic listening, challenging unconscious biases, or cultivating a culture of continuous learning, the leaders who succeed in this task are the ones who recognize that inclusion is not a side project but central to everything they do. It is a path that requires courage, commitment, and a willingness to embrace the rich tapestry of human experience. It is, ultimately, the path to a more prosperous and equitable future.

Leading Inclusively and Ensuring Equity During Global Crises

Global crises are the black swan events that test an organization's resilience. COVID-19 provided a stage where leadership faced its greatest challenge, and inclusivity its finest hour. Companies like Ford rapidly shifted production to manufacture ventilators, engaging with employees, unions, and communities in their response. The balance between commerce and compassion, strategy and empathy, revealed a path beyond profit to shared purpose.

The response to the Christchurch earthquake in New Zealand illustrates how authentic leadership can turn a crisis into growth. Prime Minister Jacinda Ardern led with empathy, inclusion, and unity, standing shoulder-to-shoulder with her people, inspiring and transforming. During the 2008 financial meltdown, banks like JPMorgan Chase faced public outrage and skepticism. The crisis handling emphasized trust-building through transparent communication and inclusive decision-making, highlighting that trust is a nurtured relationship.

The Ebola crisis showcased Médecins Sans Frontières (Doctors Without Borders) displaying empathy on a global scale. Their ground-level understanding of local cultures underscored that empathy is an actionable principle in building inclusive solutions. The 2020 Australian bushfires demanded a response that was both decisive and adaptive. The Australian government's inclusive action recognized that crises require complex and tailored responses, and that one size does not fit all.

Recent cyber-attacks revealed how technological resilience needs an inclusive mindset. Companies like Microsoft engaged with diverse stakeholders in a collective response, linking technology as a bridge in a connected world. Google's Project Oxygen emphasized the importance of psychological safety during crisis times. Leaders must create environments for open communication, which can act as a stabilizing force, turning turmoil into growth and transformation.

The global downturn brought many airlines to their knees. Southwest, however, leaned on its culture of inclusivity, involving employees in decision-making, turning crisis into a defining moment, and strengthening bonds. The gender gap often widens during crises, but Iceland's handling of the

2008 financial collapse promotes gender equality as a strategic advantage. Women's inclusion in decision-making helped the country emerge stronger and more innovative.

The Flint water crisis was a failure of leadership, empathy, and inclusion. It reminded us that environmental crises need compassionate and inclusive responses, not just technological solutions. Germany's decision to accept over a million refugees wasn't just about human rights but an inclusive vision that saw refugees as an opportunity. Inclusion became a path to mutual growth, not a zero-sum game.

The response to Hurricane Katrina emphasized local insights in crisis management. Collaboration and empathy between local government and community leaders proved effective and showcased the need for distributed leadership. IBM's response to digital transformation shows how inclusivity can be a strategic lever. Engaging diverse voices turned a potential crisis into an innovation opportunity, recognizing the essential role of diversity.

The distribution of COVID-19 vaccines became an opportunity to practice equity on a global scale. Organizations like the World Health Organization showed that equity is a practical necessity, not just a moral obligation. The rise of remote work during the pandemic has created challenges and opportunities for inclusive leadership. Companies like X.com showed that the new world of work requires flexibility and a culture that honors diversity.

Supporting small businesses during the pandemic by companies like Amazon reveals a vision of collaboration over competition. An ecosystem where diverse players thrive together places compassion and inclusion at the center of success. The narrative that emerges from weaving these strands together illustrates that global crises are opportunities to redefine leadership, practice empathy, foster inclusion, and ensure equity. In turbulent times, the way forward recognizes our shared humanity and values inclusivity as a lifeline. It calls for leadership from the heart, with wisdom and courage.

Inclusive Leadership Best Practices

Inclusive leadership is no longer a sideline conversation in the grand scheme of organizational performance; it's the very heartbeat that fuels innovation, resilience, and growth. It's not an abstraction or a feel-good initiative; it's a practical and strategic approach that is central to the evolving tapestry of global business. From multinational giants like Unilever, focusing on sustainable and inclusive growth, to startups like Buffer, embracing transparency and diversity, inclusive leadership is shaping the narrative of success in the 21st century. Let's dissect this concept, understanding its mechanics, its applications, and the best practices that can make it a part of your organizational DNA.

1. **Foster Open Communication:** Encourage every team member to express their ideas and opinions without fear of judgment. Google's psychological safety research emphasizes how teams where members feel safe to take risks outperform others.

2. **Embrace Diversity:** From gender and ethnicity to thinking styles and backgrounds, diverse teams drive innovation. Johnson & Johnson's global diversity strategy illustrates how a culture that values diverse perspectives can lead to breakthrough ideas.

3. **Cultivate Empathy:** Practicing empathy involves not just understanding others' feelings but validating them. Satya Nadella's transformation of Microsoft culture from competition to collaboration underlines the power of empathy.

4. **Encourage Participation in Decision Making:** Leaders at Warby Parker actively involve employees in decision-making, making them feel more connected and committed to the company's vision.

5. **Develop Cultural Competence:** Being aware of different cultures and how they influence behavior and communication

is essential. Airbnb's host community is a vivid example of how cultural awareness can foster a sense of belonging and trust.

6. Implement Fair Practices: Equity ensures that everyone has access to the same opportunities. Salesforces's commitment to equal pay, regardless of gender, is a compelling model of fairness in practice.

7. Build Inclusive Meetings: Ensuring that everyone has a voice in meetings is a tangible way to foster inclusion. Amazon's practice of silent reading at the beginning of meetings ensures that all viewpoints are considered.

8. Provide Opportunities for Growth: Offering tailored growth opportunities for all team members helps in building a more inclusive culture. IBM's personalized learning paths for employees underline this approach.

9. Recognize and Reward Inclusively: Rewarding not just results but also how they are achieved can reinforce inclusive behaviors. Deloitte's recognition program values collaboration and inclusiveness as much as individual achievement.

10. Evaluate Inclusion Efforts: Regularly assessing the effectiveness of inclusion efforts helps in continuous improvement. General Motors' regular diversity scorecards act as a vital tool in keeping the focus on inclusion.

❋ ❋ ❋

In the panorama of leadership, inclusiveness stands tall and proud, not as a fleeting trend but as a foundational ethos. These tools and tips are not a panacea but signposts along a path that leads to a more humane, innovative, and resilient organizational culture. It's about shifting from a mindset of command and control to one of connection and collaboration. It's not just a leadership challenge but an opportunity to redefine what leadership means in a world that is rich with diversity, alive with possibilities, and yearning for a sense of belonging and authenticity.

CHAPTER 26 - BELONGING: THE HEART OF DEIB IN LEADERSHIP

Belonging is an instinctive need, not a passive state. When we consider leadership, we often look at qualities like vision, courage, and determination. But we must not forget the essence of leadership that can bind these qualities together - the sense of belonging. In a diverse world, where global corporations operate across cultures and time zones, understanding the role of belonging in leadership becomes more than a nice-to-have aspect; it becomes a pivotal linchpin. Just like a conductor synchronizing an orchestra, the right leadership creates harmony among different notes, allowing each to resonate clearly.

What does it take to cultivate a sense of belonging within a team or organization? The answer might seem simple, but its application is an intricate art. Think of the transformation at Microsoft under Satya Nadella's guidance, where a culture shift led to a more inclusive and understanding environment. The strategies and methodologies can vary from open-door policies to structured mentorship programs. However, at the core, it is about creating a space where everyone feels seen, heard, and most importantly, valued.

Crisis moments, whether a sudden market shift or a global pandemic, are the crucible that tests the true nature of belonging within an organization. In times of uncertainty, leaders are not only strategizing on business continuity but also ensuring the emotional continuity of their teams. During the financial crisis of 2008, Howard Schultz at Starbucks refused to cut employee benefits, despite economic pressure. It was not a mere business decision; it was an act that screamed 'You belong here' to every partner within the company.

And how does one translate these ideals into everyday practices? Tools & Tips: Leadership Belonging Best Practices Guide offers not just a series of steps but a philosophy. The key lies in authenticity and connection. Leaders who embody these principles don't simply implement policies; they nurture relationships. They create opportunities for dialogues, celebrate unique perspectives, and forge connections that transcend mere work. They build an ecosystem where individuality thrives within a collective mission.

This final chapter opens the door to a deeper exploration of belonging, not as a buzzword but as the soul of leadership in the modern landscape. It provides a strategic roadmap for leaders seeking not just to manage but to inspire, not just to direct but to connect. In the end, belonging isn't a box to be checked but a melody to be composed, a melody that resonates with each member of the organization, binding them into a harmonious and resonant whole. In the words of Maya Angelou, "People will forget what you said, people will forget what you did, but people will never forget how you made them feel." Welcome to the heart of DEIB in Leadership, where belonging is the music we all long to hear.

Understanding the Role of Belonging in Leadership

Belonging in leadership is like gravity in physics - invisible, yet powerful enough to hold everything in place. It's not about creating a club where everyone fits in; it's about creating an environment where differences are embraced. Consider Adobe, a company that has actively created an environment where belonging is fostered through various inclusion programs and targeted initiatives. Here, leadership is about unifying different voices.

You can think of belonging as a bridge that connects the shores of diversity and inclusion. Diversity is about having different voices at the table; inclusion is about letting those voices speak; but belonging is about making sure those voices feel genuinely valued. When Satya Nadella took over as the CEO of Microsoft, he didn't just aim to make the workplace diverse. He aimed to create a sense of belonging, where each employee, regardless of their background, felt like a part of the Microsoft family.

At first glance, creating belonging might seem like a soft and intangible goal. However, organizations such as Netflix have shown that fostering belonging can translate into concrete business outcomes. Their culture of openness and transparent communication has resulted in an environment where employees not only feel like they belong but are also more engaged, creative, and productive.

The way a leader approaches belonging often reflects their leadership style. Elon Musk's approach at Tesla, with his direct and open interaction with employees, builds a sense of community that many describe as feeling like a part of something groundbreaking. On the other hand, Mary Barra at General Motors has fostered belonging through empathy and genuine concern for employee well-being.

One might ask, is belonging merely a product of corporate culture, or is it something more profound? Looking at organizations like Airbnb, where the culture of belonging extends beyond employees to hosts and travelers, one realizes that belonging isn't confined to office walls. It's a philosophy that, when authentically embedded, can redefine the entire ecosystem of a business.

Organizations such as Google, with their extensive resources, might be at an advantage in fostering belonging. But belonging is not about the size of the company; it's about the size of the heart. Small businesses, with their close-knit teams, can sometimes create a more profound sense of belonging. A local bookstore that operates on mutual respect and shared values can teach larger corporations a lesson or two about true belonging.

The path to belonging isn't about artificial bonding exercises. Take the case of SAS Institute, a software company known for its fantastic work culture. The leadership here understands that belonging comes from a genuine appreciation of diversity, not just team lunches. It's about the small everyday actions that show employees they are seen and valued.

In a world that's more connected yet more isolated than ever, belonging is not just a human resource agenda; it's a leadership imperative. When Adobe's leadership chose to focus on inclusion and diversity, it wasn't just about social responsibility. It was a strategic decision understanding that innovation comes from diverse minds feeling they belong.

Belonging isn't a destination; it's a continuous process. A misstep in leadership can turn a sense of belonging into exclusion. The case of Uber, where allegations of harassment shook the company's culture, shows how delicate and ongoing the process of maintaining belonging is.

Belonging doesn't mean uniformity. IBM's embracement of remote working long before it became a norm was about respecting individual preferences and creating a sense of belonging, not by making everyone the same but by appreciating what makes them different.

Leaders who have successfully fostered a sense of belonging, like Ginni Rometty at IBM, have understood that belonging doesn't start from the boardroom; it starts from the heart. They have shown empathy, openness, and a genuine willingness to connect.

What do the employees of Patagonia, a company that supports environmental causes, have in common? A sense of purpose and belonging. Belonging isn't always about what you do within the organization; it's about what the organization stands for. When values align, belonging thrives.

The architecture of belonging is as intricate as it is beautiful. Salesforce's decision to evaluate and correct gender pay gaps wasn't just about equity; it was about sending a clear message: "You belong, and your contribution matters." This is belonging in action, not words.

How does a global organization foster belonging across cultures? Companies like Unilever with a presence in multiple countries have shown that the principles of belonging are universal. Respect, empathy, and understanding transcend cultural boundaries.

Belonging is not just a word; it's a commitment. It's about creating a space where every voice matters, every perspective is valued, and everyone feels they are a part of something greater than themselves. The leadership that fosters belonging doesn't just lead an organization; they cultivate a community. They chart a course not towards profit alone but towards a shared vision where every team member is a co-traveler. It's not about walking a well-trodden path; it's about carving a new path, where the footsteps of every individual leave a mark. In the landscape of modern leadership, belonging isn't an accessory; it's the heartbeat.

Practical Strategies for Cultivating Belonging in Teams

Cultivating belonging in teams begins with an understanding that each individual is a unique mosaic of experiences, perspectives, and talents. Consider the case of Salesforce, where CEO Marc Benioff conducted one-on-one meetings with employees to truly understand their unique needs and perspectives. These insights translated into a tailored approach that went beyond general practices.

Creating belonging doesn't necessitate grand gestures. It's often the subtle, daily interactions that carry the most weight. At the coffee giant Starbucks, fostering a sense of belonging started with the simple act of using customers' names on cups. This seemingly small act communicated a powerful message of recognition and inclusion that resonated with both employees and customers.

In an era where remote work has become the norm, cultivating belonging can be challenging. GitLab, an all-remote company, demonstrates how to bridge the physical gap with intentional virtual interactions. Scheduled coffee breaks, mutual mentorship programs, and transparent communication channels have been key in building a connected team.

Transparency isn't just a buzzword; it's a tool for building trust and, consequently, belonging. Buffer's open salary policy wasn't merely a progressive decision; it was a strategic one. By removing the curtains from an often-taboo subject, they created an environment where equity was not just a promise but a visible commitment.

How does one instill a sense of belonging across different departments within an organization? At 3M, cross-functional teams work together on innovation projects, building a sense of unity and shared purpose. This collaborative approach has fostered belonging and sparked creativity, proving that innovation is often a collective endeavor.

Belonging isn't a one-size-fits-all concept. The renowned Mayo Clinic's personalized approach to patient care is an illustration of how recognizing individuality fosters belonging. By extending this philosophy to their staff, they've cultivated an environment where everyone, regardless of their role, feels an essential part of the healing process.

What about teams that face intense pressure and competition? In the high-stakes world of Formula 1 racing, the Mercedes-AMG Petronas team has shown that even in an environment defined by speed, the slow cultivation of belonging can yield championship results. Regular debriefs, acknowledgment of effort, and shared celebrations have been pivotal.

Leaders often worry about cultivating belonging

without compromising accountability. Netflix's culture memo presents a novel approach. By promoting a culture of "freedom and responsibility," they've shown that belonging and performance can indeed coexist. Empowering team members fosters not just a sense of belonging but also a drive to excel.

Is belonging an executive responsibility alone? The answer is a resounding no. Companies like Zappos have empowered every team member to be a cultivator of belonging. From the customer support team to the developers, a shared responsibility has created a sense of ownership and belonging throughout the organization.

How do you maintain belonging during times of change? IBM's transition into a cloud-focused company was not just a strategic move but a cultural one. Regular town halls, open channels for feedback, and leadership's willingness to listen ensured that employees felt part of the change, not victims of it.

The delicate balance between individuality and conformity is often overlooked in fostering belonging. Apple's culture of embracing diverse ideas while maintaining a unified vision provides a blueprint. By valuing unique insights without losing sight of common goals, they've created a breeding ground for both innovation and belonging.

Practices fostering belonging are not stagnant; they evolve with time and context. Google's continuous efforts to reassess and remodel their diversity and inclusion practices show that fostering belonging is an ongoing commitment. By being adaptive and responsive, they've kept the sense of belonging vibrant and relevant.

But what if things go wrong? In the aftermath of a failed project or a setback, how do you maintain belonging? NASA's approach after the Challenger disaster teaches a valuable lesson. Through collective grief, transparent investigation, and shared learning, they turned a tragedy into an opportunity for growth and reaffirmation of belonging.

Sometimes, belonging requires breaking away from

traditional hierarchies. The Brazilian company Semco's radical approach to management, where employees set their salaries and choose their leaders, might seem extreme. Yet, it's an illustrative example of how trusting people can create a profound sense of belonging and alignment.

In the global theater, cultivating belonging transcends borders. Accenture's seamless integration of teams across different continents has showcased how shared values, clear communication, and cultural respect can unify diverse teams. Their success in global projects underscores the universality of the human need to belong.

Lastly, it's essential to recognize that belonging is not an end but a means. Companies like Southwest Airlines have harnessed the power of belonging to create not just a satisfied workforce but satisfied customers. The correlation between internal belonging and external success is more than a hypothesis; it's a proven strategy.

In the grand tapestry of leadership, the thread of belonging might seem subtle but is foundational. From small gestures to bold policies, from daily interactions to strategic decisions, belonging permeates every aspect of team dynamics. Leaders who master the art of cultivating belonging don't just create teams; they create communities. It's not about gathering followers; it's about nurturing relationships. In the orchestration of modern business, belonging is not a silent note; it's the melody that resonates with every heart, leading to a harmonious and impactful performance.

Upholding Belonging During Times of Crisis

When crisis strikes, the intricate fabric of an organization is stretched and tested. The cracks that may have been invisible in times of calm become glaring fissures in the face of uncertainty. Consider the financial crisis of 2008, where Wall Street banks faced an existential threat. What set some apart was not just their financial acumen but their ability to create a sense of belonging among their employees, even as the foundations trembled.

Belonging during a crisis is not a luxury; it's a lifeline. New Orleans in the aftermath of Hurricane Katrina serves as a poignant illustration. The communities that thrived were those where neighbors banded together, creating a cocoon of support and belonging that weathered the storm. It wasn't the infrastructure but the human connections that were the true bulwarks.

Leadership during a crisis requires not just steering the ship but ensuring that everyone is on board. Johnson & Johnson's handling of the Tylenol poisonings in 1982 exemplifies this approach. By prioritizing the welfare of the consumers and communicating openly with the employees, they transformed a potential catastrophe into a demonstration of integrity and shared values.

Technology often plays a vital role in maintaining belonging during crises. The COVID-19 pandemic forced organizations worldwide to adapt to remote work. Companies like Slack and Zoom, which integrated virtual connection tools, not only survived but thrived. By understanding the essence of human connection, they turned virtual platforms into spaces of genuine belonging.

What about the frontline workers, the ones facing the heat of the crisis? During the SARS outbreak in 2003, hospitals that nurtured a sense of belonging among their medical staff witnessed not just less burnout but also more effective patient care. Encouraging collaboration and empathy was not a soft approach but a strategic one.

Sometimes, maintaining belonging during a crisis means admitting vulnerability. When Satya Nadella took over Microsoft, he implemented a culture of empathy and openness. During the inevitable challenges, this vulnerability became a strength, creating a resilient bond between leaders and employees that could withstand shocks.

Crisis can lead to stigmatization, further fracturing the

sense of belonging. The HIV/AIDS epidemic brought this issue to the forefront. Organizations that fostered an environment of understanding, education, and compassion ensured that those affected didn't feel marginalized but rather supported and included.

Ethical dilemmas often intensify during times of crisis. Volkswagen's emission scandal is a stark reminder that cutting corners can not only shatter a brand's image but also erode the internal sense of belonging. Upholding ethics isn't just right; it's a vital ingredient in keeping the sense of unity intact even when the pressure mounts.

Crisis leadership is not about having all the answers; it's about asking the right questions. Airbnb's response to the travel restrictions during the pandemic highlights this. By involving employees in the decision-making process and prioritizing their needs, they fostered a collective resilience that went beyond mere survival.

Cultural sensitivity plays a crucial role in upholding belonging during international crises. Toyota's response to the 2011 Tsunami in Japan was a lesson in cultural resonance. Their approach of continuous improvement and community-centric values was not just a business decision but a reflection of a deep understanding of the Japanese sense of belonging.

How does an organization uphold belonging when the very product they offer is in crisis? The Boeing 737 Max crashes put Boeing in such a predicament. By embracing transparency, continuous communication with employees, and prioritizing safety over profits, they began to rebuild the sense of trust and belonging that was shaken.

The role of external stakeholders in upholding belonging is often underestimated. Chipotle's handling of the food safety crisis shows how an organization can engage customers in the rebuilding process. By owning their mistakes and involving the customers in their recovery journey, they reestablished a sense of shared purpose and belonging.

Crisis doesn't affect everyone equally. The uneven

impact of the economic downturns often hits the marginalized communities the hardest. Companies that recognize and address these disparities, like Unilever with their inclusive growth initiatives, ensure that the sense of belonging doesn't become another casualty of the crisis.

In the volatile world of politics, creating a sense of belonging is both a challenge and a necessity. Nelson Mandela's leadership during South Africa's transition is a testament to the power of inclusion and reconciliation. By reaching across the divides, he transformed a nation in crisis into a symbol of unity.

The legacy of a leader is often defined by their handling of crises. Howard Schultz's return to Starbucks during the 2008 recession was not just about financial restructuring but rekindling the sense of belonging and purpose that had defined the brand. His open forums with employees across the country weren't mere meetings; they were a recommitment to shared values.

In the labyrinth of crisis management, the path of belonging may seem convoluted and challenging. Yet, it's not a detour but a direct route to resilience and recovery. Leaders who understand the profound power of belonging don't just navigate crises; they transform them into opportunities for growth, cohesion, and renewal. The turbulence may be inevitable, but the sense of belonging is the compass that guides through the storm towards a horizon filled with hope and potential.

Leadership Belonging Best Practices Guide

In the age where digitization and globalization continue to transform the ways we work and relate, belonging has never been more paramount. Belonging isn't merely a feeling but a necessity in the current organizational landscape. When employees feel they belong, productivity soars, innovation blooms, and loyalty solidifies. For the organizations that face the inevitable and unpredictable changes of the modern world, the concept of belonging serves as a keystone. How did companies like Pixar foster such a profound sense of belonging that it became an incubator for creativity? How did businesses like Southwest Airlines create a culture that made employees feel they were part of a larger family? The answers lie in understanding and applying specific strategies that nurture and enhance the sense of belonging within teams and across organizations.

1. Foster Open and Honest Communication: Start from the top. Leaders who encourage open dialogue and are willing to listen foster a culture where everyone feels their voice matters. Consider how Ford's CEO Alan Mulally's weekly management meetings transformed the company by creating a transparent environment where problems could be addressed without fear.

2. Implement Inclusive Decision-making: Engaging employees in decision-making processes builds a sense of ownership and trust. Adobe's regular "Hackathons" are a perfect example of how collaboration and inclusive decision-making can spark innovation and a strong sense of community.

3. Encourage Cross-functional Collaborations: Encourage interactions across different departments and roles. Steve Jobs' design of Pixar's headquarters with centralized common areas facilitated accidental collaborations that fostered an inclusive environment.

4. Recognize and Celebrate Diversity: Embrace diversity in all its forms, from cultural backgrounds to unique skill sets. Google's employee resource groups (ERGs) are brilliant in allowing employees to connect and share their diverse experiences, thus creating a culture of understanding and respect.

5. Prioritize Mental Health and Well-being: A supportive environment that acknowledges mental well-being creates a compassionate workplace. Johnson & Johnson's mental health initiatives have been groundbreaking in creating a supportive network that nurtures belonging.

6. Align Values and Actions: Integrity is central to belonging. When Howard Schultz returned to Starbucks, he closed all stores for training to realign the company's values and practices, building a renewed sense of belonging.

7. Mentorship Programs: Create mentorship programs that align employees across different levels. General Electric's mentorship initiatives have been instrumental in not only developing skills but fostering connections and a sense of belonging.

8. Community Involvement and Social Responsibility: Engagement in social causes can strengthen team bonds. Salesforce's 1-1-1 model of philanthropy is an example of how community involvement fosters a shared sense of purpose.

9. Cultivate a Sense of Purpose: Make sure every team member understands the bigger picture. Simon Sinek's "Start with Why" philosophy resonates here, making sure that everyone in the organization understands the 'Why' behind what they are doing.

10. Provide Continuous Learning Opportunities: Growth is an essential aspect of belonging. AT&T's continuous learning programs ensure that employees grow with the company, nurturing a sense of shared evolution and loyalty.

11. Handle Conflicts with Empathy and Understanding: Handling conflicts with empathy can foster deeper connections. Netflix's culture of "Radical Candor" promotes honest feedback and empathy, ensuring that conflicts become opportunities for growth rather than division.

12. Invest in Team-building Activities: Regular team-building activities strengthen bonds. Zappos's company culture, filled with team activities and celebrations, has been pivotal in creating an incredibly strong sense of community and belonging.

❖ ❖ ❖

In an era where the only constant is change, the toolset for fostering belonging is both rich and nuanced. Implementing these strategies is not about creating an artificial sense of camaraderie but cultivating an authentic connection that resonates with the very core of human nature. By embracing these principles, leaders chart a course toward a more compassionate, innovative, and resilient organizational culture. The heart of effective leadership, it turns out, beats in rhythm with the profound need for belonging. It is a compass that guides, a glue that binds, and a beacon that illuminates the path towards greatness.

EPILOGUE

We've crossed the threshold, metaphorically traversed the expanse of transformation and adaptability, scrutinizing each grain of insight along the way. This discourse hasn't been about directing your steps, but providing you with the compass and navigational tools to effectively charter your organization's course through the undulating waves of unpredictable change. It's a vast ocean out there, full of the promise of discovery and the threat of storms. But now, you're not merely a ship at the mercy of the waves; you're the seasoned captain who understands the sea's whims and knows how to chart a course through it.

Reflecting on the Path: Transformation and Adaptability

This book is an echo of a profound metamorphosis, a transformation that every leader undergoes as they dive deeper into their own potential. Each chapter has unfolded another aspect of that transformation, a treasure trove of wisdom, each nugget reflecting the multidimensional nature of leadership. Be it harnessing emotional intelligence, kindling a culture of innovation, mastering change management, or ensuring equity and inclusivity, each component comes together to paint a rich and textured landscape of resilient and adaptable leadership.

Adaptability, the art of bending but not breaking, of morphing in response to an evolving ecosystem, has emerged as the quintessential attribute of effective leadership. It's not a revelation to state that unpredictable change is the only constant, but what we've striven to do is teach you not only to survive the storm but to harness its energy, redirecting it into a force for growth, progress, and innovation.

The Significance of the Companion Workbook

While we've reached the last chapter of this book, your metamorphosis has only just begun. Your companion in this ongoing transformation, the workbook, serves as a treasure chest, brimming with tools and tips waiting to be deployed. We strongly urge you to unlock this treasure and start utilizing these actionable strategies. Let these insights seep into your everyday decision-making, not just as theoretical concepts but as practical tools you can employ right away. Like the trusted map of a seasoned explorer, this workbook will be your guide in the constantly shifting landscape of leadership, making the application of these principles not just a possibility, but a rewarding reality.

Encouragement for Readers to Apply Learned Principles

As you move beyond the pages of this book and return to the helm of your organization, bear in mind that the principles unpacked here are not mere contemplative theories; they are the tools to be used, each one with the potential to cut through the noise and carve a clear path towards a successful and inclusive future. Employ these principles judiciously, weave them into your leadership ethos, and let the transformation reveal itself.

Remember, inclusion isn't just a buzzword; it's a catalyst that ignites the dormant potential within your team. Resilience goes beyond weathering the storm; it's about building an organization that thrives amidst chaos. And innovation? It's not a luxury; it's the lifeblood that keeps your organization relevant and responsive.

Final Thoughts: The Future of Leadership Amidst

Unpredictable Change

As we reach the end of our discourse, we find ourselves on the cusp of a new era in leadership. An era characterized not by rigidity and control, but by fluidity and empowerment. An era where the leader's role is not to foretell the future but to navigate through it, not to dictate but to inspire. Amidst the unpredictability and ceaseless change, the future of leadership belongs to those who comprehend that their strength lies not in absolute certainty but in their capacity to adapt, learn, and evolve.

In this epoch of incessant change, the most formidable weapon in a leader's arsenal is a metamorphic mindset, an understanding that the crux of effective leadership isn't about clinging onto the past but continuously transforming to meet the needs of the future. As we part ways on this page, let's harness the wisdom gathered from our discourse and step boldly into an unpredictable future, armed with transformation and adaptability as our trusted allies.

INDEX

ABOUT THE AUTHOR

Suzzette Harriott, Ph.d.

Dr. Suzzette Harriott is an illuminating force in education, leadership, and personal development. With an academic background in Conflict Analysis and Resolution, she has amassed a rich, interdisciplinary skill set that also includes Human Resource Management and Psychology. An International Leadership & Life Strategist, Suzzette shapes the careers of seasoned professionals and educators, equipping them with tools to navigate modern challenges.

As an educator, Suzzette is devoted to fostering an inclusive and enriching educational environment for all stakeholders. In her role as an Executive Coach & Strategist, she focuses on essential human and organizational dynamics like Emotional Intelligence, Transformational Leadership, and Diversity, Equity, Inclusion, and Belonging (DEIB).

A published author and researcher, Suzzette's fiction teaches young readers about DEIB principles. Her nonfiction works delve into pivotal topics such as Transformational Leadership and Emotional Intelligence. Currently, her research centers on the intriguing duality of Self-Compassion and Impostor Syndrome, offering groundbreaking pathways for growth.

Suzzette's commitment to empathic leadership and transformative education resonates far and wide. Her work stands as a testament to the profound impact of human connection and the transformative power of education and self-awareness.

ABOUT THE AUTHOR

Anthony Solomon, Bs, Lc

 Anthony Solomon is a renowned public speaker, executive coach, and personal coach with a career that has spanned multiple decades and diverse platforms. His public speaking journey began during his formative years in South Florida and Jamaica, where he took to stages and arenas to inspire student athletes. Focused on key themes like resilience, family, and education, Solomon quickly established these as the foundational pillars shaping both his personal and professional odyssey.

His adaptability was put to the test during the global pandemic, a challenging period he navigated with aplomb. Transitioning his speaking engagements to online platforms, Solomon didn't just sustain his audience's interest; he expanded it. His talks served as emotional anchors for people across the globe, offering them both resilience and hope during an unprecedented time.

In recent years, Solomon has broadened his geographical footprint, accepting invitations to speak at various events in Michigan and Arizona. His distinct ability to connect with diverse audiences stems from a unique blend of experiences that range from athletics and coaching to entrepreneurship and artistic pursuits.

Adding to his impressive list of roles, Solomon has also cultivated a career as an executive and personal coach. In these capacities, he employs a holistic approach, focusing on both the personal and professional growth of his clients. Drawing upon the same themes that fuel his public speaking —resilience, integrity, and empowerment—Solomon provides individualized strategies to help clients achieve their goals.

Whether he's on stage, behind a computer screen, or in a one-on-one coaching session, Anthony Solomon consistently demonstrates a profound ability to motivate and inspire. His multi-faceted background contributes to his engaging and impactful style, solidifying his reputation as a thought leader in the realms of personal and professional development.